Armies of the Young

The Rutgers Series in Childhood Studies

Edited by Myra Bluebond-Langner, Rutgers University, Camden

Advisory Board

Joan Jacobs Brumberg, Cornell University, New York City

Perri Klass, Boston University School of Medicine

Jill Korbin, Case Western Reserve University

Bambi Schiefflin, New York University

Enid Schildkraut, American Museum of Natural History

Cindy Dell Clark, *In Sickness and in Play: Children Coping with Chronic Illness*

Donna M. Lanclos, *At Play in Belfast: Children's Folklore and Identities in Northern Ireland*

Amanda E. Lewis, *Race in the Schoolyard: Negotiating the Color Line in Classrooms and Communities*

Peter B. Pufall and Richard P. Unsworth, eds., *Rethinking Childhood*

David M. Rosen, *Armies of the Young: Child Soldiers in War and Terrorism*

Armies of the Young

Child Soldiers in War and Terrorism

DAVID M. ROSEN

RUTGERS UNIVERSITY PRESS
New Brunswick, New Jersey, and London

BP53

Library of Congress Cataloging-in-Publication Data

Rosen, David M., 1944–
Armies of the young : child soldiers in war and terrorism / David M. Rosen.
    p. cm. — (The Rutgers series in childhood studies)
    Includes bibliographical references and index.
    ISBN 0–8135–3567–0 (hardcover : alk. paper) — ISBN 0–8135–3568–9 (pbk. : alk. paper)
    1. Child soldiers. 2. World politics—20th century. 3. World politics—1989–
I. Title. II. Series.

UB416.R67 2005
355'.0083—dc22   2004016421

A British Cataloging-in-Publication record is available for this book from the British Library.

Manufactured in the United States of America

7/30/07

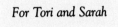

For Tori and Sarah

Contents

Preface

This book began with a quiet walk through the British Military Cemetery on Mount Scopus in Jerusalem. As I strolled among the well-ordered, manicured graves of the young soldiers who perished in Palestine during the Great War, I had a sense of the anguish, loss, and pain in these soldiers' families, feelings that have now been almost completely erased by time. The cemetery no longer radiates the raw sense of loss one feels in other military burial and memorial sites, where freshly offered tokens of remembrance bespeak the suffering of family and friends. But this walk among the graves of the fallen instilled in me an understanding that children and youth have long been consumed in the fires of war.

Many of the ideas in this book were first developed during my participation in the seminar "Supernationalism: The Ethics of Global Governance," directed by the Carnegie Council for Ethics and International Affairs and sponsored by the National Endowment for the Humanities during the summer of 2001. I thank Joel Rosenthal, the president of Carnegie Council, and Tony Lang, its program officer, who made it possible for me meet a wide variety of people involved in efforts to end the use of child soldiers. My ideas were further elaborated at the monthly seminar "Rethinking Childhood in the Twenty-First Century," sponsored by the Rutgers University Center for Children and Childhood Studies in 2002–2003. I thank my lifelong friend and colleague Myra Bluebond-Langner, the director of the center, for inviting me to participate in the seminar and for her unflagging interest in and support of this work. I also received a summer grant and release time from some of my teaching duties at Becton College of Fairleigh Dickinson University. I thank Dean Barbara Salmore for her continued support of this research.

I could not have written this book without the help and support of many people. Yossi Shavit, chief archivist at Ghetto Fighters' House (GFH) at

Kibbutz Lochamei Hagetaot in northern Israel, graciously made archival material available to me. Dalia Gai, one of the librarians at GFH, cheerfully guided me through the library's collection. I am especially thankful to Haim Galeen, the archivist of the Partisan Data Base at GFH for his personal kindness and his help with the source documents of the database. I also am grateful for his introducing me to Yosef Rosin of Haifa and Elimelech Melamed of the Irgun Hapartizanim in Tel Aviv, who gave me copies of their unpublished memoirs and, in turn, introduced me to other former partisans. Aiah Fandey of Friends of Sierra Leone provided me with valuable help in thinking through current issues in Kono District. My friends Mark Sherman, Joni Catalano-Sherman, and Ronny Perlman hosted me on numerous trips to Israel and provided me with food, good humor, and support through many difficult times. Etta Prince-Gibson, Jill Levenfeld, and Adina Shapiro graciously provided me with good advice.

Good librarians are the lynchpins of any research project. I thank the librarians and staff at the Yad Vashem Library, the Stephen Spielberg Film Archive at the Hebrew University in Jerusalem, the Central Zionist Archives, the Public Record Office at Kew Gardens in London, and the Dorot Collection of the New York Public Library for their gracious assistance. Thanks also to Eleanor Friedle and Maria Webb at the library of Fairleigh Dickinson University's College at Florham and to Grethe Zarnitz, the administrative assistant at the Department of Social Science and History, for their cheerful help with all my requests.

Portions of this book were presented at the monthly colloquium of the Department of Social Sciences and History at Fairleigh Dickinson University, College of Florham. I greatly benefited from comments and suggestions from my colleagues Gloria Gadsden, Bruce Larson, Riad Nasser, Jasonne O'Brien, Bruce Peabody, Neil Salzman, Dianne Sommerville, Irene Thomson, Peter Woolley, Robert McTague, and Roger Kopple. Special thanks to my talented editor at Rutgers University Press, Marlie Wasserman, and to my amazing copyeditor, Pamela Fischer. I also have been lucky in having many patient friends and colleagues who have listened to my constant telling and retelling of these stories. Some have also read parts of the manuscript and offered me sound and challenging comments. These readers include Phyllis Chesler, Susan Gorman, Jonny Greenwald, Leonard Grob, Randy Kandel, Barbara Kellerman, Richard Rabinowitz, and Anne Griffiths. Toby Sonneman and Helen Zelon graciously read portions of the manuscript and gave me crucial editorial guidance. Irene Nasser and Erica Schneider, two of my undergraduate students, provided important help in tracing down bibliographic and source material. Among those with whom I have discussed the ideas in this book, I would particularly like to thank Richard Langner, Enid Schildkraut, Tony Buonagura, Ingrid Freidenbergs, and Susan Bender. Needless to say no one whom I thank either endorses this book or is in any way responsible for its shortcomings.

Like many women, my wife, Tori Rosen, successfully manages a complex and demanding professional career, child care, volunteer work, and countless family obligations. Despite these responsibilities, she reviewed and commented in detail on many drafts of this book. I am profoundly grateful to her for her love, boundless energy, generosity of spirit, and deep intelligence. My twelve-year-old daughter, Sarah Rosen, constantly reminds me of the potential of children for resilience, good judgment, and understanding of human character. I thank her for being a never-ending source of love, joy, and inspiration.

Armies of the Young

Chapter 1   War and Childhood

THE IMAGES ARE burned into our minds: a young boy, dressed in a tee shirt, shorts, flip-flops, holding an AK-47, a cap pulled down over too-old eyes; a child with sticks of dynamite strapped to his chest; a tough-talking twelve-year old in camouflage. The images disturb us because they confound two fundamental and unquestioned assumptions of modern society: war is evil and should be ended; children are innocent and should be protected. So, our emotional logic tells us, something is clearly and profoundly wrong when children are soldiers. Throughout the world, humanitarian organizations are using the power of these images to drive forward the argument that children should not bear arms and that the adults who recruit them should be held accountable and should be prosecuted for war crimes. The humanitarian case, which is one facet of the general effort to abolish war, rests on three basic assumptions: that modern warfare is especially aberrant and cruel; that the worldwide glut of light-weight weapons makes it easier than in the past for children to bear arms; and that vulnerable children become soldiers because they are manipulated by unscrupulous adults. In making this case against child soldiers, humanitarian organizations paint the picture of a new phenomenon that has become a crisis of epidemic proportions. This book examines these assumptions to reveal a much more complicated picture. At the heart of this book are three conflicts in which child soldiers played a part: the civil war in Sierra Leone, the Palestinian uprising, and the Jewish partisan resistance in Eastern Europe during World War II. I chose these examples not because they are typical or representative but because they illustrate the complexities of the child-soldier problem.

The case of Jewish child partisans is salient because of the way the stories of these young resistance fighters unsettle conventional narratives of child soldiers. Many child partisans were members of Zionist and socialist youth movements that celebrated the independence and autonomy of children and youth in pre–World War II Europe. Most became child soldiers because it was the only way for them to save their lives. Had they remained civilians, they would have been murdered. At the least, this case illustrates that although being a child soldier may not be good, for some children it may be an absolute necessity.[1]

Sierra Leone is the poster-child case of the modern child-soldier crisis. But, in fact, it is strikingly unique not only because of Sierra Leone's particular history and culture but because the problem of child soldiers grew out of the breakdown and criminalization of the Sierra Leone state. The particularly horrific role that many child soldiers played in the Sierra Leone civil war was tied to their exploitation and participation in a criminal enterprise both before and during the war.

The final case, that of Palestine, also has distinctive characteristics. Palestinian children and youth have been at the forefront of radical politics and organized armed violence against Zionism since before the Balfour Declaration in 1917. The extreme actions of contemporary child suicide terrorists have their roots in an apocalyptic vision of the Jewish presence in Palestine that brought both young people and adults into radical politics long before the Israeli occupation of the West Bank and Gaza deformed the lives of Israelis and Palestinians.

The cases of Sierra Leone and the Palestinians also illustrate the complex nature of the contemporary legal and humanitarian attempts both to define the legal age of recruitment of children and youth into armed forces and to resolve the related issue of the criminal culpability of children who commit war crimes. These cases make clear that the problem of child soldiers is not merely the impetus for a humanitarian effort to protect children but is part of a global politics of age in which humanitarian and human rights groups, sovereign states, and the United Nations and its administrative agencies battle over the rights and duties of children and over the issues of who is a child and who is a child soldier. The child-soldier crisis is a part of the contested domain of international politics in which childhood serves as a proxy for other political interests.

Even before I began looking closely at the issue of child soldiers, I knew something about each of these cases. I did fieldwork as a graduate student in anthropology in the Kono diamond-mining area of Sierra Leone, which later became the center of rebel activity during the war. Since then, I have avidly followed events in Sierra Leone. I was also a lecturer in anthropology at Ben Gurion University in Israel. I lived in Beersheba, where I was active in local civil rights groups and had frequent contact with Israeli and Palestinian students. I have maintained my friendships and interest in the region by visiting and teaching in Israel since the early 1980s. I am not a formal student of the Holocaust, but as it claimed distant kin and the closer relatives of many of my friends and family, I have lived in its shadow all my life.

War is a constant companion in human life. Human societies often dream of ending war, but World War I—the "war to end all wars"—ushered in a century of human misery in which more than one hundred million people died in warfare. Now, in the opening decade of the twenty-first century, the end of war is hardly in sight. Since I conceived the idea for this book, the World Trade Center was attacked, and the United States went to war in both Afghanistan and Iraq. Elsewhere around the world, millions of people are involved in rebellions, insurgencies, and civil conflicts. Nearly every day we are confronted with pictures and stories not just of war but of children bearing arms. Indeed, Sgt. Nathan Ross Chapman, the first U.S. soldier to be killed by hostile fire in Afghanistan, was shot in ambush by a fourteen-year-old boy.

At first blush, the concept of the child soldier seems an unnatural conflation of two contradictory and incompatible terms. The first, *child*, typically refers to a young person between infancy and youth and connotes immaturity, simplicity, and an absence of full physical, mental, and emotional development. The second, *soldier*, generally refers to men and women who are skilled warriors. But where do childhood, youth, adolescence, and adulthood begin and end? For contemporary humanitarian groups that advocate an international ban on child soldiers and view child soldiers as a modern-day aberration, the answer is clear and simple: childhood begins at birth and ends at age eighteen. This view, known as the Straight 18 position, defines the child soldier as any person under eighteen years of age who is recruited or used by an army or armed group. For the rest of the world, however, it is by no means clear that that all persons under age eighteen are or even should be deemed children. The question of who is a child is important because of the indisputable fact that very young people have always been on or near the field of battle. Despite these concerns I use the term *child soldier* to refer to any person below eighteen years of age. My heuristic use of the Straight 18 position does not mean that I believe it fairly represents the idea of who is a child. To my mind, it makes little scientific or common sense to assert that every seventeen-year old soldier or bride in every society on the planet is a child. Instead I use it to highlight the difficulties of adopting this perspective.

Warfare draws in the young and the strong. We know that in preindustrial societies there is no single, fixed chronological age at which young people enter into the actions, dramas, and rituals of war. Anthropologists have had frequent encounters with children at war in these societies. Francis Deng reports that traditionally among the Dinka of the Sudan boys were initiated into adulthood between the ages of sixteen and eighteen, and they immediately received gifts of well-designed spears that symbolized the military function of youth.[2] Among Native Americans of the plains, such as the nineteenth-century Cheyenne, boys joined their first war parties when they were about fourteen or fifteen years old and slowly evolved into seasoned warriors.[3] Sometimes, as in many of the societies of East Africa, such as the Maasai and the Samburu, adolescent boys of varying chronological ages were collectively inducted into the status of warriors. The famed female warriors of Dahomey were recruited between the ages of nine and fifteen.[4] Elsewhere, even among the Yanomamo of Venezuela and Brazil, where warfare was especially valorized, adolescents largely set their own pace in determining when they wanted to take up the adult role of warrior.[5]

There is no single rule for determining when the young are fit to be warriors, although in most cultures they are in some stage of adolescence. The timing of the transition to warrior probably turns on a wide variety of practical issues because young men have to be able to demonstrate their physical and emotional fitness for these roles. In some societies, young people are deliberately socialized into highly aggressive behavior, and both individual and collective violence are highly esteemed; in others, more emphasis is based on peaceful resolution of disputes.[6] In general, chronological boundaries between childhood, youth, and adulthood are highly varied and are rooted in the historical experience of each society and culture. Indeed, some societies may not even regard childhood, youth, and adolescence as separate stages of life.

Similar issues arise in Western societies as well. Until recently, the armies of Western Europe and the United States were filled with "boy soldiers." Beginning in the Middle Ages, boy soldiers were routinely recruited into the British military, and by the late nineteenth century various institutions had emerged that organized and systematized their recruitment. In Great Britain, the Royal Military Asylum was founded in 1803 by the Duke of York and later renamed for him. The Royal Hibernium Military School was founded in 1765 for the children of so-called rank-and-file soldiers. Originally an orphanage for working-class and poor boys, it quickly established links to the military. Among the earliest recruits were twelve- and thirteen-year-olds, who were placed in regiments and served under General Thomas Gage in 1774 to suppress the growing American Revolution.[7] A wide variety of data also indicate the presence of the young on the American side of the Revolutionary War.[8] Until the twentieth century, most military service in the West was voluntary, but even with the emergence of conscription the recruitment of child soldiers continued as schools and military apprenticeship programs continued to channel boys into the military.

The Civil War in the United States was a war of boy soldiers. Throughout the Civil War, youngsters followed brothers, fathers, and teachers into war. Some lied about their age; others looked older than their age.[9] They were sometimes recruited at school, and many were brought to the recruiting stations by their parents.[10] They often had support roles but quickly graduated into combat roles. When necessary, they used weapons that were cut down and adapted for use by young people. Numerous examples abound. David Baily Freemen, "Little Dave," enlisted in the Confederate army at age eleven, first as an aide-de-camp accompanying his older brother and then as a "marker" for a survey team before finally fighting against General William Tecumseh Sherman's army.[11] Avery Brown enlisted at the age of 8 years, 11 months, and 13 days in the Ohio Volunteer Infantry. Known as the "Drummer Boy of the Cumberland," he lied about his age on his enlistment papers, giving his age as twelve.[12] Joseph John Clem (who changed his name to John Lincoln Clem) officially enlisted in the Union Army at age ten, although he had been a camp follower since age nine. He carried a pistol and a cut-down musket and was called the "Drummer Boy of Shiloh." He was given field promotions after he killed at least two Confederate officers.[13] Gilbert "Little Gib" Van Zandt, age ten, followed his teacher into the Ohio Volunteer Infantry, where he joined his father, uncles, and friends. He joined up when recruiters arrived at his school, despite his mother's pleas that he was too young to fight.[14]

The actual number of boy soldiers in the Civil War is uncertain. Some popular writers claim, probably with exaggeration, that the Civil War could easily have been called "the boys' war"; they have estimated that out of a total of 2.7 million soldiers more than a million were eighteen or under; about eight hundred thousand were seventeen or under; two hundred thousand were sixteen or under; about one hundred thousand were fifteen or under; three hundred were thirteen or under.[15] More careful historical analysis suggests that between 250,000 and 420,000 boy soldiers, including many in their early teens and even younger, served in the Union and Confederate armies.[16] On the whole, between 10 and 20 percent of recruits were underage.[17] Applying modern humanitarian terminology, the war to end slavery was in large part fought by child soldiers in numbers ever greater than those found in contemporary wars.

Numbers alone do not tell the whole story. It is equally important to see how the participation of boy soldiers in war was understood at the time. In the North, wartime funeral sermons at the burial of those killed invariably praised the sacrifice of "Christian boy-soldiers" on behalf of abolition and the preservation of the Union.[18] Writings about boy soldiers in the aftermath of the Civil War constitute a hagiographic genre that celebrates the nobility and sacrifice of young boys in battle. In the South, the nobility of the boy soldier was tied to the ideology of the "lost cause." Developmental differences between boys and men were recognized in this literature, but they were understood rather differently than they are today. Although young boys were regarded as impulsive and less mature than older men, these qualities were recast as grand and heroic. Testimonials collected by Susan Hull in 1905 describe boy soldiers as enduring battle with "patience and gaiety" and those who died as having "made their peace with God." Equally important, the experience of battle, however horrific, was not understood as destroying the lives of children but as ennobling them. Boy soldiers who survived intact were respected citizens whose contribution to civic life was enhanced by their experience of war. Of particular interest to southern hagiographers was the Battle of New Market in the Shenandoah Valley of Virginia, where the young cadets of Virginia Military Institute fought under General John C. Breckinridge. These boys, aged fourteen to eighteen, were credited with the victory and deemed to deserve respect and admiration.[19] Although it may not be possible to verify the accuracy of these accounts, they are conspicuous precisely because they put forward radically different views of children in battle than those presented in contemporary humanitarian accounts.

Hagiographic accounts also mask the brutality to which young people are exposed during war. Even individual accounts have suffered from self-censorship. The well-known British bandleader Victor Silvester wrote of his experiences as a boy soldier in World War I in his 1958 autobiography, *Dancing Is My Life*.[20] Only later, shortly before his death, did he reveal that he had participated in the execution of a fellow boy soldier.[21] Nevertheless, these not-so-distant descriptions of boy soldiers make it apparent that current humanitarian views of the involvement of the young in the military and war are different from the way that involvement was understood in the United States and Europe in earlier times. Clearly, the child soldier as an abused and exploited victim of war is a radically new concept.

In fact, humanitarian advocacy shows little or no awareness that current humanitarian views about childhood itself are historically contingent and derive from a particular constellation of ideas and practices that began to emerge in Europe during the Middle Ages. The medieval attitude toward children was generally one of indifference to age. Children were seen to be the natural companions of adults.[22] But during the Middle Ages, the germ of a set of new ideas about childhood developed. At its heart are the belief in the innocence of childhood, the practice of segregating children from adults, and the isolation and prolongation of childhood as a special protected state. These ideas and practices were virtually unknown in the preindustrial world; they developed and spread in the West with the industrial revolution, until they were established, albeit unevenly, across virtually all class and cultural boundaries. The adolescent, it has been quipped, was invented with the steam engine.[23] Outside the West there were of course chronologically young people, but childhood, as understood in the West, did not necessarily exist as a salient cultural or social category. Indeed, many of the persons we would today classify as children were classified as adults.

The emergence of formal and institutionalized schooling, which accompanied the industrial revolution, was central to the development of the idea that children are innocent and even weak. Formal schooling also increasingly segregated young people from adults and slowly replaced apprenticeship as the prime mode of education. Prior to the emergence of formal schooling in Europe and the United States, education was accomplished largely through apprenticeship. Military training was particularly tied to the apprenticeship system, and in fact the military was the most resistant of all the professions to formal schooling. In the seventeenth century, a boy destined for a career in the military—the "noble profession"—would have perhaps two or three years of separate education and at the age of eleven, twelve, or thirteen would find himself a commissioned officer in the army or navy, freely mixing with adults in the military camps.[24]

But school life and its associated ideas of childhood were not necessarily incompatible with military ideals. As schooling began to dominate educational processes, there was a union of military and school cultures as schools, which had once been primarily ecclesiastical institutions, became militarized. So, just when formal education began to separate child life from adult life and to create a special culture of childhood, that culture itself began to be shaped by a military ethos. Military discipline was thought to have a particular kind of moral virtue. Uniforms, military hierarchy, and regimentation penetrated school life, and the idealization of military officers became fused with adolescence. Officers and soldiers became "cherubim in uniform."[25] Thus, to the extent that military life was understood to be virtuous and ennobling, there was little conflict between the idea of the child and the life of the soldier. By the end of the eighteenth century, the formal relationship between children and military life was frequently organized through a variety of institutional mechanisms that combined military training, apprenticeship, and pedagogy in varying combinations according to class and status.

This pattern continued through World War I, even as the idea of an extended childhood became formally institutionalized and bureaucratized in Western life.

During World War I, young boys continued to enlist, despite official age restrictions on recruitment. Private James Martin, the youngest Australian to die in World War I, enlisted in Melbourne in 1915 at age fourteen and died a few months later near Gallipoli. His story is memorialized in the book *Soldier Boy*, by Anthony Hill.[26] Albert Cohen of Memphis, Tennessee, is reputed to be the youngest U.S. soldier to see combat in World War I. He enlisted at age thirteen and died at age fifteen.[27]

Even in more modern times, apprenticeship programs continued to find their place alongside formal schooling. In the British army, in particular, schooling and military apprenticeships were tightly integrated. Prior to World War II, the British army developed much of its skilled labor force, such as armorers (in charge of the maintenance of small arms and machine guns) and artificers (combat mechanics), in apprenticeship and technical-training programs. With the increase of mechanization in the 1930s, the British army realized that adult recruitment could not meet its manpower needs, so in 1939 it opened the Army Technical Foundation College to train boys in technical skills and soldiering. Boys still remain an important component of the British army, as both officers and enlisted soldiers.[28] For both working-class and upper-class boys, to be a boy soldier was to be part of a well-trained, highly skilled group to which society generally accorded honor and respect.

The innocence and the vulnerability of the child are the dominant theme in contemporary humanitarian discourse, but earlier ideas about children have not vanished in Western society and culture—or in the rest of the world. Various ethnic, racial, and class groups continue to hold these different ideas about childhood, although they tend to be stigmatized in U.S. society. Likewise, the ties between childhood and military culture have not been totally severed in the West; military schools and academies continue to survive even as they have taken a back seat to other forms of educational transmission. Indeed, today in the United States, almost half a million high school students are enrolled in the Junior Reserve Officers Training Corps, a program established by Congress in 1916 to develop "citizenship" and "responsibility."[29]

Contemporary Humanitarian Narratives
and the Politics of Age

Contemporary narratives reverse traditional images of the child soldier. They are part of a tendency in the contemporary world to criminalize war and to paint the military and its associated cultural and social links with the brush of criminality or deviancy (or both). The image of the child soldier—to the extent that this image is created and burnished by international humanitarian groups, agencies of the United Nations, and the policies of many national governments—vilifies military life. This characterization is targeted particularly at rebels and insurgents—the armed groups that are most dependent on younger soldiers. To this end, the definition of child soldier that is most widely accepted is the broad one found in UNICEF's 1997 Cape Town Principles. It defines a child soldier as "any person under 18 years of age who is part of any kind of regular or irregular armed force or armed group in any capacity."[30]

Humanitarian groups have had an enormous influence in shaping the international treaties that seek to ban the use of child soldiers, especially the provisions of the Rome Statute of the new International Criminal Court, which makes the use or recruitment of children a war crime. Despite considerable differences in outlook and policy among these groups and agencies, they share a common set of concepts that root the child-soldier crisis in three main sources: fundamental changes in the nature of warfare in the postcolonial era, the emergence of the small-arms trade, and the special vulnerability and innocence of children.

Humanitarian groups are part of the many thousands of nongovernmental organizations (NGOs) that collectively define themselves as "civil society." The term *civil society* has increasing come to be used alongside and sometimes to supplant the rather inelegant term *nongovernmental organization*. Over the past few decades, a unique relationship has emerged between the agencies and offices of the United Nations and civil society. The United Nations serves as the political capital of civil society, providing NGOs with an international forum and legitimacy and allowing them to influence the development of United Nations policy and the shaping of United Nations–sponsored treaties and international legal instruments. United Nations policy allows the key organizations of civil society routine access to the preparatory and working groups that both develop and grow out of international conferences.[31]

Accordingly, the leading organizations of civil society are deeply embedded in the work of the General Assembly and the administrative agencies of the United Nations. They regard themselves as partners in the United Nations system and are so regarded in the United Nations, despite the fact that they have no mandate from any political community.[32] Along with their newfound power in the international arena, humanitarian groups and other members of civil society increasingly define themselves as political actors, pursuing specific political agendas. This definition contrasts sharply with the more traditional model of humanitarian groups as politically impartial and neutral.[33] The organizations of civil society regard themselves as caretakers and upholders of the moral values of transnationalism. In the United Nations, their exclusion from the Security Council is taken as prima facie evidence that they represent the voices of international democracy, human rights, and reason against the debased interests of powerful states. The competing political agendas of humanitarian groups, sovereign states, and the United Nations and its constituent agencies have created a global politics of age, of which the child-soldier issue is only one part. Rival social, cultural, and political ideas about childhood are linked to the interests of different global polities. In the case of child soldiers, the result is pitched battles over the legal age of recruitment and use of child soldiers; the ideological and political manipulation of the concepts of childhood, youth, and adulthood; and fierce partisanship over who should be considered a child soldier.

Old Wars and New Wars: Mythologizing the Past

One of the principal conceptual pillars of the child-soldier crisis is that modern, or "new," wars differ significantly from traditional wars. Modern, new, and traditional are vague, imprecise terms, but they broadly distinguish the small-scale civil wars and ethnic conflicts that now occupy the center stage of armed conflict from previous international wars and wars of national liberation. Borrowing Robert Kaplan's notion of the "coming anarchy," or the "new barbarism," this distinction posits that traditional, or "old," wars were rule-bound and limited, while "new" wars are anomic and chaotic.[34] This analysis establishes two ideal types based on a sharp dichotomy between "traditional" and "modern" wars.

The rudiments of these ideal types can be found in reports and studies issued by the United Nations and by humanitarian and human rights groups, as well as in journalistic and scholarly accounts. The essential argument is based on the belief that traditional wars were self-limiting and rule-bound in a number of distinct ways: politically—in having clear political objectives; temporally—in having well-defined beginnings and ends that resulted in victory or defeat; spatially—in the existence of geographically bounded battlefields; humanly—in that they were fought according to a set of commonly accepted rules that, among other things, clearly distinguished between civilians and combatants.

In humanitarian discourse, new wars are said to have few if any of these characteristics. Instead, they are caricatured as aimless, formless, and without real political purpose. Such wars are frequently dubbed "hyperpolitical"— a view that valorizes past "political wars" that were fought for specific ideologies and that deems contemporary civil and ethnic conflicts as non-political and nonideological. These contemporary conflicts are demonized as purposeless modes of destruction in which "there are no victors, only victims."[35] New wars are sometimes described as a "way of life," with no purpose other than their own continuity, and as a kind of perversion of culture.[36] Sometimes they are described with metaphors of disease, such as "epidemic" or "plague." Elsewhere they are called large-scale deviant criminal enterprises, in which bandits and gangsters merely pose as rebels. These people are frequently caricatured as "self-proclaimed" or "self-appointed" rebels, terms used to stress the lack of connection between collective violence and authentic political movements. Descriptions of new wars also conflate modern warfare with terrorism, particularly the targeting of civilian populations.

But all wars are messy, and there are civilian deaths and terrorist episodes in every conflict. Still, most contemporary wars are civil wars, which almost always result in high civilian casualty rates. In addition, some recent wars are primarily terrorist in nature. In Sierra Leone, for example, one of the prime aims, if not the prime aim, of the Revolutionary United Front was the devastation of the civilian population in order to create the kind of civil strife and chaos that would bring down the government and create an opportunity for the exploitation of Sierra Leone's diamond fields. The government itself also launched attacks on civilian populations. There were also clashes between actual armies, but civilians were considered legitimate targets of violence. Likewise, in the war in Mozambique the activities of the rebel group RENAMO have involved a particularly horrifying form of terrorism, although both sides have used dirty-war tactics.[37]

Despite the terrible circumstances in which many contemporary wars are fought, neither high civilian casualties per se nor terrorist episodes constitute a real change from the way wars have been fought throughout the ages. The eighteenth- and nineteenth-century wars of the European monarchies, often cited as examples of wars conducted by "the rules," were, at best, a brief sideshow in the history of war, a highly distorted view of how warfare in Europe was usually carried out. For a much better view of war in Europe one must turn to Jacques Callot's 1631 etchings of the French invasion of Lorraine, Han

Ulrich Franck's etchings of the Thirty Years' War, and Francisco de Goya's
etchings of events during Napoleon's invasion of Spain in 1808.[38] These depictions of the horrors committed by uniformed soldiers of European monarchies against civilians, mostly peasants, quickly put to rest idealized versions
of European warfare. Moreover, "the rules" never prevented these same
European (and U.S.) armies and their postcolonial successors from extensively
and indiscriminately killing noncombatants in wars against indigenous
peoples,[39] although the genocidal killing of indigenous peoples has been
largely invisible.[40] Nevertheless, the view that the fundamental nature of war
is changing runs through virtually all the humanitarian and human rights
views of war.[41] Even if warfare could be shown to be changing over time, there
is no empirical justification for drawing a bright line between "old wars" and
"new wars" at the end of colonialism. Moreover, child soldiers have always
been present on the battlefield, so the roots of the child-soldier crises cannot be said to lie in the anomie of modern warfare as it is experienced in
postcolonial states.

The United Nations report *Impact of Armed Conflict on Children* by Graca
Machel is of particular significance in the development of the humanitarian
view.[42] This report has served as a template for virtually all human rights reporting on child soldiers since it was published. Machel herself has a long
history of participating in revolutionary politics and action. She was trained
as a guerrilla fighter in Tanzania and was active in FRELIMO (Frente de
Libertaçao de Moçambique), the armed movement that fought against the
Portuguese for the independence of Mozambique. She is the widow of Samora
Machel, who led the guerrilla war against Portugal and later became the first
president of Mozambique. She was minister of education in the first post-
independence government in Mozambique and is now married to Nelson
Mandela. Machel's revolutionary "credentials" are important because the idea
that warfare in the postcolonial world is qualitatively different from earlier
forms of war is central to the humanitarian narrative.

The Machel report characterized modern warfare in postcolonial states
as involving the "abandonment of all standards" and having a special "sense
of dislocation and chaos." Moreover, Machel describes the "callousness of
modern warfare" as resulting from the breakdown of traditional societies
brought about by globalization and social revolutions. The report cites such
phenomena as the vestiges of colonialism, internal dissent, structural monetary adjustments, uneven development, the collapse of government, the
personalization of power, and the erosion of essential services as factors contributing to a breakdown in the rules of warfare. This breakdown has led to
the loss of distinctions between combatants and civilians, especially horrible

levels of violence and brutality, and the use of any and all tactics including systematic rape, scorched-earth policies, ethnic cleansing, and genocide. The abandonment of standards has brought about human rights violations against women and children, including the recruitment of children into armed forces and groups. In Africa, in particular, the report suggests, the "strong martial cultures" no longer have rules that prohibit attacks on women and children.

In sum, the Machel report distinguishes between traditional, rule-bound warfare, including national liberation struggles, and the patterns of warfare found in postcolonial states. As she states elsewhere, "War today just simply does not match the traditional conception of two opposed armies; or even of an internal conflict pitting an armed opposition force against the established government, in which each side generally abides by the 'rules of the game,' respecting the basic inviolability of civilian non-combatants and the special protection due to the young."[43] Within this framework, humanitarians sometimes claim that children are deliberately and intentionally conscripted as soldiers or targeted as part of the strategy of war.

Many modern wars, especially the small-scale wars of Africa, are indeed taking place in the context of the collapse of the state. Nations such Liberia, Sierra Leone, and the Democratic Republic of the Congo (formerly Zaire) no longer function as de facto states even as they retain their jural international identity.[44] But the warfare that has plagued Sierra Leone, horrifying as it is, is not irrational or anomic. Quite the contrary, soldiers have fought for specific goals, in particular the control of the key resources of the Sierra Leone economy.

The collapse of the state also does not in itself explain the social and political context that allows the use and recruitment of child soldiers.[45] In Sierra Leone, this context was shaped by warlord politics, the collapse of the state, and the intrusion of criminality both within and across state boundaries. The Revolutionary United Front (RUF), the rebel group in Sierra Leone, financed the war by controlling the diamond fields. It eschewed building up a grassroots base in rural areas.[46] Indeed, some Sierra Leoneans believe that the RUF never intended to establish a state but merely planned to create a zone of terror in order to shield its criminal actions. The gross immorality of and the unspeakable crimes committed by leaders and soldiers are no more or less rational than those of the Nazis. The RUF contrasts with the revolutionary movements in Mozambique and in Eritrea, where the wars were fought by revolutionary groups that systematically mobilized the rural population. Child soldiers were present in all these struggles, but their experiences were quite different. For example, FRELIMO, the Mozambique guerilla force in which Machel played a major leadership role, routinely recruited children into its ranks. Rather than mythologize the past and render invisible the thousands of child soldiers who fought in wars of national liberation, we should ask why there was no international child-soldier crisis at that time. The answer, I believe, is that the child-soldier crisis is the crisis of the postcolonial state. For that reason the international community of humanitarian and human rights groups and of governments, once avid supporters of the armies of national liberation, have now redefined all rebels and their leaders as apolitical criminals and child abusers.

New Wars and Small Arms

A second conceptual pillar of the humanitarian narrative ties the child-soldier phenomena to the small-arms trade. The central argument is that the availability of lightweight, easy-to-carry weapons transforms the roles children play in war. In old wars, it is alleged, children served only in indirect supporting roles such lookouts, spies, or messengers, whereas in new wars light weapons enable children to be used as combatants. The Organization of African Unity's 2000 Bamako Declaration on Small Arms Proliferation states, "We must recognize that the widespread availability of small arms and light weapons has contributed to a culture of violence."[47] UNICEF claims that the widespread availability of small arms is one of the primary reasons for the disturbing phenomenon of child soldiers. According to UNICEF, because children can use these arms without much prior training and because the weapons require little maintenance and support, it is easier than in the past for children to become direct combatants. UNICEF also claims that the presence of these weapons creates a "culture of violence," while others argue that it has served to create a new form of mass slaughter.[48] Human Rights Watch echoes this view, declaring, "Technological advances in weaponry and the proliferation of small arms have contributed to the increased use of child soldiers. Lightweight automatic weapons are simple to operate, often easily accessible, and can be used by children as effectively as adults."[49] A grimmer picture is painted by William Hartung: "When an army composed largely of ten- to fourteen-year-old children armed with automatic rifles that can fire 600–700 rounds per minute is set loose on the civilian population, the results can be devastating."[50]

But there is virtually no hard evidence that the spread of small arms has anything to do with the use of children, even if some advocates describe it as "self-evident."[51] The most popular weapon for child soldiers, the Kalashnikov assault rifle, or AK-47, has been available since 1949; it was the key weapon of national liberation groups, rebels, and insurgents long before the child-soldier crisis. In addition, there is the weight itself. At 9 pounds and 7 ounces, the AK-47 is similar in weight to or even heavier than many of the rifles used in the U.S. Civil War.[52] The U.S. rifle musket of 1861, which went into mass production during the Civil War, was a simple and durable weapon at 8.88 pounds.[53] Hundreds of thousands of British Pattern 1853 Enfield rifles were smuggled into the South during the Civil War; this rifle weighed just under 9 pounds.[54] Another widely used Civil War weapon was a carbine rifle produced by Sharps, which at 8 pounds weighed less than many modern weapons.[55] The British Lee-Enfield 303 rifle was about 9.5 pounds—virtually identical to the AK-47 in weight—and was considered a heavy weapon.[56] It was developed during the Boer War and was used in the British campaign to suppress a late-nineteenth-century in-surgency in Somalia led by Mohammed bin Abdullah Hassan, whom the British dubbed the "Mad Mullah of Somaliland."[57] This rifle was part of the flood of weapons that entered Sudan after World War II, became a staple weapon of the Nuer during the first civil war (1955–1972), and presumably was used by Nuer of all ages.[58] The 6 pound–5 ounce U.S.-made M-16 rifle is considerably lighter, but there is no correlation between its availability and the presence of child soldiers.[59]

It is rare to find factual references to the firepower or weights of any of these weapons in humanitarian discourse on small arms or even descriptions of how they might be used. My conversations with former soldiers in the U.S., German, and Israeli armies indicate that the use of these weapons presents a more complex picture than do simple descriptions of their technical weights and capacities. For example, although the M-16 is a light weapon, it is not widely used by child soldiers. Some soldiers consider it too long and unwieldy to be used by children. However, children do use weapons that are consider-ably heavier. For example, children recruited into the Hizbollah in southern Lebanon routinely used rocket-propelled grenade launchers (RPGs) against Israeli soldiers. Sometimes referred to by the Israeli soldiers as the "RPG gen-eration," these children held the weapons against their stomachs while they fired them, sometimes causing considerable injury to themselves. The RPG-7, the most widely used of these weapons, weighs over seventeen pounds, and the grenade weighs an additional five pounds.[60]

In addition, weapons are only a small part of the weight that soldiers bear. Victor Silvester, mentioned earlier, who joined the British army in World War I at age 14 years 9 months, remembered the exhaustion induced by carrying a rifle and a ninety-pound pack during twenty-five- to thirty-mile training marches.[61] In more recent years, Tim O'Brien's novel *The Things They Carried* memorialized the total weight—material and psychological—carried by soldiers during the U.S. war in Vietnam.[62]

In theory, weapons such as the AK-47, the M-16, and the German G-3 can fire hundreds of rounds per minute, but in fact there are severe practical limitations to their use. Continued firing overheats and destroys the barrel of the gun, and rapid firing of the weapons is inaccurate because they start to ride upward. In fact, combat training in the West stresses the economy of weapons use and firepower. Soldiers are trained to use only one or two shots at a time. In the United States, the M-16 has been modified to allow a soldier to fire three short bursts of fire in order to maintain accuracy. Soldiers themselves usually carry only six to eight clips of ammunition, with up to thirty rounds per clip. A well-trained soldier can perhaps fire 150 or more rounds per minute but will quickly run out of ammunition. These modern weapons have a great deal more firepower than the weapons of the nineteenth and early twentieth centuries, but the weight has not changed substantially since then.[63]

No doubt, modern small arms can be used to kill and terrorize civilian populations, but most of the people killed and maimed in countries like Sierra Leone and Rwanda were killed with knives and machetes, not with guns. In sum, small arms can be terrifying weapons of destruction, but their role as a factor in the child-soldier crisis is, at best, indirect. A small number of organizations that specialize in tracking the small-arms trade have begun to retreat from their previous position that there is a causal relationship between the availability of small arms and the existence of child soldiers.[64] Nevertheless, this presumed link remains a staple of humanitarian discourse.[65]

The Vulnerability of Children

The third conceptual pillar of the humanitarian narrative asserts that children are recruited and conscripted as child soldiers because they are vulnerable and can be easily manipulated. Much of the emphasis in the humanitarian narrative is on the forced recruitment and abusive exploitation of children who are used as child soldiers. Soldier Child International portrays children in Uganda as being "harvested" by the various armed factions fighting in northern Uganda. It alleges that children who resist are beaten or otherwise forced into service and are sometimes killed.[66] The compulsory recruitment of child soldiers is frequently described as being linked to specific acts of terror and horror such as forcing new recruits to kill family, friends, or co-villagers in macabre ritual acts designed to ensure that the child soldier will be permanently alienated and separated from family, home, and community life. In addition, once they are recruited into armed forces, child soldiers are said to suffer from the worst forms of child abuse, including forced labor, sexual slavery, the forced use of drugs, and outright murder.[67]

Some of these accusations are true. In addition, much evidence indicates that the dramatic use of terror has played an important role in many contemporary wars, and so episodes of this kind have no doubt occurred. Nevertheless, the vast majority of child soldiers are not forcibly recruited or abducted into armed forces and groups. Indeed, in Liberia, children were among the first to join the armed groups, and in the Palestinian intifada they have often been the catalysts of violence.[68] Even the Machel report argues that not all children in combat should be seen merely as victims. Indeed, perhaps for children, as well as adults, it may be true, as Nordstrom argues, that the "least dangerous place to be in a war today is in the military."[69]

The relatively few published interviews with current and former child soldiers carried out by anthropologists in the field make plain that the experience of children at war has scant connection with the depictions in the humanitarian literature. Paul Richards's interviews with male and female child combatants in Sierra Leone show that "many under-age combatants choose to fight with their eyes open, and defend their choice, sometimes proudly. Set against a background of destroyed families and failed educational systems, militia activity offers young people a chance to make their way in the world." Krijn Peters and Paul Richards argue that, given these circumstances, child soldiers should be seen as "rational human actors" who have a "surprisingly mature understanding of their predicament."[70]

Harry West's interviews with adult women who served as children in FRELIMO's Destacemento Feminino, or Female Detachment, show that many of them saw their participation in combat as empowering and liberating, and they continue to see it this way as adults.[71] For these women, revolutionary ideologies played an important role both in organizing the meaning system in which they operated as child combatants and in helping them create new roles and identities in postcolonial Mozambique. Many of these women interpret their war experiences as freeing them not only from colonial rule but also from male structures of dominance in "traditional" Mozambique society. The revelation that these former child soldiers understand their participation in combat and other revolutionary acts as threshold events that led to participation as full citizens in the political life of Mozambique is reminiscent of the hagiographic portraits of child combatants in the nineteenth-century United States. Yet virtually every activity these girls participated in, from cooking to transporting war materials and supplies to learning to use weapons and attacking civilian settlements and Portuguese soldiers, would nowadays be recast as criminal forms of child abuse under the humanitarian narrative.

In much the same light, Virginia Bernal's study of schoolgirls and peasant women who joined the Eritrean People's Liberation Front shows that many
were deliberately recruited for combat roles and temporarily enjoyed rough
equality with male combatants. Sadly, after independence, they were denied
the benefits of full citizenship and were pressed back into extremely conservative gender roles. Nevertheless, Bernal interprets their experience under
arms as having endowed them with both "critical perspectives" toward
Eritrean society and the skills to engage in collective action.[72] She makes it
abundantly clear that participation in war, even for schoolgirls, is not a wholly
negative experience.

Finally Angela Veale's short study of female ex-combatants from Tigray
Peoples Liberation in Ethiopia shows these women to be more self-confident,
independent, and politically aware than those who did not serve. All the
women studied had been recruited as child soldiers at ages ranging from 5 to
17, with an average age of recruitment of 12.68 years. None of the women
regarded themselves as having been powerless or having been victimized.[73]
All this evidence points to the strong need to evaluate the situation of child
combatants in context and of giving due weight to history and circumstance.
Studies such as these can help break through the ideological posturing that
often characterizes academic and political debate and can orient us toward
the reality of children's lives, even under extreme circumstances.

Chapter 2   Fighting for Their Lives

Jewish Child Soldiers of World War II

AMONG THE MOST memorable stories of the Holocaust is that of Motteleh the child soldier. Motteleh, age twelve, was hiding in the forests of Belarus—then part of eastern Poland—when he was rescued by and joined a partisan group. Disguised as a local villager and carrying false identification papers, he became well known as a player of Ukrainian folk melodies on his violin and was hired to play at a German army hostel. Over time he used his violin case to smuggle explosives into the cellar of the hostel. One evening when an SS division on its way to the eastern front was billeted at the hostel, he blew it up, killing everyone. The violin is on display at the Yad Vashem Holocaust memorial in Jerusalem.[1] Motteleh did not survive the war, but his story is memorialized in the novel for young people titled *Uncle Misha's Partisans*.[2]

Another tale, "The Glass Eye," is probably apocryphal, but I have often heard it read or told on Holocaust Remembrance Day in Israel. The story goes that the Germans captured an eleven-year-old partisan. The German officer in charge had one glass eye and offered to spare the boy's life if he could determine which of the officer's eyes was made of glass. After gazing into the officer's eyes, the boy chose the correct eye and was spared. When the officer asked the boy how he knew which one was the glass eye, the boy replied that it was the glass eye that still retained a trace of humanity.

The stories of Jewish child soldiers during the Holocaust force us to address the question of how children can defend themselves when faced with a genocidal enemy that targets every person for death regardless of age or condition. The murders of countless children during the Holocaust make painfully clear that genocide is always redressed after the fact. When a people or a community is at the edge of an abyss, the choices are hard and few. There are no places of safety for children. Some hide, while others take up arms in self-defense. For Jewish children and youth, joining the armed resistance against genocide was a matter of life or death. To be left outside the protective umbrella of self-defense was a death sentence. Under such conditions, the conventional thinking that child soldiers are victims of their recruiters is turned on its head. The recruiters may be their only saviors. Indeed, during the Holocaust, the survival of many Jewish children depended on whether they could join the armed resistance against the Germans and their allies.

The problem of self-defense under conditions of genocide is not like the problem of self-defense in the context of ordinary crimes. During peacetime, the criminal law limits the right of self-defense to the moment when an attack is underway. Once an aggressor breaks off the attack and retreats, the victim has no right to pursue the attacker. Self-defense can neither be too early nor too late. A preemptive strike against an aggressor is illegal because force is used too soon; retaliation against an aggressor is illegal because it is force that is used too late.[3] The rationale behind this restriction is that when the attack abates, the police or other civil authority can stand between the attacker and the victim and provide the victim with protection and justice. But when genocidal rage prevails, the victim is under perpetual attack even if the immediate violence is broken off for the moment. No civil authority or zone of safety stands between the attacker and the attacked. Victims cannot survive without creating forms of protection and resistance. Moreover, self-defense cannot be organized on an ad hoc basis. It requires a sustained effort under the constant threat of annihilation. In the reverse of ordinary law, it may require that the victim attack the attacker.

World War II began with the German invasion of Poland on September 1, 1939. The war unleashed a reign of terror that resulted in the destruction of six million Jews—most of the Jewish population of Europe. The murder of world Jewry was a principal objective of German war policy.[4] Jewish armed resistance to Germany's policy of genocide took different forms. Most prominently, groups of Jewish partisans, or "ghetto fighters," formed in the cities of Eastern Europe, and individuals and groups of Jews throughout Europe fled into forests and rural areas where they either formed or joined partisan forces. Some of these forest partisans retained their specifically Jewish identity, while others joined with non-Jewish groups.

How many child soldiers fought among the ghetto fighters and partisans? Hard figures are elusive, but one study of a thousand Jewish soldiers of the Lithuanian Division of partisans suggests that more than one-third of the division's Jewish soldiers were fifteen to twenty years old. Many had been involved in youth groups prior to enlisting in the division, and a large number of people were related to one another—brothers and sisters, fathers and children, married couples. The Lithuanian Division obtained its recruits from the flight of refugees.[5] Likewise, anecdotal evidence in the memoirs and autobiographies of partisans and ghetto fighters consistently points to the pervasive presence of children.

The surviving children and youth who fought are now elderly. Most have died in the years since the war. Many others were killed during the war, despite the fact that the survival rate for partisan fighters was higher than that of the Jewish population as a whole. Many former Jewish partisans are both literate and energetic. As a result, Jewish partisans, including children and youth, have been able to create a treasure trove of memoirs, autobiographies, and reports that provide a window into the lives of child partisans during this era. These former fighters are also able to control the telling of their own stories, adults' personal recollections of childhood and youth under arms. Among these survivors is Haim Galeen, manager of the Partisan Data Base at Ghetto Fighters' House in Israel, who has published his book *An Eye Looks to Zion* in Hebrew.[6] Haim introduced me to Havka Folman Raban, the author of *They Are Still with Me*, and to Yosef Rosin, Elimelech (Misha) Melamed, and others who have provided me with written unpublished accounts of their experiences.[7] Many former partisans have urged me to collect their stories before it is too late and all of them, even those who were young children during the war, have died.

These stories are important because children and youth played a major role in partisan resistance against the Germans. They formed the core of the urban partisan units and were an important component of many forest partisan groups. Some children and youth provided indirect support: they served as couriers, helped manufacture crude weapons, distributed resistance publications, or delivered basic support services such as making food or taking care of animals. But in most instances children and youth served directly in combat. Young fighters and resisters did not necessarily regard themselves as children. Often they referred to themselves as "youth," a term normally used in Hebrew, Yiddish, and Polish to describe young people from about thirteen to twenty-one years of age. At other times, young people described themselves as children but saw little conflict between the life of the child and the serious business of resistance.

The participation of children and youth in armed resistance emerged from the unique political role they played under German oppression. Observers of life in the Warsaw ghetto in Poland made it clear that children and youth sustained much of the political life of the ghetto: "It is no exaggeration," said one observer, "to state that the only environment in which political movement still pulsates with life, in which the will to act has not utterly failed and in which action takes place—is that of the youth. Nobody but the youth publishes and distributes illegal publications nowadays; nobody else engages in political and idealistic activity in Jewish society on a large scale."[8] Despite the horrific conditions of ghetto life, children and youth imagined themselves as a revolutionary vanguard. As the underground newspaper *Neged Hazarem* (Against the Stream), published in the Warsaw ghetto by the socialist-Zionist youth movement Hashomer Hatzair (Young Guard), proclaimed, "We the children aged 13 to 18, will be the ones to lead the Jewish masses to a different future, a better future."[9]

Necessity, Honor, and Duty

That children were among the Jewish youth fighters and partisan groups should not be surprising. Children were part of virtually every partisan and resistance movement in World War II. But Jewish partisan units, especially the ghetto fighters, were distinguished by the disproportionate number of women and children in their ranks. The reason was simple: all Jews were targeted for death. Genocide, in singling out an entire people for death, makes no distinction between soldier and civilian, combatant and noncombatant, male and female, infant and elder. Jews and the Roma were the only ethnic or national groups targeted for total extermination by the Germans. Individuals from other ethnic and national groups who sought to resist German control could join armed groups in the forest and leave their families in comparative safety, although admittedly under brutal German occupation. For these groups, civilian life and noncombatant status provided a partial, if inadequate, zone of safety. But for Jews there was no safe harbor from war. Civilian life was a guarantor of extermination. For all its brutality and danger, armed resistance was one of the few zones of relative safety for children. It offered the hope of survival as a fighter in the face of the virtual certainty of civilian death.

Armed resistance also provided the possibility of sustaining personal and national dignity and honor in the face of the horrors of the Holocaust. As the destruction of the Jewish community unfolded, youth, especially organized youth, quickly recognized the German intention to bring an end to all Jewish life in Europe. They observed Jews being herded into cattle cars, starva-

tion in the streets, public hangings of resisters, and beatings and random killing of the innocent. As the awareness of the fate of Jewry began to grip the
community, children and youth increasingly regarded passive acceptance of
death at the hands of their oppressors as a form of national and personal dis-
honor. The idea of dying with honor began to emerge as a guiding ideology.
Children and youth preferred to live, but if they were going to die anyway,
they preferred to die in a way that gave meaning to their deaths. Armed resistance, even when futile, presented children and youth with a way to man-
age and control identity and destiny in the face of murder. These children
and youth, termed "romantic phantasiasts" by the Warsaw ghetto observer and
secret archivist Emmanuel Ringelblum, were the only ones who remained on
the field of battle.[10]

Marek Edelman's story of the humiliation of an old Jew on the streets of
Warsaw makes clear how an assault on the honor and dignity of this man led
him to join the resistance. Edelman, one of the leaders of the uprising in the
Warsaw ghetto, writes:

> I once saw a crowd on Zelzana Street. People on the street were
> swarming around this barrel—a simple wooden barrel with a Jew on
> top of it. He was old and short, and he had a long beard.
>
> Next to him were two German officers. (Two beautiful tall men
> next to this small, bowed Jew.) And those Germans, tuft by tuft,
> were chopping off this Jew's long beard with huge tailor's shears,
> splitting their sides with laughter all the while.
>
> The surrounding crowd was also laughing. Because, objectively, it
> was really funny: a little man on a wooden barrel with his beard
> growing shorter by the moment as it disappeared under the tailor's
> shears. Just like a movie gag.
>
> At that time the Ghetto did not exist yet, and one might have
> not sensed the grim premonition in that scene. After all, nothing
> really horrible was happening to that Jew: only that it was now
> possible to put him on a barrel with impunity, that people were
> beginning to realize that such activity wouldn't be punished and
> that it provoked laughter.
>
> But you know what?
>
> At that moment I realized that the most important thing on
> earth was going to be never letting myself be pushed onto the top
> of that barrel. Never, by anybody.[11]

Even when children found safety hiding among civilians, some saw it as
their moral duty to join partisan units. Marek Herman, born in Lvov, then
in Poland, in 1927 is but one example. When Lvov was invaded and occupied

by the Germans in 1941, Herman's entire family was murdered. Because he looked Polish, the fifteen-year-old Herman took off his armband with the Star of David and passed as a non-Jew. By luck he was befriended by a troop of Italian soldiers stationed in Lvov. Although allied with the Germans, the Italians decided to bring a number of "orphans" back with them to Italy. Herman was saved. He was adopted by an Italian family and could have lived out the remainder of the war protected by local residents and peasants in Italy. At age sixteen, however, Herman observed a truck of Czech partisans entering his town. The Czechs were trying to join up with an Italian partisan unit. Seizing an opportunity, he translated for the Czechs and Italians and quickly volunteered for the communist Forty-Ninth Garibaldi Brigade, an Italian partisan unit. Herman immediately informed his adoptive parents that he would not return until the end of the war. "I didn't need to think further about what to do," Herman recalled. "It was natural to join the partisans; that had been my dream. It was like a gift from heaven for me." Commenting on Herman's choice, the writer and Auschwitz survivor Primo Levi remarked that Herman "doesn't hesitate for a minute: he understands what is right and what is wrong and he understands the debt he must pay. He became a partisan, while only a few centimeters taller than a rifle."[12] For Levi there is no doubt that even a child has moral agency and that for Herman the only legitimate choice was to take up arms.

The Geography of Resistance

As Germany evolved into a fascist state, it invaded, annexed, and occupied neighboring countries. Following the German invasion in 1939, Poland, which was the center of Jewish resistance, was divided into two parts: Germany occupied the western portion of the country, and the Soviet Union occupied the east. The Polish Jewish community was split in half. Cities such as Lublin and Warsaw came under German control, while the eastern cities, such as Bialystok and Grodno, fell under Soviet occupation. Other Polish cities such as Vilna to the north were incorporated into Lithuania and remained free of German or Soviet rule until 1941. These changes created a massive flow of Jewish refugees who streamed toward eastern Poland, the Soviet occupied zones, or north toward Vilna. This torrent of refugees included most of the Jewish leadership of the prewar political parties.

As German control over Poland tightened, the geographical proximity between city and forest made the forest a natural place of refuge. Many Jews, but particularly young people and children, fled into the forests from the towns, cities, and villages of rural Poland. Flight into the forest became one of the few ways to survive following the 1942 German decision to locate and kill all the Jews in occupied Poland in an operation known by the code name Erntefest, or Harvest Festival. Jewish underground forces in the ghettos were aware that the forests contained a growing partisan movement and that one option for urban partisans was to abandon the ghettos and take up arms in the forests. It was the official view of the Communist Party that the ghettos were undefendable because fighting groups would forever be hampered by the presence of civilians. The communists urged all people of fighting age and ability to escape from the ghettos and to join the forest partisans. Most Jewish fighting groups in the major cities rejected this position. They argued that Jews and Jewish honor should be defended where Jews lived—in the ghettos. But in the end fighting strategies were mixed: in some ghettos, such as Vilna, fighters made the decision to take a stand in the ghetto, but, recognizing that they would ultimately lose, they prepared to move out to the forests. In Warsaw, the dominant strategy was to do battle within the ghetto, although after the destruction of the ghetto, the remaining fighters did make their way into the forests.

The Climate of Resistance among Youth

Within the Jewish community it was the young who were most determined to challenge German control directly. Most prominent among the youth groups were the Zionist and socialist youth movements, which were a central part of Jewish life in prewar Poland. These groups served as a ready-made platform for organizing resistance.

ZIONIST AND SOCIALIST YOUTH MOVEMENTS

Zionist youth groups emerged in Europe between World War I and World War II, especially in Poland, Lithuania, Belarus, and the Ukraine. For the most part they brought together largely secular Jewish youth for social and cultural activities. They created strong and coherent organizations that relied on scouting as a model for their basic structure. All tended to recruit children from about thirteen to eighteen years old, and sometimes they created groups for younger children. Most of the Zionist youth groups combined the ideas of socialism with the more ancient Jewish tradition of return to the Land of Israel (Eretz Yisrael). They advocated the immigration of Jewish youth to Palestine and the creation of socialist communal and collective settlements (kibbutzim). They stressed the reading, writing, and speaking of Hebrew as the language of the new Jewish culture. They believed that leaving Europe and living as socialist farmers in Israel would be the solution to centuries of European anti-Semitism and oppression.

The most important of these groups were Dror (Freedom), which was tied to the Zionist Workers Party in Poland and the United Kibbutz (Kibbutz Meuchad) movement in Israel, and Hashomer Hatzair (Young Guard), which was linked to the National Kibbutz (Kibbutz Artzi) movement in Israel. Some significant differences divided these groups. Dror tended to draw its members from working-class youth, had a less dogmatic and liberal view of socialism, and was skeptical of the Soviet Union. Hashomer Hatzair's members were better educated and wealthier Jews, but the organization was far more Marxist and tied to the policies of the Soviet Union. However, Hashomer's active promotion of scouting activities brought it into contact with non-Jewish scouting organizations in Poland—contacts that would serve it well when the war broke out.

Many other youth organizations played a role in the resistance. These included Gordonia, named after A. D. Gordon, an intellectual follower of the Russian novelist and utopian socialist Leo Tolstoy, and the nonsocialist Akiva, named after a rabbi and scholar of the Talmudic era. Others like Hanoar Hazioni (Zionist Youth) were nonpolitical and humanist in their orientation, while still others, such as Betar, attracted right-wing Jewish nationalists. Just prior to the outbreak of World War II the main Zionist youth groups had almost sixty-seven thousand members spread over more than nine hundred branches in Poland alone.[13] With the non-Zionist youth wings of the Socialist and Communist parties, organized youth movements boasted a membership of about one hundred thousand just prior to the outbreak of the war. Of these some two thousand youth were active members of the ghetto fighting organizations in Poland.[14]

THE DEVELOPMENT OF YOUTH CULTURE

In the years prior to the war these groups forged an oppositional culture among youth. Zionist youth not only criticized the long history of European anti-Semitism but also rejected much of adult Jewish life and culture, which they viewed as distorted and corrupted by European persecution. Although they adopted scouting as an organizational model, they imbued it with Jewish and socialist values. The key local chapter or group was termed the *ken*, literally "nest" in Hebrew. Among the Noar Hazioni, each *ken* was divided into troops (*gedud*), and each troop was further subdivided into groups (*kivutzot*). The members or cadets (*chanichim*) were divided by age, and the group as a whole met formally, sometimes in uniform, lining up and reporting much like contemporary scout troops.[15] In Hashomer Hatzair the *ken* was usually divided into age groups; the youngest were eleven to fourteen (*b'nai midbar*); a middle group of scouts (*tsofim*) were fourteen to sixteen; and an older group of "seniors" (*k'shisim*) were seventeen and older. The *ken* became the operational center for the oppositional movement. As the war went on, the *ken* evolved first into a political and residential unit and finally into an underground cell.

The combination of scouting, socialism, and Jewish culture turned the youth organizations into a distinctive social force. The groups occupied the central place in a youth- and child-centered utopian movement that promoted the immigration of young people to Palestine and the creation of socialist, egalitarian communities. Their critique of "bourgeois society," adult authority, and traditional family organization was tied to a utopian vision of a life in the Land of Israel free of injustice and inequality. Youth censure of family life was not merely theoretical. Youth leaders actively promoted the immigration of young people to the Land of Israel, actions that involved them in the breakup and separation of Jewish families. As they prepared for immigration, they fashioned, in Poland and elsewhere, model communities of the kind they hoped to create in Israel. Youth groups established urban collective living groups, also called kibbutzim, where members met, hosted delegations from Europe and Palestine, and sometimes lived together, sharing labor and resources according to socialist principles. At agricultural-training kibbutzim in rural areas of Poland, members learned to live and farm in preparation for the life of collective farming in Israel. Indeed, those who had not joined a training kibbutz in preparation for immigration by age twenty-one usually left the movement.[16]

The Jewish youth groups that developed in Eastern Europe and the utopian dreams at their core were linked to the worldwide emergence of youth movements in the late nineteenth and early twentieth centuries, including such movements as the Boy Scouts in the United States. Virtually all these movements were influenced by a late-nineteenth-century German youth movement—the Wandervogel, usually translated as Birds of Passage. This highly romantic movement began as way for young people to break away from parental authority through hiking and expeditions into the German countryside. The leadership of the Wandervogel remained largely in the hands of the youth themselves. The German youth movements had an important influence on the Jewish youth movements such as Hashomer Hatzair, whose kibbutzim in Israel were comprised mainly of youth from Poland. Jewish youth from Poland came into contact with the Wandervogel movement right after World War I as refugees in Vienna. Jewish youth converted much of the romantic esprit of the German youth movements into a far more practical design for living. They were, as one kibbutz member argued, "spoiled children" who had to create a real community.[17]

As German traditions were incorporated into the Jewish youth movements, they took on a particularly Jewish political and cultural coloring. Like
the German youth movements, the Zionist movements regarded adolescence
not simply as a developmental stage in the progression toward adulthood but
as an autonomous and pure state in which it was possible to fully realize one's
humanity. Youth culture rejected the world of adult values in order to build
a world around the values of youth. Autonomous and intimate groups under
the leadership of young leaders stressed the development of physical fitness,
scouting, and connection to nature. In addition, the Jewish movements en-
visioned a world of youth guided by the ideas of Zionist pioneering, socialism, and romanticism. Although Hashomer Hatzair and Dror were most
devoted to the mix of Zionism, socialism, and Marxism, all the youth groups
were inspired by the idea of universal social justice. These notions transformed
the idea of a separate youth culture into a belief that Jewish youth were a
distinct revolutionary vanguard.[18]

The organizational and ideological strength of the youth groups was bolstered by the newspapers they published and their creation of a complex cultural and quasi-communal life built around meetings, group singing of Hebrew
and political songs, political discussion, poetry, and guest speakers from Europe
and abroad. These activities gave each *ken* the sense of being a distinct, intimate, and separate community with a unique sense of destiny. A sense of secrecy pervaded many meetings, partly because middle-class and professional
parents often viewed the utopian dreams of their children with suspicion and
concern and partly because the youth themselves sought to distance themselves from the problems and complexities of everyday life in Poland. Secrecy
created an atmosphere of transcendence that linked personal identity to the
idea of personal and political redemption in the Land of Israel.

Avraham Mussinger, for example, describes a typical meeting of his
Hashomer Hatzair *ken*:

> We would get together twice [a week] . . . at 8:00 P.M. and we would
> spend two or three hours together in our narrow room with our
> counselor, in order to hear from his mouth descriptions of collective
> life in the Land [of Israel]; on the accomplishments in turning
> uncultivated soil into agricultural land; on the ideal character of the
> Jewish person, a worker on the land who lives from the work of his
> hands, free from the customs and complexes of the exile, brave in
> the face of difficulty and danger; and on the formation of a new
> society, etc. We knew that the day was not far off when we would
> be able to help our brothers in exile.[19]

Similarly Sara Altman describes her experiences:

The chapter had its headquarters in a two story house . . . on a noisy, narrow, closed off alley. . . . At first, I was careful that none of my father's acquaintances would see me going to the den. . . . There were two perhaps three small rooms. The chapter at that time had about 200 members. There was much noise, tumult and conversation in the rooms. Groups of boys and girls sat in each corner, with their backs to the center of the room and their faces inwardly turned to their circle, surrounding their counselor. . . . From the partial sentences that one could make out coming from all corners, one would immediately realize that in one of the older groups, one of the members was lecturing about Fourier's *Utopia*, . . . and in the oldest group, they were discussing the Arab question. . . . It did not bother anyone that in the next room, a group of girls was singing "How Pleasant Are the Nights of Canaan" in a clear voice. Another counselor was teaching her group to dance the Hora. Here everything was clear, sparkling and certain.[20]

The intimate and ideologically charged atmosphere of the *ken* drove a wedge between the world of children and the world of adult authority. Youth leaders encouraged young people to abandon the urban Jewish world of professionals and workers, shopkeepers and journeymen, rabbis and teachers to become farmers in the Land of Israel. Adults saw these young people as childish, irresponsible, and threatening. However, with hindsight, we realize that the "irresponsible children" who abandoned their lives in Europe survived the war. Those who clung to their family responsibilities largely perished.

YOUTH GROUPS AND SELF-DEFENSE

The rapid spread of anti-Semitic attacks in Europe in the 1930s triggered a concern for self-defense among the youth groups. In Poland, the center of the youth movements, the problem was especially acute. The growth and intensification of anti-Semitism in Poland paralleled developments in Nazi Germany, and by 1935 at least one girl had been shot and killed by unknown attackers at a youth-movement lecture. But by 1939, shortly before the outbreak of the war, only about five hundred youth-group members had received some self-defense training. Moreover, the fact that Jews could not lawfully obtain weapons seriously hampered arms training.[21]

The Arab Revolt (1936–1939) in Mandatory Palestine also played a small part in promoting Jewish self-defense in Poland. Kibbutz and youth-movement emissaries from Palestine coming to Poland between 1936 and 1939 stressed the importance of self-defense training for anyone considering immigration. In fact, until the outbreak of the war in 1939, the focus of the youth groups remained immigration to Palestine. As they understood it, the fundamental issue for Zionist youth in 1939 was not the possibility of war but the British White Paper effectively shutting down twenty-two years of lawful immigration to Palestine. Only the outbreak of war radically transformed the youth groups into fighting units.

The Outbreak of the War and the Development of Armed Resistance among Youth

The outbreak of the war surprised many leaders and members of youth organizations. As German bombs fell on Bialystok, Poland, nineteen-year-old Chaika Grossman met with the fifteen- and sixteen-year-old members of her Hashomer Hatzair ken. She was deeply concerned that the young people could not grasp the dangers of war.[22] Misha Melamed, age fifteen, caught unawares when the war reached his town of Ivye in Belarus, tells us, "I returned home from a party in school celebrating the end of the year of study. It was quite late, but I walked slowly knowing that the following day I could sleep and did not have to get up early. The next day . . . I awoke at 7:00 in the morning to the sound of noise in the streets. . . . Tanks of the Red Army moved in easterly and westerly directions and there was a sense of panic."[23] Havka Folman Raban, age fifteen, a member of Dror in Warsaw, went to summer camp in 1939 and returned home a few days before the German invasion of Poland. She writes: "Around the campfire with my friends, I felt myself belonging to a wonderful world; life seemed beautiful. Now I can say we lived in a bubble. The world was erupting around us and I, like my friends, was busy with who liked whom."[24]

The Germans erected ghettos in Eastern Europe to gather together the Jewish population for the long-term goal of extermination. But the systematic murder of millions could not be accomplished overnight. The prelude to annihilation was the creation of an isolated and compliant population, which the Germans accomplished by murdering most of the Jewish political leadership and terrorizing the remaining population through countless acts of murder, sadism, and torture. Jewish armed resistance developed within an aggressive "culture of terror" created by the occupying power.[25] Terror was the prime means used to concentrate and ghettoize the population, to create conditions of starvation and disease, to facilitate the deportation of the population to concentration and death camps, and to carry out the final liquidation and razing of the ghettos. But the huge managerial task of bringing about mass murder provided resistors with a thin temporal and political space in which to organize.

Resistance groups began to fully organize in the period between the concentration of the Jewish population into ghettos and the final deportation and liquidation of the Jews in 1942 and 1943. As we have seen, Jewish youth groups in Poland organized self-defense forces even prior to the creation of the ghettos, and self-defense remained the main concern of these groups until reports of the systematic murders of Jews by the Germans became commonplace.[26] But, as the communists had predicted, direct armed resistance was constrained by the willingness of the Germans to murder innocent civilians in reprisal. Because resisters feared that they would do far more harm than good, direct attacks on German forces were few until the deportations began. In some instances ghetto fighters attacked German forces outside the ghettos in order to deflect blame. In July 1942, for example, Vitka Kempner led her small group of Hashomer Hatzair youth fighters out of the Vilna ghetto to blow up a German troop train twelve miles distant, an attack that killed some two hundred German troops. Because it took place far outside the ghetto, the Germans attributed the incident to Polish partisans. Although a young girl in Kempner's unit was killed, this became the fighting strategy of the Vilna ghetto fighters.[27]

Resistance was also slowed because of the position of Jews as a disenfranchised minority. Jewish resistance groups were cut off from the usual sources of support. Normally, guerilla and underground resistance movements take root in places where the local population provides food, weapons, moral support, concealment, and protection.[28] But Jewish armed resistance units were a hated minority, situated in a territory noted for extreme anti-Semitism. With notable exceptions, the local population was as hostile to Jewish self-defense as it was to the German occupation. In Poland, some groups affiliated with the main Polish nationalist resistance force, the National, or Home, Army (Armia Kracowa, or A.K.), were actively involved in the extermination of Jews, although this behavior was not typical of the Home Army as a whole. In fact, during the uprising in the Warsaw ghetto, the Polish Home Army was a main source of arms to the fighters. Other underground organizations, such as the Polish Communist Party's People's Army, or People's Guard (the Armia Ludowa, or A.L., which in its earlier development was known as the Gwardia Ludowa, or G.L.), were much smaller and were able to provide only occasional support to the Jewish resistance.[29]

Political conditions also worked to thwart resistance. Two types of organizations, both run by adults, emerged in the ghettos. The first was the Judenrat, the official local administrative structure established by the Germans in every ghetto. Members of the Judenrat were surviving prewar social and religious leaders. Many Jews imagined the Judenrat as a protective buffer between the German occupiers and the Jewish community. Others hoped that Jews would be permitted to live relatively autonomously under the Judenrat, even if isolated and ghettoized. There was no room for young people in this structure. The Judenrat was simply an instrument of German oppression, created to carry out German orders and to mask the true intent of German policy. The second type of organization was a broad network of Jewish self-help groups that created public kitchens, food-distribution centers, schools, music groups, libraries, and cultural groups. These organizations provided an alternative community, a public zone of civility within the culture of terror.[30] They did not directly challenge German power, but in providing personal aid and preserving a small part of prewar Jewish life, they sought to fend off the destabilization of cultural frameworks that is inherent in a terrorized population.[31]

Outside this framework of adult organizations were the Zionist youth groups and the organized youth wings of the left-wing political parties. The Zionist, socialist, and communist youth were radically divided ideologically and politically. But in the context of the German occupation they created an underground oppositional community designed to organize resistance and promote armed opposition. In addition to the Zionist youth groups, which played a leading role in armed resistance, the youth movements of the socialist Jewish Labor Bund (the Bund) and the Communist Party quickly organized to oppose the Germans. Like many political parties of the prewar era, they also had paramilitary militias composed of the toughest older youths and adults of their largely working-class constituency. But the youth wings, especially the Bund's youth wing Tsukunft (officially Yugnt Bund Tsukunft, or Youth Bund— The Future), were central to organizing armed resistance in the Warsaw ghetto and played a dominant role in others. Nevertheless, in general, the Zionist youth groups dominated armed Jewish resistance to the Germans.[32]

In the Warsaw ghetto, the principal fighting groups of the Jewish Fighting Organization (the Zydowskie Organizacja Bojowa, or Z.O.B.) were combat units drawn primarily from the Zionist socialist youth groups and the youth movements of the left-wing political parties: Dror (five units), Hashomer Hatzair (four units), Akiva (one unit), Gordonia (one unit), Hanoar Hazioni (one unit), Jewish Labor Bund (four units), Communists (four units), Left Labor Zionists (one unit), Right Labor Zionists (one unit). In addition to this main fighting organization, the right-wing Jewish Military League (the Zydowski Zwiazek Wojskowy, or Z.Z.W.) served as the underground army of the Zionist Revisionist Party and its youth wing, Betar.

Despite the sudden onset of war and the initial organizational disarray, youth movements rapidly responded to the danger. The house owned by the Dror movement in Warsaw was quickly transformed into a center of communal living, clandestine education, and underground activity. Disguised as a center for refugees, it was a residence for leaders and members of Dror and other youth movements who met to develop a response to the German occupation, prepared and distributed papers and publications of the underground, and reestablished Jewish educational programs suppressed by the Germans. With the creation and sealing of the ghetto, activity within the house intensified. As food became scarce, members moved in together to share resources.[33] The need for resistance became apparent. An article in the underground newspaper *Dror*, published in Warsaw in August 1940, called for the creation of a "cadre of Jewish youth that is prepared for battle."[34]

At first, resistance was nonviolent and centered on the creation of an underground press and the dissemination of anti-Nazi materials. Many girls served as couriers and created an information network of youth groups in different cities and regions. For the German occupiers any form of resistance, especially the underground press, was punishable by death. To make the point clear, on April 18, 1942, the Germans carried out a mass execution of printers and distributors of the underground papers.

Zionist youth groups owed their ability to rapidly resist the German occupation to the organized youth subculture they created prior to the war. Their success was due not merely to the fact that they were rebellious or even that they were Zionists but rather to the fact that the armed resistance to the Germans was, in essence, a realization of their values.[35] Zionists were a minority in prewar Poland. Distanced from much of the Jewish mainstream, Zionist youth functioned as an oppositional and countercultural movement. Moreover, for most adults, Zionism meant giving monetary and moral support to the developing Jewish community in Palestine. Young people who created a quasi-communal way of life and who intended to move to Israel and live in socialist collectives were deemed childish, nonconforming, eccentrics and kooks. But turning inward toward the strong and coherent utopian ideologies provided youth with a vision around which to organize resistance. In addition, the youth groups had long functioned as surrogate forms of family and kinship for their members, relationships that were strengthened during the occupation. The occupation also generated a move toward communal living as young people left their families to live with friends in the movement. The intimacy and trust built over the years allowed local chapters to be converted into clandestine cells of resistance that could take advantage of movement resources such as meeting places and mimeograph machines for the creation of an underground press.[36]

Another significant factor was that the youth-movement leadership system remained intact, and leaders were committed to not abandoning the groups. They differed considerably from most of the leaders of the Jewish political parties in Poland, who fled to the safety of the Soviet umbrella, leaving the rank and file with a significantly less experienced and less able leadership, unable to decide on a course of resistance. In stark contrast, in early 1940, many important youth activists from Hashomer Hatzair and Dror returned from the relative safety of Soviet-occupied Poland to German-occupied territory to ensure the continuity of the youth movements.[37] As a result, the youth groups had a leadership cadre with both the discipline and the courage to mount armed resistance.

But even this dedicated leadership might have foundered had the youth movements not retained their dynamism in the absence of formal leadership. Before the war broke out, Chaika Grossman, mentioned earlier, was sent by the senior youth leadership in Warsaw to prepare the youngsters in her *ken* for underground activity in the event of German occupation. When the war broke out, Bialystok was occupied by the Soviet Union, and Grossman was sent to Vilna in Latvia—then still a free city—to help organize immigration to Palestine for the stream of Jewish refugees fleeing German-occupied Poland. When the Germans occupied Vilna, she helped set up the underground organization there and finally returned to Bialystok in January 1942, some six months after the Germans had occupied the city and ravaged the ghetto, killing thousands of Jews. When she arrived in Bialystok virtually nothing remained of the strong Jewish life of that city. Yet the youth group she led still retained much of its prewar vitality. In her view, youth were the only ones who senses had not been dulled by the oppression.[38] Before her first meeting Grossman worried that her "kids" might have given up socialist and revolutionary politics, but instead she found them uncompromisingly committed and militant. Her task, as she described it, was to turn this youth group into a disciplined underground army.

The youth groups were, finally, the only Jewish organizations able to maintain a consistent network of contacts across Poland. Using teenage female couriers, who carried forged identity papers and documents, the local chapters of the youth movements maintained contact with one another across Poland, Lithuania, and Belarus. As a result they bypassed the communications and information blackouts imposed by the Germans. The adult leadership of the Judenrat, by contrast, was isolated and locked into the ghettos, unable to communicate with the outside world. As a result, youth groups controlled a wider information network than other groups in the ghettos and had a far better sense of German intentions than the adults did. Youth leaders were the first to recognize and fully understand that German policy called for the total extermination of the Jews. The ideas and underground proclamations and manifestos of these groups called for both armed and unarmed resistance against the Germans, and in hindsight it is clear that they had the most accurate understanding of German policy of anyone within the Jewish community.

The Struggle between Generations

Jewish political leadership in the ghettos was radically split by both age and ideology. Adult leaders claimed authority and knowledge while in fact they functioned in a state of ignorance and denial; they favored a mixture of accommodation and attempts to ameliorate Jewish suffering through cooperative but ultimately futile strategies. The youngest and the most radical leaders were better informed but lacked political legitimacy. However, young people did not necessarily rebel because they had better information. In many instances their actions were simply the result of sheer bravado. As Folman Raban put it, "We did everything that was forbidden because it was forbidden. That is how the resistance began."[39]

The budding militancy of youth put them into direct conflict with the politics of the Judenrat. Grossman describes her early conflicts with the Judenrat as she tried to raise money for arms within the Bialystok ghetto. She writes that she was able to exploit the hazy identity of the youth groups to obtain some support from the Judenrat. Even if marginal, Zionist youth groups were a legitimate part of the Jewish community, and historically their focus on "pioneering" life in Israel meant they were perceived as nonpolitical. Nevertheless, the Judenrat was flooded with rumors that the youth groups had taken a militant turn and were organizing armed revolt. Grossman's task was to convince the Judenrat that the youth groups should be perceived as responsible children—still childlike and not aggressive. By portraying Hashomer Hatzair as Zionist and hiding its partisan identity, she was able secure support. Grossman's description shows that popular ideas about childhood innocence were invaluable in masking the formation of an underground army within the ghetto. Children and youth could be mobilized because they were still seen as children. The Germans and their allies had no compunctions about killing Jewish children when ordered to do so, but when the underground cells of the Bialystok ghetto formed, the ambiguity of childhood provided an opportunity for organizing and recruiting fighters.[40]

One theme that persistently threads its way through Grossman's narrative is how ghetto authorities invariably tried to portray youth militancy as "childish." Youth leaders were frequently admonished not to behave like children. A chorus of ghetto officials chided them to behave "responsibly," which basically meant being cooperative and nonconfrontational with the Judenrat and the Germans. Yet, as "children," they found that their militancy was not taken too seriously. In one instance Grossman tells of a meeting with a Judenrat official from whom she hoped to obtain a permit to open a public kitchen for the poor. This permit would allow Judenrat funds to flow into the movement, and the kitchen could serve as a front for clandestine activities. A good relationship with the Judenrat could also help her obtain exit permits that would allow youth-group members to leave the ghetto and make contact with other resisters. The official was a Jewish leader whose young daughter was a member of Hashomer Hatzair but who was now safely in Moscow. Despite misgivings about the militancy of Grossman's group, he agreed to fund the soup kitchen. "He was," as Grossman puts it, "not too enthusiastic about Hashomer Hatzair but he thought its members nice children who, in the course of time, would awaken from their childish dreams."[41]

Grossman portrays this struggle between generations as an ideological struggle that, by happenstance, fell along generational lines. But it is hard to untangle these issues. The idea of armed resistance was unacceptable to the Judenrat. Had the Judenrat leadership fully perceived the youth groups as communists or partisans (or both) they would have been immediately spurned and repressed. Partly because of their youth and the continuing legitimacy of their Zionist aspirations, they received limited support from the Judenrat. Youth were deemed by adult authority to be both militant and malleable. Childhood mitigated a crystallization of attitudes and opened up opportunities for action. The youth groups took themselves seriously even if, for a while, the Germans and the Judenrat did not.

The Judenrat was not alone in feeling threatened by the militancy of youth. Many Jewish families did also. Halina Birenbaum, who was ten years old in 1939 and about to enter the third grade, describes the winter of 1942–1943 following the deportation of most of the Jews from the Warsaw ghetto. Her brother was a member of Hashomer Hatzair, and there was intense conflict at home over his underground activities. "We had a typewriter at home, so I often saw Hilek using it to copy various materials for the resistance movement. My father opposed this, and kept telling Hilek that the Nazis would take us all to Auschwitz (Oswiecim) to our deaths on account of his illegal scribblings. Even before the war, my father refused to let Hilek go to meetings. He was furious when he came home late from them in the evenings. Now there was no end to the shouting and quarreling. But Hilek dismissed the pleas and demands in silence and went on with his business."[42] Birenbaum makes clear that the wedge that had been driven between parents and children even before the war was exacerbated by the occupation. Militant youth, once willing to immigrate to Zion over their parents' objections, would now resist the Germans in much the same way.

The Recruitment of Children

Most of the approximately two thousand young people who made up the ghetto fighters were already in their mid-teens or older, but some were younger. Most of the fighters were recruited from the youth groups, but others were recruited as well. Ruzka Korczak, who did much of the recruiting for the underground fighting forces in Vilna, spent considerable time contacting children on the streets of the Vilna ghetto for possible recruitment. She focused her efforts on orphans who showed a sense of defiance.[43] In some respects it was probably easier to recruit orphans because their ties to their families had already been destroyed by the war.

Despite the ideologies of the youth movements, family and community loyalties continued to hold the fighters hostage to the needs of the larger community. Ghetto youth were generally unwilling to openly engage the Germans as long as their communities or families might be killed in reprisal actions. Indeed, in no ghetto did armed resistance break out until the final liquidations of the ghetto were underway and the community was already doomed. The problem of family loyalties challenged recruitment efforts. In Vilna, for example, potential recruits were asked whether they could abandon their families and were rejected if they felt they could not.[44] Abba Kovner, one of the commanders in Vilna, made it clear how serious this question was. He turned away his mother from his bunker in Vilna because he could not let in all the mothers of members of his unit. She was ultimately captured and killed by the Germans.[45]

There are few statistical data on the age distribution of the ghetto fighters, but a wide variety of testimonial evidence points to their youth. A description of a fighting group's Passover seder in the Vilna ghetto in 1942 shows how the group had become the family. The dinner table was decorated with wildflowers smuggled in by one of the girls. The meal itself consisted only of beet salad and beet juice, and a fourteen-year-old boy, the youngest of the fighters at the table, read the four questions, the traditional ceremonial opening of the seder.[46] Shlomo Schuster, considered one of the bravest fighters in the Warsaw ghetto during the uprising of April 1943, was thirteen years old when the Germans invaded Poland and fifteen years old when he joined the Dror fighting unit in Warsaw in 1941. He was seventeen when he was killed in 1943.[47]

The question of how to handle even younger children troubled ghetto fighters. Attempts at organizing the Grodno ghetto in Belarus involved coping with the mix of children and youngsters who desperately wanted to be recruited. Despite the fact that the ghetto had fallen into the hands of the Gestapo and liquidations were being carried out, the youth groups still managed to function. The older members of the youth groups were organized into fighting groups, and they recruited some of the younger children into dangerous activities. Even the youngest children, such as those belonging to B'nai Midbar, a preteen part of Hashomer Hatzair, sometimes found a way to participate. As Grossman puts it: "The B'nai Midbar children's groups were dispersed. There was no point in maintaining any organizational contact with them. These little ones, who came knocking at the doors were sent away empty-handed; we couldn't maintain fighting units of 12 year olds. Some of them stubbornly accompanied the underground, were couriers, carried information and demanded to participate in more important activities."[48]

These words point to the moral dilemma facing the recruiters of the youngest of children. The leaders believed they were too young to be used effectively in fighting units, and they therefore rejected most of them. But information provided by couriers about mass executions of Jews throughout Poland and Eastern Europe led youth leaders to believe that the Germans were planning to exterminate all Jews. For ghetto fighters and partisans, cutting off the youngest from recruitment came with the awareness that these unarmed children would, in all probability, be murdered.

But many, if not most, youth did not join in the fighting. Janina Bauman, as a girl of seventeen, hid behind an oak cupboard with fourteen other people for four days during a forced deportation. She described the death of a young couple during the armed resistance in the Warsaw ghetto in January 1943 and the conflict it created about her decision not to join:

> At dusk when . . . we emerged from the hiding place, we learned
> that a handful of armed Jews had attacked the German troops that
> morning. . . . When I ventured out the dead bodies of a girl and boy
> were lying on the pavement just outside our gate. I felt a strange
> urge to see their faces. I could see in the faint light of the early
> sunset how young they both were. The girl's hair was spread over the
> snow, which was stained with her blood. I knew her. I knew a lot
> about her. Her name was Halinka; like myself she was a doctor's

daughter, a year my junior. In the ghetto she had attended [meetings of] a younger group of the "Bond" students. My friends, even myself, used to gossip a lot about her with confused feelings of outrage and envy; at less than fifteen she had already had a lover. This lover, a dark handsome boy of eighteen, now lay dead in the snow next to her. My heart contracted with pain. In helpless agony I cried for them and hated myself, a righteous virgin hiding like a coward while others fought and died.[49]

Sex and Sexuality

One of the main issues in the contemporary debate about child soldiers is the sexual exploitation of female child soldiers. This was a significant problem in the civil war in Sierra Leone, where the rape and abuse of young women was widespread.[50] No evidence indicates that this kind of sexual exploitation occurred among the ghetto fighters, although as I show below, some young women and girls traded sex with forest partisans for food and protection. But for the most part ideas about sex and sexuality that existed in the prewar Jewish community continued to inform sexual behavior among the fighters throughout the war.

Traditional attitudes toward sex in both the religious and the secular Jewish communities encouraged restraint but were not particularly repressive. Sexuality within the youth groups was marked by a strong sense of Puritanism coupled with a critical attitude toward conventional forms of family and marriage. The youth culture encouraged camaraderie, egalitarianism, and intimacy yet feared the disruptive effects on group cohesion of overt sexuality. At the same time, war created the possibility of shedding sexual conventions with little consequence. These views coexisted uneasily, but, on the whole, sexual relations were governed by a great deal of restraint.

Both the Zionist and the socialist movements were antibourgeois in attitude and often attracted rebellious and unconventional children and youth into their ranks. Bauman's reaction to the deaths of her young friend Halinka and her lover—both members of the Bund youth group—shows that unconventional partnerships existed. Kovner is reported to have lived together with two women for much of the war.[51] But the Zionist youth movements in particular were governed by notions of asceticism and purity that discouraged open expressions of sexuality.

In the youth movements sexual restraint played an important role in maintaining group cohesion. Social and personal relations flourished within each *ken*. Couples formed, young men and women engaged in sexual relations, but there was always a looming sense that sexual bonding between couples undermined group cohesion. In some respects it is a rather surprising story. It was wartime, and teenagers who had often separated both physically and emotionally from parents were trapped in ghettos and were preparing to engage in armed combat against insurmountable odds. Yet in seeking physical and emotional companionship with their peers these youth still found intimacy largely within the tenets of the youth movements. Simcha Rotem, a member of a Dror fighting unit in the Warsaw ghetto, described the situation as follows: "It was hard to tell who were 'couples': the leaders of the . . . movement were loyal to 'sexual purity,' and affairs were mostly platonic. Couples talked a lot, exchanged feelings, dreamed." As to relationships with his own girlfriend, Rotem went on to say: "I loved Irena with all the fire of my youth, and we spent every free minute together. . . . We spent the whole war together. Perhaps our behavior didn't always please the 'mothers and father of the movement' with whom we lived or suit their notions of sexual purity. I must admit that they really were different from us and practiced what they preached and believed."[52] Rotem was originally a member of the non-socialist Akiva youth group and seems not to have relished the disciplinary zeal of the Dror youth group in which he fought.

Another, perhaps more typical, experience was that of Folman Raban, a member of Dror and a courier in the Warsaw ghetto. She writes: "I fell in love. I found a boyfriend. . . . A young man of 21 and a girl of 16. He left his girlfriend for me, which embarrassed and flattered me at the same time. . . . We would go for walks in the moonlight. We were as close as holding hands; young people, we kissed with heat and desire. The truth is that I was looking for intimacy, real closeness with a mate, a man to whom I would belong, but was afraid of the possible consequences and didn't dare sleep with him."[53]

There are dozens of examples such as these. Plainly there was little or no sexual exploitation. Within the youth groups, sexual relations remained largely under the control of youth peers. Young women seemed, for the most part, to be in control of the degree to which they entered into romantic or sexual relations with young men. Indeed, if Rotem is correct, the older leaders, mostly young men and women in their late teens and early twenties, were even more restrained about sex than the younger fighters.

The Problem of Arms and of the Use of Violence

The most pressing problem for ghetto fighters, outside the war itself, was the shortage of weapons. Given the glut of small arms in the world today, it is hard to imagine launching a resistance movement without weapons, yet this was essentially the case in the ghettos. In the Warsaw ghetto, the Jewish Fighting Organization (JFO), led by Mordechai Anilewicz of Hashomer Hatzair, had virtually no arms when it was formed in 1942. Initially, the fighters obtained a few weapons from the Armia Ludowa, but they received their first important shipment of ten pistols from the Armia Kracowa in December 1942. Using this small supply of arms, the JFO offered the first armed resistance in the ghetto on January 18, 1943. Following this first act of the resistance, they received a shipment of fifty pistols and fifty hand grenades from the Armia Kracowa. With the liquidation of the ghetto at hand the JFO was able to arrange a larger purchase of arms, explosives, and gasoline for the manufacture of Molotov cocktails. By the end of March 1943, shortly before the final German attack, every fighter in the ghetto had one pistol with ten to fifteen rounds of ammunition, four to five hand grenades, and four to five Molotov cocktails. The few rifles were assigned to different defense areas. There was one automatic weapon, a machine pistol, in the entire ghetto.[54]

One of the main problems for the ghetto fighters was raising money for arms. In the Warsaw ghetto, the youth movements used "sniffers," or intelligence agents, to find rich Jews who were forced to make cash "donations." Other times they would break into apartments at night and "requisition" what they could. In one instance Rotem posed as a Pole and kidnapped the daughter of a rich Jew in order to extort money from her father. When her father arrived, Rotem staged a mock execution of the father, who finally agreed to "contribute" a large sum to pay for his and his daughter's release. Rotem describes these actions as "necessary." "These actions," he states, "weren't exactly my pride and joy. . . . [But] without money we couldn't prepare for the uprising, acquire weapons and support the fighters."[55]

Grossman's youth-group members raised money by making and selling forged documents to other Jews: "We sold them to people we knew well, and used a go-between to hide the sources. We were strangled then by a lack of means to maintain the movement, apparatus, and especially the purchase of arms. We decided that this dirty money, the price of the modern Jewish right to live, would be devoted to arms. Our comrades were hungry in the ghetto, frozen because we lacked clothing and wood for the stove, but we did not take one penny of this money."[56]

The young fighters felt anguish when circumstances forced them to engage in what they would have once regarded as criminal acts. Even though their behavior might have been crucial to survival, it engendered guilt and shame. The German occupation eroded the boundaries between law and lawlessness, so that although it might be thought that German violence against the Jews was "lawless," the opposite was the case. Germany used the entire force of the law to criminalize everyday life and ultimately to criminalize the very existence of Jewry. Because nothing in the law imposed by the German state or the German occupation could serve as a reference for ethical or moral behavior, there was a complete breakdown in the boundaries between law and lawlessness and a total disjuncture between law and morality. Law stood in total opposition to morality.

Under this regime every act of resistance was a criminal act punishable by death. To be Jewish was criminal per se, but even non-Jewish resisters or partisans were, in the German view, "bandits." All the media participated in painting a picture of resistance to German rule as a deviant criminal conspiracy. Jews found themselves confined to a world where they were constant prey to state-sponsored gangsterism, thuggery, and murder and were surrounded by petty criminals and thieves of every sort. It was impossible to organize even the most meager resistance to the Germans without violating the law at every turn. The testimonies of participants in the resistance make clear that the boundaries between criminal and noncriminal behavior virtually disappeared. To resist at all required descending into a world of criminal acts. Yet within this world Jewish fighters continued to strive to maintain a sense of morality and natural law so as to give collective justification and meaning to their struggle.

The Forest Partisans

Jewish partisans were only one of many groups inhabiting the forests of Eastern Europe. The forests were a hiding place and refuge for armed groups of every kind: criminal gangs, Red Army soldiers who had escaped from the Germans, the nationalist Polish Home Army, the Polish Communist People's Army, the National Armed Forces (Narodowe Sily Zbrojne, or N.S.Z., a fiercely anti-Semitic fascist group that hated Germans and Jews with equal passion), and the Polish Peasant Battalions, which were tied to the Polish Peasant Party.

Surviving in the forest required both luck and skill. Many, perhaps most, of the individual Jews who fled the ghettos for the forests died or were killed. Some, however, even young children, were recruited or found a safe haven in partisan units and began to participate in the fighting. In some circumstances groups that fled the ghetto were able to establish independent Jewish partisan units.

The size of the resistance in the forest gives some idea of its complexity. Belarus had the most partisans in Eastern Europe.[57] The Baltic states, especially in the forested areas near Vilna, and parts of western Ukraine were also major areas of partisan activity.[58] Some twenty to thirty thousand Jews were in fighting partisan units in these areas. In the thinly forested areas there were about two thousand Jewish partisans; the most famous unit was that of Yechiel Grynspan, which was based in the Parczew forest. Jews appear to have made up between 10 and 15 percent of the total number of partisans in Eastern Europe. Mass escapes of Jews into the Polish forests began in 1942. In all, more than fifty thousand Jews fled into the forest. Although the majority were killed, the survivors formed the basis of partisan resistance. The escapees came from ghettos, transports, labor camps, and some even from death camps; they were frequently the surviving members of communities that had been exterminated. Because they were escapees, they were actively hunted and had to organize and arm themselves quickly, ever mindful of a rural population that was hostile or indifferent to their fate.[59]

It is not easy to estimate how many children took refuge among partisan groups in the forest, but when the war came to an end a virtual river of children poured out of the forests of Eastern Europe, looking to rebuild their lives. Lena Kuechler, a young psychologist interviewed in 1946, described the children who came to her home for displaced children in Zakopane, Poland.

> The children whom I have collected came from various parts. A great many come from forests, mostly the older boys and girls. Older to me means fourteen . . . and fifteen year old children. The main center of the partisans was in eastern Poland. I have a boy here by the name of Nathan Schacht. . . . He fought together with the Russian partisans. He lived in the forest for two years, and he was only eleven years old. He got a horse. . . . I had several such boys who kept the bridle in their mouths, and in their hands revolvers, fighting on horseback. These boys, naturally starved the same as all the soldiers. They made raids . . . from the forest, put mines under bridges, blew up bridges. . . . Then when they knew that the army was about to pass by, they would loosen up rails, and the like. I had many such boys who had fought with the partisans.[60]

Most of the children in the partisan armies were running for their lives. One of these was Nathan Schacht, mentioned above, who fled into the forest at age eleven and joined a partisan unit. He was living with his family in Lamberg in north central Poland when they were seized by the Germans. His mother told the children to run, but only he ran away. He fled to a farm where for a brief time he hid with a local peasant. "I worked in the field," said Schacht. "I worked everywhere, whatever he asked me to do. I worked in the forest. And then [he] . . . did not want to hide me. I had nothing to give him. He wanted me to give him something for hiding me. . . . He did not want to keep me, so I left. So I ran away to the forest. I went to the partisans."[61]

He ran deeper into the forest and was found and taken in by Russian partisans: "When I came there I did not see anybody. . . . I walked toward the river, about two kilometers, I noticed a Russian partisan. I saw him. . . . He took me to the captain. . . . He introduced me. He gave me food, everything he gave me. I was there eighteen months. . . . I was then . . . eleven years old." At first Schacht was involved in expropriating food from local peasants, but he quickly began making and planting mines. "We made mines," Schacht related. "[We] put mines under trains. We put mines . . . under everything, whatever we could. The front lines were not far from the forest." Schacht's worst moments were during a German offensive on July 21, 1943. "When the Germans made an offensive, they bombed the forest terribly . . . so that the trees flew in the air. [Many] were killed. . . . I threw hand grenades. I planted mines."[62] Schacht was badly wounded; he was released from the partisan group and taken to a Russian hospital for treatment. After eight months in the hospital, he was taken to a children's home in Cracow. By April 1946 he had made his way to a home for displaced persons in Bellevue, near Paris, where at age fifteen he was awaiting transfer to Palestine.

Schacht was only one of countless young children who fled into the forest alone or with one or two companions. Michal Weilgun was forced into a ghetto and fled after his parents were taken away. He was eleven years old and wandered around in the forest, cold and hungry, until he was taken into a partisan unit in which he served until 1944.[63] Berta Bertman was ten years old when the war broke out and was forced into the ghetto in Minsk along with her family. Realizing that she would soon be killed, she broke out of the ghetto with two of her friends in 1943 and made her way to a partisan unit some sixty or seventy kilometers from Minsk.[64] Leah Rog was eleven years old when the war broke out; she and her sister escaped into the forest near her village, where they were helped by some villagers. Later, they joined a group of Jews in the forests; they managed to survive there for two years and finally joined a partisan group in 1943.[65]

These stories and others make clear that for children becoming part of a partisan fighting group was one of the main avenues to survival. But it was not simple to join a partisan group. Early on in the war partisans frequently refused to accept anyone who did not have a weapon. Those who had no arms were left to their fates. Later on in the war, as partisan armies grew and Germany's defeat was foreseeable, a growing supply of arms from the Soviet Union allowed for wider recruitment. But many partisan groups, especially

Polish and Ukrainian nationalists, were anti-Semitic. They not only did not accept Jews but frequently murdered every Jew they encountered.

Some escapees, particularly older boys and youth, organized their own partisan groups. The story of Nahum Kohen provides a typical example. When the war began, Kohen took flight from Warsaw and made his way into Soviet-occupied Poland. Once Germany declared war against the Soviet Union, he fled into the forests near Trochenbrot-Ignativa. In the forest he met a number of orphan boys from scattered villages. Together they decided to form a partisan unit. At first the group had only two rifles, but they were able to steal some from Polish forest rangers and to buy others. They finally organized a group of eighteen "boys." Although Kohen doesn't enumerate the ages of all his "boys," it is clear that many were quite young. One, Avram Druker, is described as a "broad-shoulder[ed] 16-year old." Another, identified only as "Schwartz," was also sixteen years old. These two boys were not the youngest; the youngest was often used as a scout because of his age.[66] This group fought independently; most were killed, but the rest, including Kohen, were ultimately absorbed into a larger Soviet partisan group.

As Kohen's narrative also makes clear, becoming a partisan was one of the few ways of staying alive in the forest. Kohen describes a day when his unit came across what remained of a Jewish family hiding in the woods. The family—a father, a mother, and a young boy—were living underground in a covered hole, one meter deep, that they had lined with moss. All three were naked. They had escaped a German execution squad that forced the victims to undress before killing them. Two daughters had been executed. At first, the family thought Kohen's group was going to kill them. Kohen describes their panic and how they begged and screamed for mercy and tore their hair out. Kohen's group managed to calm them down, and members of the unit gave them their own clothing to wear. The family had survived only because the father crept out each night to steal rotten food from a peasant's pigsty. He was afraid to steal clothing from the peasants for fear of revealing his family's presence. The parents begged Kohen to take their son into his unit to save his life, but the partisans could not. The boy's feet had started to rot, and he couldn't walk even with the aid of crutches.[67]

Other youngsters were part of larger mass escapes into the forest. Misha Melamed was fifteen years old when war broke out and his town of Ivye in eastern Poland (now Belarus) was invaded by Germans. He was immediately pressed into forced labor cleaning German cannons but the worst was yet to come. On May 12, 1942, all the Jews of Ivye were assembled in the town square by German SS units and Polish and Lithuanian police. Of these, some twenty-five hundred were selected out and forcibly marched out of town. In a short while those remaining in the square heard the sound of machine gun and rifle fire in the distance. An SS officer addressed them: "Jews, do not worry, your lives are spared." "For the time being," said another SS officer, "you will remain alive and you will pay for your lives by your work for the German government." Soon Melamed and some fifty young people were seized by Polish police, given shovels, and marched to the execution site, an area of deep pits about thirty-five meters long.

> When we got to the pits . . . a most horrible sight was revealed
> before our eyes—that of some 2,500 bodies partly or completely
> naked, men, women, children and the old. . . . The Polish police and
> the German gendarmes circulated among the victims and when they
> saw signs of life among some of them, they shot and killed them in
> cold blood. I recognized some of the victims, friends, neighbors and
> neighbors' children. The shock was overwhelming. We worked in a
> stupor as if under hypnosis. We worked . . . until we covered the pits
> with earth and chlorine.[68]

By the summer of 1942 rumors reached the Ivye ghetto that partisans were organizing in the forest, and an underground was set up whose leadership included Melamed's father, a physician. "The goals of the organization [were] to acquire weapons, establish contact with the partisan units and attempt to escape the ghetto to join with the partisans to fight and wreak vengeance on the Nazi enemy. The young people, including myself, enthusiastically joined this underground." On December 31, 1942, the Germans surrounded the ghetto. Fearing the worst, Melamed determined to escape. Over the next few days, under heavy snowfall, four hundred people got away. Most were young people and members of the underground, but Melamed's family was also able to escape. His father managed to bring with him clothing, food, and medications. Some of the escapees had rifles and pistols. Melamed was armed only with a kitchen knife, and his brother Efraim had only a bottle of sulfuric acid.[69]

Despite the escape, the freezing cold took its toll. "After searching for the partisans for several days and nights . . . more than half of the Jews who fled returned to the Ghetto." Not long after, Melamed and his family were able to find shelter at the home of a villager who had been his father's patient and who agreed to make contacts with a local partisan unit. A few days later five partisans from the Stalin Brigade under the command of Yasha Horoshayev came to the house. "Efraim and I immediately joined Horoshayev's company and my father was appointed the head doctor of one of the battalions of the Stalin Brigade. Efraim received a rifle immediately as he had undergone pre-army training in the Vilna Gymnasium. There was no limit to my joy when I received, after a short period of training, a rifle with fifty bullets. After physical and spiritual humiliation, after [the] beating and murdering [of] my fellow Jews, I was able to fight and take revenge. I was willing to sacrifice my life in the struggle against the Nazis. I was free, a partisan with a rifle, thrilled and ready for any battle."[70]

The partisan groups that formed in the forests were supplemented by small groups of fighters who had managed to escape the destruction of the ghettos. Jacob Celemenski, a young courier for the Bund, was outside the Warsaw ghetto during the uprising in 1943 and attempted to locate and regroup some of the surviving fighters. He and Yitzchak Zuckerman, a Dror commander, drove through the forests disguised as non-Jews, attempting to find those who had escaped. Celemenski describes his first encounter with the remnant of the ghetto fighters: "The driver stopped and we jumped out. I expected to see a comrade behind every bush, but only a few silhouettes emerged from behind the trees and approached us. Before me stood the last remnants of the ghetto heroes: as former members of our children's and youth organizations, students of secular schools and clubs they were well known to me. The young people were emaciated and dirty. We greeted each other warmly but sadly. I wept unashamedly as I saw around them the ghosts of those who had fallen behind the burning walls." The surviving fighters Celemenski found were a broken collection of children and youth. "Jurek," he tells us, "lay on the cold, wet ground covered with a military coat. He had a high temperature and complained of being cold. Next to him sat his close friend Faygele Goldsztain. A few paces away, his sister Gute Blones, also unwell, lying on the ground, was comforted by her young brother, the 13 year old Lusiek."[71]

This account and others make clear that everyone, children and adults alike, knew that other than by participating in an armed partisan group there were few ways to survive in rural Poland. The genocidal rampage of German forces, the roving bands of predatory bandits, a hostile peasantry, and armed groups of Polish and Ukrainian partisan nationalists placed everyone on the thinnest edge of existence.

The Treatment of Children in the Forests

As in the ghetto, the context of genocide meant that there was virtually no space not to be a soldier. Children may in fact have been especially vulnerable to genocide. Some 1.5 million Jewish children were killed in Europe, and as the liquidation of Jewish communities progressed, the Germans took special pains to ensure that children were killed. Many young children, at least those above the age of eleven, survived by joining partisan units. But even younger children were arriving in the forests, and, if not immediately killed by Germans and their allies, they sometimes found themselves face to face with partisan units. For most partisans, the presence of very young children was an undesirable burden. They had little inclination to absorb anyone who could not serve as a combatant in the partisan ranks, and most of these children were probably abandoned. But sometimes even very young children found their way into partisan units.

Between 1942 and 1944, Faye Schulman was a combatant and a nurse in the Molotov Brigade, a Russian partisan unit operating in eastern Poland. The brigade consisted of over two thousand people, most of whom were former Soviet prisoners of war who had escaped from German prison camps. With great difficulty she persuaded the commander of her unit to let her allow her to take care of Raika Kliger, an eight-year-old orphan girl. She reports how difficult it was to care for a child under the conditions of partisan warfare. Raika was apparently willful and caused a lot of trouble. She often crossed the guard lines while playing, creating alarm within the camp. Schulman had to fend off rumors that both she and Raika were spies, and some of the partisans apparently wanted to kill them both. The partisans, Schulman reports, were concerned mainly that the girl would be captured by the Germans and would give them vital information. One of the partisans almost shot the child in order to take a watch that she possessed, and later on, while Schulman was away on mission, Raika's coat was stolen, and the child was completely neglected by the group. When Schulman returned to camp she found Raika shivering, suffering from weight loss, and covered with lice. Later Schulman learned that Raika had an uncle in a nearby partisan unit. Although he was glad to know Raika was alive, he did not want to take her because of the conditions in his own partisan base. Nevertheless, Schulman managed to take care of Raika for over a year and was finally able to get her evacuated to Moscow. Yet there were also very young fighters in the same group. Schulman tells the story of an eighteen-year-old partisan who, dying because of a stomach wound, passed his rifle on to another Jewish boy age twelve. This boy, who had been working on kitchen detail because he did not have a weapon, was now able to join the fighting force.[72]

Harold Werner's small group of partisans initially consisted of six to eight people who fled from the Wlodawa ghetto in Poland, although later in the war they affiliated with the Armia Ludowa. Initially, the only weapons they had were a revolver and a flare gun, but they managed to purchase a sawed-off shotgun from a peasant and, thus armed, began to forcibly take arms from local villagers. Among their group was Itzik, a ten-year old orphan who came across them in the Maloska forest and who pleaded to be taken along, saying that he "would not be a bother and that he could get a gun and that he could run very fast." One woman in the group, whose entire family had been massacred, took pity on the boy, and they decided to take him with them. Itzik was treated kindly. The boy called Werner "Uncle Hershel," and the entire partisan group functioned like a small family. Itzik's entire family had been killed, and he himself had narrowly escaped death. He and his family had been detained by the Germans and shipped by train to the Sobibor death camp. En route his mother pushed him out of the moving cattle car through a small opening she had made in the side of the car. He survived the fall and made his way into the forest. Itzik described himself as a lucky boy.[73]

There was no weapon for Itzik, but after the group attacked a force of ten Germans, he obtained a rifle from one of the dead Germans. Because the rifle was so heavy, the other partisans took turns carrying it for him. When Itzik developed a foot infection that made it impossible to walk, they left him with a Polish farmer. The boy recovered but had to run away from the barn where he was kept when the Germans searched the area. He managed to hide with another peasant family and eventually was found by a small Russian partisan group, the "Shustka," which brought him back to Werner's group. Itzik was now eleven years old and carried a pistol given to him by the Shustka. Werner tells us that Itzik "had not had a haircut since we left him . . . and his hair hung down to his shoulders. He looked to be half-child and half-adult." Because the Shustka was crossing over to the Russian side of Poland's Bug River, Werner decided Itzik would be safer with better organized and more numerous partisans on the Russian side; despite Itzik's pleading Werner made him go with the Shustka.[74]

By the spring of 1944 Werner's group had grown to about four hundred partisans under the leadership of a larger Russian partisan group that crossed the Bug River to push against the German forces. Among these forces Werner once again met Itzik. A heavily armed partisan army under the command of a General Kolpak came through his area. Werner estimates that there were more than ten thousand people in Kolpak's army. Werner's description of Kolpak's partisan army suggests it consisted of children and youth: "As Kolpak's soldiers passed through the village, we saw that the force was composed of many nationalities. There were dark faces, light faces, and Asian faces, but the most noticeable thing was that they were all young faces, often in their mid- to late teens. The soldiers were dressed in all kinds of clothing, some wearing half-German uniforms and half-civilian garb." In this force Werner noticed a young boy of about thirteen riding a horse and carrying a

rifle and a pistol. It was Itzik. The boy called out "Uncle Hershel" and leapt
from his horse, and they kissed and hugged. Itzik told him that General Kolpak
was like a father to him and had made him a cavalry soldier. As he left with
his cavalry unit, Itzik told Werner that he was still a lucky person.[75]

Not everyone was lucky enough to get into Kolpak's army. The young and
healthy often struggled to find a place. When Kolpak attacked the Ukrainian
town of Skalat in 1943, the Jews of the town, all of whom were in the town's
concentration camp, believed that the hour of their salvation had arrived and
they would join Kolpak's army. The army blew up bridges, military and police buildings, freed all prisoners, and took as much stored food as they could
find. But the partisans wanted only the strong and healthy fighters and abandoned the Jewish inmates to the revenge of the Germans and Ukrainians.
Nevertheless, some thirty healthy men, women, boys, and girls followed the
partisans out of town. At first the partisans drove them off with sticks. But
persistence paid off, and after a few days they were eventually given weapons
and included among the partisan ranks. Those left behind perished.[76]

Werner's group also found other small children in the forest. They were
able to absorb these children or help them because the circumstances of partisan warfare were changing. In 1943, the Germans still controlled Poland,
but Jewish and other partisan groups were making their power felt in the
countryside. Peasants who might otherwise have routinely turned over Jewish
children to the Germans for a bounty—usually a bag of salt—now had to take
into account the existence of armed Jewish units in the countryside and the
real possibility of deadly reprisal for collaboration with the Germans. Itzik's
temporary placement with the peasant family mentioned above, for example,
was carried out under threat that Jewish partisans would retaliate if he were
not well treated. But children were sometimes discovered and killed anyway.

Older children were much more common within partisan ranks. Michael
Temchin, one of the many physicians who joined the partisans, was the chief
medical officer for the Armia Ludowa in the Lublin region of Poland. His
communist partisan unit was a mixed group of Jews and Poles, and his personal medical assistant was a thirteen-year-old girl (he does not describe her
as a "girl" but as part of a group of women whom he trained as nurses). But
her relative youth did surprise him as he states: "It was odd to see this teenager with an automatic gun on her shoulder and a bag of bandages in her hand.
She used the gun and the bandages equally well whenever the need arose."[77]

Young partisans like this girl were occasionally assigned noncombat roles,
but these appear to have been idiosyncratic decisions on the part of local
commanders. Kopel Kolpanitzky, a fifteen-year-old member of the Betar youth
movement, went into the forests following the revolt in the ghetto of Lahva,

a village in Poland (now Belarus) west of Pinsk. His brother also sought refuge in the forests but was murdered by Polish partisans because he was Jewish. In the forest Kolpanitzky tried to join a partisan group but was rejected because he had no weapon. In June 1943, he finally joined a group under a General Komerov. Komerov had been a friend of Kolpanitzky's father and may also have been the commander in control of the area where the partisan group killed Kolpanitzky's brother. In any event, possibly out of a sense of responsibility for the boy, Komerov decided not to place him in a combat position but rather in a support role. At age seventeen, Kolpanitzky joined a much larger multiethnic partisan force. Kolpanitzky, afraid that he might be rejected because of his age, lied and said he was eighteen.[78] This is the only instance I found in which an older teenage partisan felt he had to lie about his age, but perhaps when Kolpanitzky joined the partisan group, it was a well-organized partisan army under Soviet command and control.

The Brutality of Partisan Warfare

Child partisans had a quick and brutal introduction to the realities of warfare. Sixteen-year-old A. Romi Cohn made his way into a Slovak partisan unit where he was the only Jew. Born in Bratislava in 1929, he was a student in a yeshiva when the war broke out. Most of his family was murdered, and after years of hiding he escaped into the forests of Slovakia. The commander reluctantly accepted him into the unit; the commander's main concern was not Cohn's age but the need to hide Cohn's Jewish identity in the Slovak unit. The day after Cohn arrived he was given a submachine gun and sent on patrol with older partisans who trained him how to shoot. The training was strict and unforgiving, and the partisans assigned to train him were angry and impatient men. He had never handled a weapon before and was surprised at its weight, but he managed. His fellow partisans made it clear that if he were not able to keep up he would be abandoned.[79]

Cohn's introduction to partisan warfare was harsh. In his first action he helped set a trap for an unarmed peasant so as to interrogate him about German troop movements. After trapping the man, the partisans put a knife to the peasant's throat and a gun to his head and threatened to kill him and his family, including his children, if he was lying. Cohen was shaken by the cruelty of the interrogation even though the peasant was not physically harmed.[80] But Cohn makes it abundantly clear that even though he was a boy, he was expected to conform to the demands of battle.

Partisan warfare in Europe was cruel, and as a rule no quarter was given. The Germans tortured and executed all captured resisters regardless of whether they were combatants. The Germans preferred method of execution was hanging. The executions were organized as public spectacles of terror that were widely photographed. The hanging itself was really a slow and painful strangulation with no drop. One of the most infamous photographs of the Holocaust is the German execution of the young partisans Masha Bruskina (age seventeen) and Kiril Truss (age sixteen) along with Volodia Shcherbatsevich, an older partisan. All were members of the resistance in Minsk, Russia. With their hands tied, the victims were marched to a gallows set up in front of a yeast factory. Bruskina was forced to wear a sign on her chest saying: "We are partisans and have shot at German soldiers." Resisters were made to wear such signs at their executions regardless of whether they were combatants.[81]

Partisans, when they could, repaid their enemies in kind. They killed virtually every captured German soldier. German dead were the major source of supplies, and the bodies of dead Germans were stripped of anything useful: weapons, ammunition, boots, hats, and scarves. Captured Germans were interrogated and executed. Some partisan groups ceremonially stabbed captured soldiers and allowed them to die slowly and painfully. The task of carrying out the stabbing was deemed a great privilege. Cohn, who was given the "honor" of executing a German prisoner, recounts the grim details of putting the man to death. After the prisoner was interrogated, he was tied to a tree, and his blindfold was taken off. Partisan tradition, according to Cohn, dictated that his belly be slit open and he be left to die. "I looked into his eyes and he began to plead pathetically 'Please don't kill me.' He cried. Tears streamed down his cheeks. . . . Standing in front of the prisoner, I thought of my mother and my family. . . . As I pulled the knife out, I could see the faces of my mother, sisters and my brothers. All I had to do was use the knife and I would have had some measure of revenge. Looking at this whining creature though . . . I was repelled by the whole idea. I knew I could never kill this way. But even if Cohn could not bring himself to stab the man to death, his fellow partisans could. "I turned to [my friend] Franti and handed him my knife. All I could say to him was 'You can have the honor.' As I walked away screams of pain and anguish told me that Franti had accepted."[82]

This execution of prisoners took place even with regular army units. Marek, one of the young Vilna partisans, reports that at the end of the war his unit became affiliated with the Red Army, and he was given custody of a boy who was a member of the German SS. The boy pleaded for his life, and Marek, now part of a regular Red Army unit, assured him that he would be treated as a prisoner of war and not executed. The next day Marek received an order to execute him. Having spent time getting to know the boy, he could not bring himself to do it, but someone else did.[83]

Family Camps

The one major exception to the general pattern of Jewish partisan resistance was the development of so-called family camps. Most partisan units believed that their main obligation was to do battle with the Germans and their collaborators. However, a few partisan groups saw their primary obligation as the rescue of those who had fled into the forests. These partisan units created the family camps.

Family camps developed primarily in the largest and most inaccessible forests, such as the Naliboki forest of western Belarus. The most well known of these were the family camp established by Tuvia Bielsky, which sheltered about twelve hundred people, and that of Shalom Zorin, which had about eight hundred. Family camps coexisted with partisan units; in some respects they were symbiotic, and the members of family camps regarded themselves as partisans. The differences were largely a matter of emphasis. Although the prime goal of the family camp was rescue, not partisan warfare, from time to time armed members of family camps did participate in partisan warfare alongside other partisans units.

Descriptions of life in Bielsky's camp show that its social organization was different from that of most partisan units. At its core was a group of armed men and dependent women and children. Women were required take care of the children. Unlike regular Jewish partisan units, the Bielsky camp did not have women fighters. Men dominated, and prestige and status were linked to male control of arms and fighting. The social hierarchy of the family camps reversed the class order of Jewish life in Poland. Youth, strength, and practical skills were highly valued, while those with intellectual and professional skills were of little use. Virtually all the men with prestige were armed youth from the working class. Because young women attached themselves to powerful men, working-class men entered into relationships with upper- and middle-class women with whom they would never have had contact in peacetime. But these attachments were relatively stable; many of the partners survived the war and remained in long-term marriages.[84]

Attachments to men had important advantages for women. Such liaisons enhanced their personal safety and gave them increased access to food. In the Bielsky camp armed men went on food-gathering expeditions, a dangerous activity that involved expropriating food from hostile rural communities. In addition, the camp was sometimes in competition for food with fighting partisan units, both Jewish and non-Jewish. It was expected that food gathered on these expeditions would be shared with the whole community. This was a matter of principle because many of the people—the elderly and young

children in particular—were unable to help find food. And, in fact, most of
the food gathered appears to have been distributed to the whole community.
But men involved in the expeditions also set aside additional food for themselves and the women who were attached to them. These people fared better
in the family camps than others. There is no evidence that women were
coerced into sexual and domestic liaisons with armed men. In fact many
women, by choice, remained unattached. But the decision to remain unattached had clear disadvantages.[85]

Unattached women could sometimes find other means to improve their
status and access to food. Riva Kaganowicz-Bernstein, who joined the Bielsky
partisan group when she was fourteen years old, was able to obtain small
supplements of food by performing specific jobs. By volunteering for guard
duty she significantly boosted her status and access to food because a special
store of food was earmarked for those on guard.[86]

The inequality in the family camps generated some resentment. But these
fighters, unlike their urban partisan counterparts, were not ideologically committed to socialism or egalitarian relationships between men and women. In
the end, Bielsky and other leaders of family camps saved the lives of many
by making the difficult moral decision to protect and defend even those who
could not fight.

Despite the term *family camp* only between ten and thirty children were
at any time at the Bielsky camp. There was a least one four-year-old boy, but
few children were younger than ten; most were in their teens. In fact, many
of the children in the Bielsky camp could have been combatants in other
partisan units. Adolescents were mobilized into the workforce, tending cows
or serving as apprentice shoemakers and carpenters.[87] These and other tasks
grew in importance as the Bielsky camp came to serve as a support base for
fighting partisan units. Thus, some teenagers, probably the youngest, had
a more childlike status, while older teenagers had more adult duties.
Kaganowicz-Bernstein was probably in the older category. But this division
of labor was not universal. Yosef Rosin, who in 1944 spent some time as a
partisan with both the Bielsky and the Zorin camps remembers that the Zorin
camp had a group of children from age eleven through fifteen who served in
the extremely dangerous role of guides for hundreds of escapees from the
Minsk ghetto.[88]

The Bielsky camp kept the youngest children out of direct combat by
creating a life for them that was a faint echo of European childhood, even to
the extent of creating a "school" without textbooks or writing materials. In
addition, members of the camp who had lost their own children doted on
camp children.[89] Many partisans longed for a life in which their images of

childhood would once again be a possibility. Rosin reminds us of the power of this longing when he tells of his first encounter with the children of the Bielsky camp on May Day 1944: "The First of May celebration took place in [a] . . . big shed. A stage was constructed and a short show in Yiddish was performed. There were speeches in Russian and Yiddish and a choir sang. But the climax was a group of little boys and girls, who danced the popular Jewish Dance 'Sherele' to the well known melody sung by the choir. Even today it is difficult to explain the emotion I, and I believe also my friends, felt seeing a group of Jewish children singing and dancing in those horrible times. For years after this event I have had tears in my eyes when telling about it."[90]

But the lives of children in the family camps were the exception. Elsewhere children and youth were routinely found in battle. And the lives of children in family camps depended on the existence of fighting partisan units where children as young as those in the family camps fought against their enemies.

Conclusion

The participation of Jewish children and youth in warfare was driven by a combination of necessity, honor, and moral duty. Necessity was the central consideration. Jewish children and youth wanted to live, and no one could or would save them. Armed resistance offered them the slim possibility of survival in a world where the murder of Jews did not matter to anyone. But even in this terrible context children and youth also struggled to control their own identity and destiny. They took up arms as individuals, but they also fought as Jews, Zionists, socialists, and communists. If they were almost certain to die, they wanted to die under circumstances of their own choosing. They wanted to die in a way that would give meaning to their lives. As soldiers, children and youth fighters made it clear that they would be killed with impunity.

Yet necessity and honor were not enough to sustain resistance. The energy, flexibility, and brazenness of children and youth provided the means to build fluid structures of resistance that older Jews could not create. These strengths grew out of the robust youth movements, whose organization and world-view allowed children and youth to develop capabilities without the supervision of adult society. Within these movements the beliefs and ideologies of self-determination, egalitarianism, and universal justice helped sustain children and youth during the most horrible times. Likewise, the partisan units that accepted children and youth had to be willing to find a role for them under the harsh conditions of warfare. None of these strengths completely protected children and youth from the necessity of making impossible and terrible choices. Children ran away from parents who were facing certain death, chose between resistance and restraint when the lives of others were at stake, and faced down the moral authority of a frightened and oppressed adult society that labeled armed resistance dangerous and criminal. In the end these child soldiers made dignified and honorable choices, and their lives serve as a reminder of the remarkable capability of children and youth to shape their own destinies.

Chapter 3   Fighting for Diamonds

The Child Soldiers
of Sierra Leone

W̲HEN HE WAS EIGHT, Tamba Fangeigh was kidnapped in Kono District in eastern Sierra Leone by soldiers of the Revolutionary United Front (RUF), the rebel army in the civil war (1991–2001), and was placed in the so-called Small Boys Unit of the rebel fighters. The joy he took in the killing of local militia and civilians is chilling: "We came, we surrounded them and cut some of them, killed them, put tires over them and burned them. . . . I killed some, put tires on them, beat them, including the civilians who were with them. We took some of their properties and after that we went to Magburaka. We were shooting, advancing. We were shouting, we were happy, we were clapping."[1]

Abbas, a young student at Saint Francis Primary School in Freetown, describes his own contribution to the terror: "When we caught *kamajors* [progovernment militia], we would mutilate them by parts and display them in the streets. When villagers refused to clear out of an area, we would strip them naked and burn them to death. Sometimes we used plastic and sometimes a tire. . . . I saw a pregnant woman split open to see what the baby's sex was. . . . Two officers, '05' and 'Savage,' argued over it and made a bet. Savage's boys opened the woman. It was a girl."[2]

In the early 1970s, I lived in Kono District, the center of Sierra Leone's diamond-mining industry. I was doing research as a graduate student in anthropology in Njaiama, the capital of Nimi Koro Chiefdom. During the war, this town was heavily attacked. Between 150 and 600 people were murdered or were reported massacred in and near Njaiama by the end of August 1995.

In writing this book, I made and renewed ties with many Sierra Leoneans. I still do not know what became of most of the people I knew in Njaiama. No doubt some were killed, many fled, and others have been able to return home to resume some semblance of their former lives.

I lived in Njaiama during a tense time in Sierra Leone history. Siaka Stevens, the president of Sierra Leone, striving to create a dictatorship, had declared a national state of emergency. Youth thugs of the president's All People's Congress roamed Kono District and the Mende chiefdoms to the south, harassing and murdering political opponents. Illegal diamond mining and banditry were endemic. People were fearful. Accusations of witchcraft against women, combined with rumors that "big men"(politically and economically powerful adults) were involved in ritual cannibalism, added to the general apprehension. My friends in Freetown sometimes asked how I could do fieldwork in a region renowned for political violence. But with one exception real violence passed me by. I had no idea that I was witnessing the prelude to a terrible civil war.

Today, the ten-year civil war in Sierra Leone is a symbol of the horrors of modern war. The bloody and notorious role of child soldiers in the rural and urban killing fields is emblematic of the brutal character of the war. Armed children and youth spread unspeakable fear throughout Sierra Leone. They were responsible for thousands of murders, mutilations, and rapes, and for torture, forced labor, and sexual slavery. The war has become the prime example of the "new barbarism," a terrifying kind of warfare predicted to be the signature style of modern conflict.[3]

Why were children and youth recruited into armed forces and armed groups in Sierra Leone? How did they become involved in the appalling atrocities committed during the war? The exploitation of children in this war, especially those in rebel ranks, was part of the wide-scale abuse and destruction of the population as a whole. The maltreatment of children and youth was only part of a sweeping pattern of misuse and cruelty that characterized the rebel movement throughout the war. To begin to understand, perspectives must shift from the old model—which assumes that war and peace are antitheses—to a new one that sees both peace and war as alternating expressions of the same social and political order. Put simply, the violence of peace spawns the violence of war.

The war in Sierra Leone illustrates the extraordinary difficulty of separating peacetime from wartime because the manner in which children and youth were drawn into warfare grew directly from Sierra Leone's particular history and culture. Far from being an aberration, the war in Sierra Leone demonstrated Karl von Clausewitz's celebrated dictum that war is politics by other means. The seeds of civil war were sown in the prewar peacetime politics that mobilized large numbers of children and youth in the years following Sierra Leone's independence in 1961 and turned them into political thugs. Youth violence was encoded into the normative structure of everyday political competition in Sierra Leone. Its legitimization opened the door to unrestrained bloodshed.

Youth thuggery in peacetime Sierra Leone derived from Sierra Leone's patrimonial political system, in which adults, children, and youth depended for their livelihoods and social standing on the big men. In this system children and youth, like adults, provided services in exchange for economic support. Young men provided the big men with the physical strength, energy, and fearlessness needed to intimidate and murder political rivals.[4] In the despoiled circumstances of Sierra Leone's economy, the ties of dependence and violence among big men, young men, children, and youth rippled through rural and urban communities, disrupting and distorting ties of family and kinship.

At a more fundamental level, the war recapitulated in modern form some of the worst excesses of precolonial and colonial slavery, which transformed Sierra Leonean men, women, children, and youth into forced laborers, sexual slaves, and slave soldiers. The history of slavery in Sierra Leone, with the exploitation of youth and youth labor as its primary objective, became a template for the brutality of wartime oppression. In wartime, the extreme forms of dependence and violent control of children and youth that existed in peacetime often devolved into this brutally modern form of slavery. Nowhere was this more apparent than in the RUF strongholds like the diamond fields of Tongo in southeastern Sierra Leone and in the Kono diamond-mining district of eastern Sierra Leone. Male captives, including children and youth, were enslaved as soldiers and diamond miners, and female captives were forced into sexual slavery and domestic service.

Orlando Patterson reminds us that the principal mark of the slave is not that he or she is treated as human property or is physically abused but rather the "social death" of the slave as a person.[5] Every slave is torn out of his or her community and culture, and family ties are thus destroyed. In Sierra Leone, the kidnapping of children and youth, the permanent tattooing of child soldiers with the mark of the RUF, the reports of gruesome rites in which children were forced to publicly murder family and community members to ensure their alienation from them show the trademark violence of a slave regime. Even now, in the postwar period, hundreds, perhaps thousands, of children and youth who once served in rebel armies continue to work as slaves or near-slaves in the diamond fields of eastern Sierra Leone.

Paradoxically, the rebellion sometimes afforded children and youth a kind of terrifying freedom of action, with the RUF goading them into devastating the country and its peoples with little restraint. But the children and youth who entered this moral vacuum were free of the constraints of custom and law only as long as they complied with the dictates of the rebel forces, who punished or killed those who failed to conform. Many youth were little more than slave soldiers, abducted and forced into rebel ranks; they were abused, exploited, and murdered just as they abused, exploited, and murdered others. Sixteen-year-old Ibrahim Barry Junior, also known as General Share Blood, makes this point with absolute clarity in describing how he used terror to rule the Zebra Battalion of the Small Boys Unit of the RUF:

> My men knew I had to drink human blood every morning. If we had a prisoner, I would kill him myself. I would cut off his head with a machete. Otherwise I would send my boys out to find a prisoner or capture a civilian. . . . I had a wife, named Sia Musi; her [other] name was Queen Cut Hands because her specialty was cutting the arms and hands off prisoners. She was our queen. . . . Queen Cut Hands died in battle last year[;] . . . that night I killed three of my boys to punish them. They should have died instead of Sia Musi. . . . [Also] if one of the boys committed a crime, if he refused to obey an order, I would put burning leaf on his eyes. It would blind him. And if one of my boys tried to escape and was caught, my fighters would murder him themselves, because they knew it would even worse if they brought him to me.[6]

The RUF became infamous for maiming and killing by chopping off the arms, breasts, hands, legs, tongues, and heads of their victims, and it was responsible for the deaths of untold thousands of innocent people. Initially a radical student movement, the RUF evolved into one of the worst agents of terror in contemporary Africa. The RUF has been especially reviled in international human rights circles for its forced recruitment of children as combatants, use of forced labor, and the sexual exploitation of children.[7] Without doubt, the RUF and its allies were responsible for most of the human rights abuses during the war.

A shorthand key to the carnage can be found in the nicknames, or "bush names," the self-styled noms de guerre of the RUF fighters: Black Jesus, Captain Backblast, Body Naked, Blood, Colonel Bloodshed, Commando around the World, Commander Blood, General Share Blood, General Bloodshed, God Father, Commander Bullet, Captain Cut Hands, Queen Cut Hands, Captain Bonus, Dry Gin, Mohammed Killer Boy, Major Cut Throat, Mr. Die,

Nasty, Pepper, Rebel Baby, Sgt. Burn House, Superman. Members of other fighting groups such as the West Side Boys, usually regarded as a gang of criminals and bandits recruited from other armed forces, had names such as Colonel Cambodia, Brigadier Bomb Blast, and Mohammed Kill Man without No Law. RUF leaders dubbed the rebel invasion of Freetown in 1999 "Operation No Living Thing," and the systematic mining and looting of the diamond fields of eastern Sierra Leone, "Operation Pay Yourself." Like many perpetrators of terror, the RUF also photographed its atrocities, proudly displaying the severed heads and arms of its civilian victims for the camera.[8] The names of the RUF fighters are more suggestive of bandits and pirates than of soldiers, and they reflect the fact that this was a war virtually without ideology. It was not separatist, reformist, radical, or even a warlord insurgency. In the end, it had the support neither of the peasantry nor even of the students among whom it originated.[9]

Once war broke out, the factors that drew children and youth into combat became even more complex. The violence seeped so deeply into society that the old anarchist antiwar adage—"You may not need war but war needs you"—certainly applied to Sierra Leone. Some children and youth were bored and attracted to violence. Others felt safer as fighters and armed soldiers than as defenseless civilians. Some came for economic reasons, others because they wanted to defend their homes and villages against rebel actions or to exact revenge for the killing of family members. Many joined local militias as volunteers and fought with the support of their kin and community. Some found freedom in the anarchy of war and the suspension of the rules of civilian life, while others were simply abducted and forced into armed service. No single common social denominator or personal motive links all the children who were in combat. The participation of child combatants cuts across the entire armed struggle in Sierra Leone and cannot, in itself, serve as a simple yardstick for distinguishing good from evil. What sets Sierra Leone apart from many other recent wars in Africa is, according to the U.S. Agency for International Development mission there, the difficulty of distinguishing perpetrators from victims.[10]

No reliable data exist on the numbers and ages of the child soldiers who fought in the civil war. Although very young soldiers are said to have served, many appear to have been teenagers between the ages of sixteen and eighteen. Most estimates are that at any time during the war some five thousand children were serving as soldiers, fighting on all sides of the war. In February 2002 the Sierra Leone government reported that a total of 45,844 ex-combatants had been demobilized since July 1999, including 5,596 child soldiers.[11] Some argue that there were more child soldiers in the rebel ranks than in government armies and militias.[12] By some estimates half of all RUF combatants were between eight and fourteen years of age.[13]

Why did all parties to the conflict make use of child soldiers in combat? First, in some respects, it would be far more surprising if child soldiers had not been widely involved in the war in Sierra Leone. Certainly, the presence of child combatants in the fifteen- to eighteen-year-old range represents no seismic shift in the involvement of children in warfare in Africa or elsewhere. Youthful soldiers or warriors were present in many precolonial African societies and were part of the military in virtually every anticolonial war of liberation on the African continent from the Mau Mau rebellion in Kenya through the struggles of FRELIMO against the Portuguese in Mozambique.

Second, whereas Western countries have increasingly large numbers of the elderly, a large proportion of the African population is young, and they now constitute the majority of the population. Fully 55 percent of the total population are nineteen years old or younger. In the United States, this same age group constitutes only 28 percent of the population.[14]

Third, the social and cultural boundaries between childhood and adulthood are quite different in Sierra Leone than in contemporary Western society. In Sierra Leone's subsistence, market, and service economies, children constitute a large part of the labor force. Large numbers of children and youth live and work in ways that in the Western world are the exclusive domain of adults. Moreover, a great many of Sierra Leone's children reside in Freetown or in smaller urbanized cities and rural towns, where poverty, unemployment, and poor education have created massive discontent among children and youth. With children thus marginalized, the boundaries between childhood, adolescence, and adulthood have been systematically eroded.[15] Although humanitarian groups often proclaim that the war "robbed" children of their childhood, the biggest thefts took place during peacetime. In any event, the allegedly purloined childhood of young Sierra Leoneans should not be confused with childhood as it is understood in middle-class London, Paris, or New York.

All these factors—demography, the culturally diverse configurations of childhood and adulthood, the erasure and redrawing of the social and cultural boundaries of childhood and adulthood during peacetime—help explain why children and youth throughout Africa have been thrust into the public space in ways that disturb and threaten panicked elites.[16] But these general factors alone do not fully account for the specific ways in which children and youth were drawn into conflict. At least part of the explanation lies in the special circumstances of Sierra Leone, where for centuries children were exploited in the slave trade, which in its domestic version lasted until 1929. Additional understanding comes from examining the contemporary political processes that mobilized children and youth for political violence and military action.

Slavery and Premodern Warfare in Sierra Leone

Warfare and terror in Sierra Leone have deep historical roots. In her *Memories of the Slave Trade* Rosalind Shaw describes how premodern Sierra Leone was dominated by the terrors of the Atlantic slave trade. By the eighteenth century up to two hundred slaves a day were being dispatched from Sierra Leone. The provision of people for the slave trade was inseparable from warfare. The quest for slaves brought the small chiefdoms in the interior into a state of continuing warfare, as they sought to capture slaves for both the Atlantic and the domestic trade.[17] Local peoples were both perpetrators and victims in a system that created anarchy and dislocation throughout Sierra Leone.[18] Less well-remembered is the fact that although the British began to outlaw and suppress the Atlantic slave trade in the early part of the nineteenth century, slavery was permitted to continue within rural Sierra Leone until 1929. Thus slavery and the warfare associated with slavery are not simply a dim historical memory but a system of practices that endured well into the modern era. As Shaw puts it, in Sierra Leone, "terror had become a taken for granted aspect of the environment in which people's lives unfolded."[19]

While the Atlantic slave trade flourished, most of the slaves traded to the Americas were men. In contrast, women and children primarily fed the domestic slave trade. For women, slavery usually meant a life of agricultural labor as a wife who was also a slave. With the decline of the Atlantic slave trade, slaves were taken up as agricultural laborers and as fighters in trade wars in the Sierra Leone hinterland. If Shaw's account of slave wives and slave soldiers disturbingly resembles the exploitation of men, women, and children during the civil war in Sierra Leone, it is her intention. That a young Sierra Leonean soldier in 1992 was able to treat his wife in much the same manner as if she had been a nineteenth-century slave, kidnapped and stripped of virtually all the protections of community and kinship, drives home Shaw's point about the long-term continuity of the predatory economy and society.[20] For Shaw, the exploitation, kidnapping, and murder that underlay the slave trade became inscribed into the cultural patterns and practices of life in Sierra Leone.

Kenneth Little's classic ethnography, *The Mende of Sierra Leone*, also shows that children were routinely used in combat. The Mende, one of the most important ethnic groups in Sierra Leone, used a predatory style of warfare designed for plunder and slave taking rather than for territorial expansion. Mende towns were stockaded fortresses encircled by concentric rings of war fencing. Warfare was pervasive; fences were stormed, and fighting was usually hand-to-hand combat using swords and spears. Mende leaders gave strong palm wine to their leading warriors to bolster their courage. Captured women and young children became valuable slave labor, important in the expansion of the rice economy. No quarter was given to males; the victors—dancing around the town—led the male captives outside and stabbed them to death. The wholesale slaughter of male captives suggests the pattern of Mende warfare following the end of the Atlantic slave trade. At that time, women and children were still being taken into slavery, while male captives, who could no longer be sold off to the Americas, were of no value.[21]

Although Little does not provide specific information about chronological age, it is clear that men, youth, and boys physically able to fight constituted the Mende fighting forces. Mende boys made the simultaneous transition into both manhood and warrior status when, at puberty, they were initiated into the Mende male secret association, the Poro. Boys emerged from the Poro initiations as warriors. The youngest recruits, or "war sparrows," served as bearers but also fought when called on. Although the Mende did not reckon age with precision, the youngest warriors were in their early teenage years. The West today regards such young people as boys or children, but the Mende saw them as young adults with the rights and duties of adulthood.

The organization of nineteenth-century Mende warfare was typical throughout much of the forested area of Sierra Leone. Similar patterns appeared among the Kono and other Mende neighbors.[22] Few, if any, Western ideas about the rules of war applied. Women and young children were not direct combatants not because they had a protected status as civilians but because they were to be reduced to slavery. Adult male prisoners and captives were executed as a matter of course, and drugs—in this case alcohol—were used to bolster a warrior's courage. Combatants were primarily male, from young boys to adults. Although the modern use of child soldiers in Sierra Leone is not merely a projection of nineteenth-century warfare into the present period, the historic link between warfare and human exploitation makes it clear that the involvement of children in war is not simply a modern-day abhorrence.

The Origins of Youth Violence

Children and youth have played an important but often hidden role in Sierra Leone's political development over the last century with the rise of urban youth culture, the role of youth in secret associations, and the eventual spread of urban youth culture to the diamond-mining areas of eastern Sierra Leone. All these developments contributed to increasing violence among youth.

URBAN YOUTH CULTURE

Freetown, the capital of Sierra Leone, was founded in 1792. Its earliest settlers were liberated Africans from England, Jamaica, and Nova Scotia, as well as Maroons who had taken part in the rebellion in Jamaica. This nonnative population formed the core of Freetown's residents, but as the principal city of the Colony and Protectorate of Sierra Leone Freetown also attracted migrants from the hinterland. By the end of the nineteenth century, Freetown was a sharply stratified, multicultural city. A small number of British colonists controlled most of the significant positions in government and commerce; next were the Creoles, or Krio, largely the descendants of liberated Africans, whose unique culture and society encouraged the formation of a strong professional class of lawyers, physicians, and clergy that controlled most of the administrative positions in government. The elite of Freetown dubbed it the "Athens of Africa." Like Athens of old, it was built on an underclass— in this case, one composed largely of poor and young African immigrants from the hinterland along with a significant number of the less successful descendants of early settlers.

The poorest and youngest segments of this society developed their own youth culture beginning in the early part of the twentieth century. Organized youth gangs such as Arms Akimbo, Foot-A Backers, and A-Burn-Am (led by a Generalissimo Yonkon) were present in Freetown by 1917.[23] A young working-class culture emerged with a pool of young people who worked alongside adults as domestic servants, drivers, dockworkers, hawkers, laborers, night watchmen, peddlers, petty criminals, pimps, and shoeshine boys, along with school dropouts and the unemployed. Alienated and hostile toward traditional and governmental authority, they were apolitical, antisocial, and violent, and they lived at the margins of society.[24] These youth, and the organizations they created, became a platform from which political violence was launched.

Freetown grew steadily in the early twentieth century. Like many cities in West Africa, it experienced exponential growth following the end of World War II as migrants came hoping for economic prosperity and anticipating political independence from Britain. The influx of migrants coupled with growing social-class stratification gradually turned youth into independent social actors who were less subordinate to adult authority than they had previously been. Youth and youth organizations, although not necessarily identified as such, were central to the social and political life of urban Freetown.

In the first systematic anthropological study of Freetown, conducted in the 1950s, Michael Banton noted the importance of youth associations among literate migrants from rural Sierra Leone who were excluded from urban Creole social institutions.[25] Banton's study shows that among the Temne (one of the main ethnic group in Sierra Leone and the focus of Banton's study) youth groups such as Boys London and Ambas Geda provided a social venue for these migrants. These new groups created a crisis in political authority as young people, who regarded themselves as a modernizing force and whose levels of literacy set them apart from their elders, evaded or rejected the authority of the chiefs. These young people also came into conflict with colonial authority as they encountered the inequities of modern forms of stratification. Ethnically based, and hardly radical, these youth associations concerned themselves with policing the morality of their members; they gave financial help to those who had minor scrapes with the law but expelled those who had multiple offenses or a felony conviction. Banton saw Freetown as an ethnic mosaic of transformed tribal groups and religious associations. He paid scant attention to African organizational groupings that cut across ethnic groups and boundaries. Not surprisingly, in the wake of the strikes and riots in Freetown in 1955 he claimed "everyone's ignorance of the laboring classes in Freetown was revealed by the outbreak of rioting . . . which caught the government by surprise."[26]

Even more surprising is his silence regarding Freetown's long history of labor strife and the militant organization of labor. In truth, prior to World War II, youth played a pivotal role in the West African Youth League, a Marxist organization with extensive support as a multiethnic, anticolonialist, nationalist movement. In the late 1930s, the Youth League held mass meetings, formed trade unions, published a newspaper, contested elections, and was open to all sections of the working class in Sierra Leone.[27]

The Youth League was founded by I.T.A. Wallace-Johnson, a Krio who was born in Sierra Leone but who emerged as a youth leader and critic of colonialism when he moved to Ghana (then the Gold Coast) and Nigeria. Wallace-Johnson was a Marxist trade unionist who had studied in Moscow.[28] He started a chapter of the Youth League in Nigeria, but in 1938 the colonial administration charged him with sedition and deported him to Sierra Leone. The Youth League attracted teachers, clerks, workers, the self-employed, and the unemployed with its message of socialism and its tactics of mass mobilization.[29] With a strong teenage following the League made rapid electoral gains in the Freetown city-council elections of 1938; this success put Wallace-Johnson on a collision course with the colonial government and the affluent ruling sectors of the Krio community.[30] The electoral victory of youth representatives from the lower and working classes overwhelmed the Krio elite, led by Dr. Herbert Christian Bankole Bright (dubbed "Banky" in the street). The youth victors passed out mock obituary notices of Krio domination that proclaimed the victory of youth over the Krio "Uncle Toms" and that included the following poem, sung to the tune of "Pussy in the Well."

Ding Dung Dell
Banky's in the well
Who put him in?
A little youth in teen
Who'll put him out?
No! never to be out.
Oh what a jolly sight for Youth to see
Big Banky in the Well.
OKAY[31]

Wallace-Johnson's nationalist movement believed in and built on the power of youth. It wanted the radical leadership of youth to transform Sierra Leone. But the Youth League's electoral successes were short-lived. Wallace-Johnson was branded an "evil-doer" by the established press. The Krio community and the colonial government actively sought to suppress the Youth League and rid Sierra Leone of its leader via a deportation bill specifically directed at Wallace-Johnson. Fearing that no jury would ever convict Wallace-Johnson, they championed draconian legislative bills that curtailed freedom of the press and ended trial by jury in Sierra Leone. At first, Wallace-Johnson was detained under emergency wartime regulations, but in the end he was convicted of criminal libel (without a jury), imprisoned, freed, and later incarcerated again by the colonial government. The outbreak of World War II and the sense of emergency it created legitimized the suppression of the West African Youth League. But the despotic use of law to suppress democracy and dissent was astonishing even by colonial standards. As a result, Sierra Leone may be the only country in Africa where World War II effectively stalemated the development of African anticolonial nationalism.[32]

The West African Youth League, effectively died with the internment of Wallace-Johnson. The League was the first major democratic challenge to colonial power. An entrenched elite that used law to criminalize political opposition crushed it. The dictatorial and suppressive manipulation of law and legislative processes by a colonial regime purportedly preparing Sierra Leoneans for democracy became a template for the use of law as a cudgel to bash all opposition to entrenched power. The emergence of the West African Youth League was part of a larger story of the mobilization of youth in Sierra

Leone. The suppression of the League made it plain to urban youth that democratic electoral politics was the exclusive province of the elite and that the political mobilization of youth would be suppressed.

YOUTH AND SECRET ASSOCIATIONS

Secret associations hold a prominent place in Sierra Leonean politics and youth culture. The political life of many societies in the forested areas of West Africa's Upper Guinea Coast was dominated by such associations, which usually serve as an adjunct to established power and lend a sacred dimension to political violence. But, at times, secret associations also served as a basis from which to challenge political power. The existence of secret associations and the violent history of the region are intimately linked. The Poro, which held a central place in the government of many rural and traditional societies of Sierra Leone, is widely credited with having organized armed resistance to the British from the late nineteenth century through much of the colonial period.[33] The Poro also played an important role in the political socialization of youth by fusing sacred and secular power and orchestrating the rites of passage through which boys were socially and culturally transformed into men. In more recent years, many urban youth organizations borrowed the symbolism and cultural trappings of secret associations. During the civil war, secret associations were a means of organizing youth for combat.

The Poro was part of a dual system of political power. Formal political power was centralized in the largely secular office of the chief (or the paramount chief, as some of them were called under colonial rule). The Poro, in contrast, was charged with maintaining the social order through control over the sacred. But because the chiefs and other secular leaders were usually high-ranking members of the Poro, it is wiser to think of the Poro as a sacred and secret dimension of political power than as a separate and discrete political institution. Although the exact role of the Poro has never been fully delineated, the sacred power exercised by the Poro often involved terror and violence.[34] The sacred power of the Poro (sometimes referred to as its "medicine") was symbolized by a spirit, a masked figure often termed the *Gbeni* among the Kono and Mende.[35] *Gbeni* is usually translated as "devil" in English or "debel" in the Krio language. These terms describe both the masked spirits and the power they embody.

Secret associations did not disappear from the political and social life in Sierra Leone with urbanization and modernization but flourished in an attenuated and modified form. A host of secret associations exist throughout Sierra Leone, each of which has its own "debel." In Freetown, for example, a secret society of civil servants called the Hunters Societies emerged among the middle-class Krio and served to defend Krio status and privilege. By the 1970s, the function of the Hunters was fulfilled by various Masonic orders that took on a distinctively Sierra Leonean structure and tone.[36] These largely middle-class associations occupied a bounded and segregated cultural and social space that offered little room for poor and working class youth.

For these youngsters, the main secret associations were the *odelays*, sometimes known as "devil societies"; *odelay* refers to both the organized masquerading that these associations did as well as to the groups themselves. By the early 1960s there were more than sixty of these associations in Freetown, all founded by boys between the ages of ten and seventeen.[37] These associations were quite different from their rural or urban middle-class counterparts. First, they were competitive and aggressive, operating at times like inner-city gangs. Second, they were less segregated by gender than their rural counterparts, so girls could participate with boys in the same societies, sometimes as members and sometimes as followers.[38] Third, membership was flexible, and young people could belong to more than one society, a fact that apparently reduced fighting between societies. Finally, and perhaps most important, the youth secret associations were composed almost entirely of young people. Unlike the Poro and other secret associations of rural Sierra Leone, whose initiates were politically and ritually subordinate to adult authority, a hierarchy of peers governed the *odelays*.

Because these secret associations were composed mainly of youngsters, they had little political power. They generally functioned as gathering places where young people cooked, ate, drank beer and distilled palm wine, and prepared for special events in which each society's elaborately dressed "devil" paraded down the streets of Freetown accompanied by dancing and singing. Major parades were held on Christmas, Easter, and Whitsuntide (the seventh Sunday after Easter, commemorating Pentecost). By the late 1970s parades were held during Eid Ul-Adha, the Islamic holiday celebrating the sacrifice of Ishmael by Ibrahim.[39] Parades promised excitement, which took the form of organized fighting among different youth groups that battled each other and sometimes the police with a variety of weapons, including bottles, knives, whips, battery acid, daggers, and swords. Once fighting erupted, the elaborately dressed devils often withdrew and were replaced by more utilitarian devils with simple dress and sharp axes.[40]

Organized violence thus became a major factor in the lives of urban youth. Locally known as *rarray* boys, they prized skill and courage, and good fighters were highly esteemed. Indeed, a prime role of youth leaders was to organize fighting. The initiation ceremony for new members lasted two to three days and stressed endurance to pain. Boys were beaten, kicked, cut with glass and razor blades, and sometimes hung from a tree or above a fire. Boys who were especially good fighters paid reduced membership dues.[41]

In the last decades of the twentieth century the *odelays* became even more violent and political. As the economy weakened, *odelays* became a magnet for alienated and displaced youth, including high school students, dropouts, and youngsters from the working class.[42] Self-styled student revolutionaries from Fourah Bay College joined the mix, bringing about a confluence of violence and politics. The *odelays* became more deeply criminalized, internationalized, and characterized by greater intergenerational authority and hierarchy.[43] *Odelay* masqueraders began to dress in military garb and carried real or carved guns. The members of one *odelay*, Education, carried knives in textbooks while masquerading.[44] More contemporary portraits of urban youth associations are strikingly Dickensian: highly authoritarian and Fagan-like big men (*agbahs*) in their later twenties and early thirties and somewhat younger big brothers (*bras*) control groups of young boys and provide them with food, money, protection, and shelter in exchange for stealing and pimping.[45] Their activities became so tied to prostitution and drug use that the basic relationship between boys and girls was often one of pimp to prostitute. But some *odelays* had important female officials called mammy queens, who during the civil war were some of the most violent and powerful female combatants. The tropes of secrecy and violence that knit together the lives of poor urban youth via these secret associations often became the basis from which they challenged power and authority.[46] Many joined illegal mining operations and became miners or soldiers or both.

It was not only the urban secret associations that expressed the discontent of youth. During the time I lived in the Kono diamond-mining district in the 1970s I found that Poro ceremonies inadvertently amplified the widespread sense of economic despair in the diamond areas. For Kono youth, the diamond resources that later allowed the rebel forces to underwrite their rebellion were a mixed blessing. The iron law of natural-resource expropriation in Sierra Leone meant that all Sierra Leonean governments (colonial and postcolonial) walked away with most of Kono's diamond wealth, leaving local people mired in poverty. Sentiments surrounding Poro initiation rites reflected the frustration of rural youth who faced an uncertain future. As in the past, Kono teenagers were initiated into the Poro in a highly orchestrated ceremonial rite of passage conducted in a sacred forest grove. Traditionally these ceremonies took place over a period of weeks or even months. By the early 1970s these rites were diluted and adjusted to meet school and work schedules, and the rites hardly provided (if they ever did) a seamless transition from childhood to adulthood. Kono children, living in a world of diamond mining, smuggling, and broken dreams, faced a future with few real opportunities. If anything, the ceremonial transition from childhood to adulthood underscored the sense that the road to adulthood was a perilous journey filled with insecurity and disappointment.

A Kono schoolboy, Aiah Baiama, told me:

> When I was young, before I went into the [Poro] association, everyone told me of all the beautiful buildings that were in the [initiation] grove. You know, I asked many questions when I was a child, and my brothers, they would lie to me about the Poro. I often asked them why it was that when they emerged from the Poro they looked so fat and manlike. They would tell me about all the beautiful buildings that were in the grove which were small in size so that they could not be seen from the outside. They told me of white women who feed people. They said there was a white woman in each of those buildings, and because she fed them white man's food they became fat. They said that those women would take out my heart and cook it and give me the heart of a man.[47]

"But of course," said Aiah, "it wasn't like that at all." Aiah emerged from the Poro grove with the full realization that it was not a secret magical place where all the riches of the world could be found. No white woman transformed his life and turned him into a well-fed and courageous man. Instead, he emerged with a greater sense of the realities of life in the diamond region. Like all young men in the region, whether they graduated from school or dropped out early, he faced a life of grappling with joblessness and poverty.

By the early 1970s, a sense of economic despair had seeped into Kono society, soiling the most sacred precincts. The notion that a magical white woman would provide sustenance and ritually transform scrawny boys into healthy men reflected the extensive pessimism of youth about their fellow Sierra Leoneans. Aiah's story is a childhood story, but it was told at a time in which personal success and failure were attributed to malevolent forces, especially the powers of witchcraft. These stories often contrasted the supposed behavior of Europeans and whites with that of Africans and Sierra Leoneans. The material success of whites was attributed to the willingness of white witches to produce a material world of abundance for all, while the failures of Sierra Leone were attributed to the personal malevolence of Sierra Leoneans. Unlike the white witches, whose magic was said to serve the public good, the witches of Sierra Leone were deemed to have accumulated their wealth in secret and kept it hidden. They harmed and exploited one another and ruined and destroyed their neighbors. "In the world of the witches," a youngster told me, "there is everything: airplanes, cars, cement houses, diamonds, and other riches. There is everything you white people have in your place. You see these witches here. They are just as powerful as your white witches are, and they can make anything by virtue of their power that can be made in your world. But they are selfish and evil and keep it all for themselves and hate others for their success."

The idea of secrecy and secret associations is so deeply embedded in Sierra Leone society that it became a template for action by all parties to the conflict. In response to RUF attacks on defenceless rural communities, the government encouraged the formation of "community vigilance units," some of which grew out of the secret associations such as the Poro and hunting societies. Poro authority was crucial because of the breakdown of other forms of civil authority and protection. Rashid Peters, a former Mende child soldier, reports that he was recruited at twelve to join the Mende Civilian Defense Forces, the Kamajors. Peters recalls, "We were in support of the government, the people, and the local community. The government recruited us to flush out the rebel enemies. We young local hunters were called *kamajors*. We became spies for our people and took the risk of getting secrets on the enemy side. Our leaders told us that we should fight for our land and freedom. They told us the secrets of the village during our conscription in the thicket of the bush. We were told that these secrets must be kept strictly if we wanted to avoid the enemy's bullets when they attacked."[48]

The RUF also made use of Poro or Poro-like rituals. RUF recruits were often sworn to secrecy and took oaths of loyalty, the violation of which was said to result in the magical death of the violator. Some assert that during the wars in Liberia and Sierra Leone, the role of the Poro was "bastardised."[49] The U.S. State Department cited unconfirmed reports that in March 2001 RUF fighters forcibly conscripted civilians into the Poro.[50] Similarly, a report of the European Commission claims that the RUF's use of the Poro was a way of manipulating the cultural "infrastructure" of rural life in Sierra Leone. Arguing that the Poro is the "main idiom of transition from childhood to adulthood in forest society," the report interprets the use of the Poro by the RUF as a way of abusing a traditional sacred rite to convert children to a radically new way of life.[51] This perspective promotes a Pollyannaish view of the premodern Poro, mischaracterizing it as a benign institution of adolescent enculturation and socialization. In fact, it always was a political force that employed sacred terror. Not surprisingly, many fighting groups seized on these powerful symbols as a means to organize and control youth.

THE NATIONALIZATION OF YOUTH CULTURE

By the late 1960s and 1970s, youth discontent, inflamed by extreme economic inequality, was evident throughout Sierra Leone. The urbanization of the countryside was accompanied by the spread of youth violence, which fanned out from Freetown to the diamond-mining areas of eastern Sierra Leone. Here, only a decade after independence, a small and wealthy European, Lebanese, and Sierra Leonean elite had created an affluent enclave where young and ambitious bankers from the United Kingdom rubbed shoulders with European diamond-company managers, government officials, and Lebanese diamond dealers. The elite played tennis at courts on the grounds of the National Diamond Mining Company, which also ran a local medical clinic that was off-limits to Africans. Government officials and diamond dealers rode the streets in Mercedes Benzes. In well-guarded houses, they ate imported, thick-skinned oranges from Lebanon (not the thin-skinned, sweet oranges sold by local street hawkers) and dined on tenderloin beef from Europe. They proudly displayed photographs of their frequent tours of urban nightclub haunts in Belgium and France. Private gasoline-powered generators kept the lights on, the beer cold, and the steaks frozen.

Surrounding this tiny islet of public affluence was a sea of migrants who had poured into the diamond fields from all over Africa since the end of the World War II. Koidu, the central town of Kono District, boasted a vibrant local African economy. Near the bright pink central mosque sat dozens of market women, shielding themselves from the sun under hand-held umbrellas or makeshift awnings of bright fabric and selling rice scooped out of great enamel pans. Others sold beans, bread, boiled and mashed yams (fufu), dried fish (bonga), cassava, peas, potato leaves, peppers, tins of tomato puree, bottles of palm oil and peanut oil, and the ubiquitous tins of Carnation evaporated milk, snidely known as "white man's snot." Neatly stacked for sale were matches, soaps, kerosene, plastic buckets, medical charms, herbs and roots, and wicker baskets. Behind the street vendors, tin-roofed stores provided space for sellers of clothing and finished goods. Tailors with pedal-operated sewing machines worked under the eaves of the roofs. At the edge of town, Fula herdsmen marketed cattle they had driven from the tsetse-fly free north for slaughter in town. Koidu itself was awash with people from all over West Africa—from Mali, Senegal, Guinea, the Gambia, and Liberia.

Diamonds and the quest for wealth and prosperity were the driving force behind the emergence and growth of Koidu. Koidu has often been described as having the character of the Wild West with the diamond miners the equivalent of the miners of the California Gold Rush. But the analogy is superficial and masks important differences. In reality, the situation in Koidu was more like the era of Prohibition in the United States. During the California Gold Rush, anyone could stake a claim. In Sierra Leone access to the principal resource—diamonds—was restricted by law to a select few. The rest of the population was indifferent or hostile to a legal and political system that siphoned off the riches for a national and international elite. As a result, large groups of men and boys devoted themselves to the illegal mining of diamonds. Some were successful, but for most the lure of diamonds was a hollow promise.

Large deposits of riverine diamonds were discovered in Sierra Leone in 1930. Mining diamonds in rivers and streams, unlike mining operations in other areas of Africa, can be carried out with shovels, pails, sifters, and other simple and rudimentary equipment.[52] The most extensive deposits in Sierra Leone are found in Kono District and the forested areas of the Gola forest in Southern Province near the Liberian border. For twenty years after diamonds were discovered, the Sierra Leone Selection Trust (S.L.S.T.), a De Beers–controlled British mining company, had a monopoly over mining and prospecting. By 1952, however, news of the riches of the diamond fields had spread, and young migrants from all over West Africa came to Sierra Leone and threatened the S.L.S.T. franchise. All mining by individuals was illegal, and the diggers posed a powerful challenge both to the S.L.S.T. and to the stability of Sierra Leone. The Diamond Protection Force, a company-owned paramilitary, protected the diamond deposits and routinely faced off against the young miners. Despite the suppression, the productive output of the illegal diggers at that time was twice that of the S.L.S.T. and may have amounted to 20 percent of world production per annum.[53]

Prompted by riots and bloodshed in northern Sierra Leone and faced with widespread lawlessness among young miners throughout the diamond fields, the colonial government promoted a plan to give Sierra Leoneans a limited stake in the mining. The government reduced the S.L.S.T. monopoly to an exclusive area of about 450 square miles of the richest deposits. The remaining reserves, largely undeveloped, were made available for limited mining by individual Sierra Leoneans under a licensing system that required the consent of local tribal authorities. The government believed that this plan would curtail illegal mining because local tribal authorities would be involved in the regulation of mining and individual Sierra Leoneans would be granted some access to legitimate mining.

To knit this scheme together, in 1956 the colonial government enacted the Alluvial Diamond Mining Ordinance and the Diamond Industry Protection Ordinance, which created a series of diamond protection areas and gave the government broad powers to arrest and expel "strangers" from these areas.

A *stranger* was basically any person who wasn't specifically exempted from the law. Strangers were subject to arrest, expulsion, a fine, and up to six months in prison, and if they were found in possession of a sieve, shovel, a shaker, pickaxe any other tool that could be use for prospecting or mining they could receive up to twelve months in prison with hard labor.[54] In 1956, with much fanfare, the government launched "Operation Parasite," designed to drive all illegal miners out of the diamond areas.[55]

But these measures were too little and too late. In many areas the migrants outnumbered the local people. In Kono District, the heart of the diamond fields, migrants overwhelmed the Kono, the local inhabitants of the region. In 1963, the Sierra Leone census reported that Kono District had a population of 167,915, with only 90,000 identified as Kono. The rest were migrants.[56] By 1970, the population of Kono District had expanded to about 249,000, and in the districts where diamonds were heavily concentrated the numbers of migrants often greatly exceeded those of the local Kono.[57] In addition, because tribal authorities granted so few individual licenses, and the system of granting of licenses was perceived to be so corrupt, the whole plan had little effect on illegal mining. Operation Parasite was thus a failure. Instead of clearing the mining areas of strangers, it generated a protracted, low-level war of attrition among government authorities, paramilitaries, and illicit miners. Long periods of hide and seek were followed by massive operations designed to move strangers out of the diamond protection areas.

Operation Parasite was followed in 1969 by Operation Exodus, and so-called stranger drives—the forced arrest and deportation of migrants—began to dominate the political landscape. By this time, the struggle over diamonds was generating chaos and violence throughout the region. A report from the Eastern Province Intelligence Committee to the Ministry of the Interior on the impact of Operation Exodus on the Kono diamond protection area tells the whole story. The committee noted widespread episodes of assault and extortion carried out by the Sierra Leone army. It cited massive popular resentment against the government that stemmed from the belief that the government condoned the atrocities carried out by the army. The committee recommended that the army be withdrawn immediately.[58] Military operations in Kono established a pattern of predation by the Sierra Leone army. This pattern was repeated over and over again during the civil war, when renegade troops called Sobels—Soldiers by Day and Rebels by Night—plundered the people and resources of the diamond areas. But even in 1969 the army was not the only problem. Illicit mining also created widespread banditry, with thieves raiding villages and mining offices in search of gems. By 1970, the Tama Forest Reserve, later an RUF haven, was nicknamed "Katanga Province" after the lawless secessionist province of the Congo known for its thievery and violence.[59]

Kono's pervasive economic and political problems led to numerous anticolonial and antigovernment political movements, which were suppressed by the central government.[60] One major movement of the 1950s and 1960s, the Kono Progressive Movement, tried to forge political links with migrants, but on the whole, even within this movement, the Kono regarded themselves as victims of predatory governments and greedy migrants. In the end, Kono grassroots political movements subscribed to the formula that the diamonds of Kono District belonged to the Kono people and not to anyone else. This hostility soured the relationship between the rural Kono and the non-Kono migrant urban populations developing in their midst.

When rebel forces invaded Sierra Leone in 1991 and started their drive to seize Kono District, their goal was to control the diamond fields, the major single source of resources in the country. From the Kono perspective, the rebels were an extreme version of the kinds of migrants and bandits that had been part of life in the District for decades. The attitude of the RUF was equally hostile. It did little or nothing to try to organize the dissatisfied subsistence farmers, miners, and struggling schoolboys. The rebels came to Kono not to create a revolutionary force but to gain access to the same resources that had been drawing migrants and bandits since the 1950s. The Kono, if anything, were in the way and were useful only to the extent they could be exploited.

The Atrocities of Peace: Youth Violence and the Political System

The violence and corruption of the politics and economics of diamond mining deepened when Stevens was elected president of Sierra Leone in 1967. Stevens's election ended the rule of the Sierra Leone People's Party (SLPP), which had ruled Sierra Leone through the transition from British colonial rule and during the first few years of independence. Stevens and his political party, the All People's Congress (APC), created a one-party state in Sierra Leone by immediately destroying the power of the SLPP. Destroying the SLPP not only meant shutting down the national party but also controlling the rural elite. Especially targeted was the system of local rule by paramount chiefs, which had considerable importance in Sierra Leone. Next, Stevens sought to control the key resources of Sierra Leone, especially diamonds. Controlling diamond production not only allowed Stevens and his followers to amass personal fortunes but also provided the means for rewarding and punishing political supporters and opponents.

William Reno argues that Stevens created a "shadow state," which combined patronage and violence and became the effective system of political rule in Sierra Leone. During Stevens's rule and that of his successor, Joseph Momeh, the formal and public institutions of government devolved into an empty carapace, occasionally animated by private patronage networks. However, this empty shell of a government continued to serve as a symbol of international authority and legitimacy and was used to channel the funds of international institutions into private hands. Because so many state-level institutions had been gutted, control over the key resources of society was transferred to private strongmen and their followers. From the point of view of ordinary Sierra Leoneans, the government continued to be the main source of organized violence, although an increasingly weakened military began to be overshadowed by private paramilitaries.[61]

Early in his presidency, Stevens and the APC leadership realized that children and youth could play a major role in maintaining political control. Violence was spreading through the diamond areas and the network of small towns and villages that surrounded the region. In the larger towns such as Bo and Kenema, displaced and unemployed youth were concentrated in pockets of poverty and despair. Stevens himself had a background in trade unionism, and he and the APC deliberately began to organize youth, stressing the links between the APC and Wallace-Johnson's West African Youth League. But this connection was a sham; the APC was interested only in mobilizing youth for its own narrow political interests.

The SLPP had already provided Stevens with a model for political thuggery. During the 1967 elections the SLPP made use of "action groups," bands of teenage males dressed in white bandannas and vests bearing the palm-tree symbol of the SLPP, to intimidate the voters. Aminatta Forna, in her autobiography, *The Devil That Danced on the Water*, describes the rampages of the SLPP youth when the military staged a coup to thwart the transition of power from the SLPP to the APC. Having been victorious in the elections, Stevens was being sworn into office at State House when he was arrested. That night, the army shot down a crowd in Freetown that was protesting the coup, and the wounded were taken to Conaught Hospital. The hospital was raided by SLPP youth bearing automatic weapons, who had come to finish off the victims, but they retreated when the physician in charge confronted them. Under the APC, youth violence multiplied. Stevens began using youth violence to create an atmosphere of anarchy and terror in order to bring about a one-party state. S. I. Koroma, nicknamed Agba Satani, Satan's chief disciple, who later became vice president of Sierra Leone, led this effort. The youth groups were his power base.[62] Koroma's start in politics came when he was supported by Rainbow, an *odelay* in central Freetown, for the 1962 city-council elections.[63] Koroma was explicit about his belief that violence was inseparable from politics.[64]

Throughout Sierra Leone, members of the APC youth wing (APC Youth), wearing red berets and red tee shirts bearing the logo of the rising sun, became the political muscle whenever the APC wanted to display its power. In 1968, key members of APC Youth became the leaders of the two important *odelays*—Firestone and Eastern Paddle—symbolizing the fusion of politics and street violence.[65] Under the APC, citizens and soldiers who had served under previous governments, opposition politicians, and rivals within the party were subject to the ravages of the youth supporters. Youth set people on fire, burned down their houses, shot children, paraded citizens about naked and beat them, brought opponents before youth-run kangaroo courts, and hacked men and women to death with machetes. In Ginger Hill, a neighborhood in Freetown, APC Youth members threw sticks of dynamite into the houses and shops of Mende and Fula residents, killing people in their beds. Youth thugs controlled official public spaces, routinely menacing and abusing citizens. Forna describes them as "lupine youth in red T-shirts and bandannas[,] . . . cruel and confident as predators."[66]

The Kono District was one of the many places in Sierra Leone where APC Youth concentrated its attention. I had a dramatic encounter with APC Youth in 1973 in Nimi Koro Chiefdom, where the APC was making a concerted effort to depose the local paramount chief, Dudu Bona, an opposition-party member. At the time Sierra Leone was under a state of emergency that prohibited opposition-party activity, and Chief Bona was charged with calling secret meetings with opposition-party leaders. Charges began to pile up, some bordering on the fantastic. It was claimed that the chief was training subversives in the nearby Nimini mountains, confiscating property, misusing chiefdom revenue, maltreating elders, using forced labor, arbitrarily appointing village chiefs, and engaging in cannibalism.[67] An inquiry was held at the local court in the town of Njaiama. I had obtained permission from the local court president, an APC official, to attend and tape-record the hearings. But on the third day of Bona's "trial," several pick-up trucks carrying members of APC Youth roared up to the courthouse and surrounded it. The party was showing its muscle. A number of people were picked out, kicked out of the courtroom, and threatened. I was at the courthouse at the time, and I did not see anyone beaten up, although there were widespread reports of beatings and other abuses. I was pushed out of the courthouse by a member of the APC Youth who looked about sixteen or seventeen and who was screaming at me in Krio and in English: "Who are you? Fuck you! Fuck you! Give me the tapes." Two or three others surrounded me, my tape recorder was smashed, and I was detained.

The youth leader claimed I was a spy and threatened to kill me, but in the end they forced me into one of the trucks and drove me to the police station at Yengema near Koidu. An officer of the Criminal Investigation Division, who declared that this was a "police matter" and that he would deal with me, took me into custody. I was released, without charge, a few minutes after the youth left, with a warning from the officer to "be careful." Soon after this episode I was told by the local court president that the government decided that the public trial of the chief had been a mistake and the entire matter was adjourned to the district officer's office in Yengema, where it was settled outside the public eye. Chief Bona remained in power.

What I witnessed was a minor episode in the transformation of youth thugs into a government-sponsored paramilitary. The template for the contemporary child soldier in Sierra Leone was forged under the APC regime. Virtually every atrocity visited on the people of Sierra Leone during the civil war (save the amputation of limbs) was part of the peacetime repertoire of political violence. Prewar political violence was the training ground for warfare. Marauding bands of youth first learned in peacetime that they could kill and maim civilians with impunity and that the "rule of law" was a club for bludgeoning political enemies. Similarly, the sexual exploitation of young women and girls had peacetime roots. The destruction of the Sierra Leone economy pushed women and girls into prostitution. Many of the young girls who were sex slaves during the war had been actively working as sex workers prior to the war. The term *rarray girl* came to mean prostitute or sex worker.[68] Teenage girls, known as "fresh pick," were especially prized by big men—in this case, government officials, APC party bosses, and anyone who had access to wealth via government- and party-controlled patronage networks.[69] The Sierra Leone government's role as a decades' long promoter of youth violence has not been subject to public inquiry. It has also not received much attention in the United Nations because the ideology and structure of the United Nations are not amenable to scrutiny of intrastate, government-sponsored violence.

But most Sierra Leone youth were not involved in thuggery. The young political thugs I observed were clearly not from Kono. They did not speak Kono to anyone. They were *rarray* boys in political drag. All the screaming and intimidation that I saw and heard was in Krio, the lingua franca of the region. APC Youth was clearly a hostile and alien presence in Nimi Koro Chiefdom even given the fact that the chiefdom was at the center of the illegal diamond-mining activities. Indeed, although I knew many Kono boys and young men who were involved in illegal diamond mining, for most of them it was part-time or occasional work. Their lives were still partly rooted in both agriculture and in the possibility of achievement through education.

But it is a mistake to believe that the APC did not have local supporters. The system of local rule by paramount chiefs, known as the Native Administration, was built around favoritism and corruption. Chiefs were involved in the awarding of individual diamond-mining licenses and in contract mining schemes that allowed them to nominate persons to develop joint operations on the mining company's leasehold area using tribute labor. Money and the chance to work were political favors dispensed by the Native Administration.[70] These inequalities divided loyalties within Kono District and elsewhere in Sierra Leone, creating widespread discontent wherever local rulers monopolized employment and resources.[71] This discontent was the reason, in part, why some Kono and Mende youth joined the RUF.[72]

The Radicalization of Youth

Youth violence became a basic building block of political life in Sierra Leone. The widespread poverty, the personal enrichment of the elite, the failure to use the wealth of Sierra Leone to develop a robust market economy, and the lack of education and job opportunities ensured an endless supply of unemployed, unemployable, and alienated youth. Sierra Leone was, and still is, a country filled with unwanted youth. Some portion of this youth were always available to be recruited into any setting—legal or criminal—that offered a hint of economic opportunity. Yet these poor and alienated youth would most likely have remained at the margins of society had they not been drawn into a revolutionary setting developed by their more privileged counterparts, university and high school students.

Not long after the APC came to power, students from the elite high schools in Freetown and from the University of Sierra Leone began to dabble in revolutionary ideologies and politics. Much of their revolutionary ardor was centered on opposition to the APC and was grounded in the tenets of Pan-Africanism, socialism, and revolution. Students developed study groups and read the writings of Marcus Garvey, Kwame Nkrumah, Karl Marx, V. I. Lenin, Fidel Castro, and, most important, newer works such as the *Green Book* of Libya's Colonel Muammar al-Qadhafi.[73] College students and unemployed high school graduates also began to drift into the pubs of Freetown, where they mixed with local toughs.

As Sierra Leone slid deeper into economic crisis, a volatile mixture of poor youth and radicalized students emerged. In 1977, student demonstrations at Fourah Bay College against the authoritarian rule of the Stevens regime resulted in severe government repression of student and faculty leaders. But the demonstrations helped forge a connection between students and working-class and poor youth. Some radical students began to imagine themselves as a revolutionary vanguard, and their willingness to openly confront authority earned them support in Freetown and other cities. But student radicals were heavily sanctioned: student leaders were arrested or detained, students were locked out of the campus, and all student political activity was eventually curtailed. By the mid-1980s the crackdown on student radicalism pushed radicals off campus and into the cities of Freetown, Bo, Kenema, and Koidu. Joining with the violent youth of the *odelays* these students helped shape the development of a political culture that stressed the necessity of radical violence as the cure for all the ills of Sierra Leone. At the same time the ritual use of drugs became central to youth radicalism, and those who did not use drugs were excluded from radical politics.[74]

The student revolutionary movement was transformed and subverted by events that drew student leaders into contact with Libya. In 1983, a delegation of faculty and students, including the student-union president, Abdul Gbla, and the anthropologist Moses Dumbuya, were invited to participate in the celebration of the Libyan revolution.[75] From that time on Libyan cultivation of student radicals grew with the continuing oppression in Sierra Leone. Between 1987 and 1988 between twenty-five and fifty Sierra Leoneans, including students led by Alie Kabbah, the leader of the 1977 student demonstrations, were in Libya training in the use of weapons with the idea of launching a rebellion in Sierra Leone.[76]

Here the picture becomes murky. Foday Sankoh, the late leader of the RUF, was among those who received military training in Libya. Sankoh, a member of a revolutionary cell in Kono District, was a former army corporal and television cameraman. He had been imprisoned for several years for his involvement in an attempted coup against Stevens. He replaced Kabbah as the leader of the revolutionary movement. Most important, Sankoh was an ally of Charles Taylor, leader of the National Patriotic Front of Liberia, who was leading his armies in a civil war in Liberia and seeking to extend his control into Sierra Leone. Sponsored by Taylor, Sankoh established the RUF. Only three of the initial student revolutionaries who went to Liberia joined the RUF, and a year after the RUF was formed only Sankoh was still alive.[77] Initially fueled by violent revolutionary rhetoric against the corruption of the Freetown elite, the movement rapidly degenerated into a bloody scramble for diamonds and power.

The oral history of the revolution portrays Kabbah as having betrayed the movement. Whatever the truth, Kabbah eventually abandoned revolutionary politics and left for the United States. Sankoh took over his role of recruiting new members for training in Libya, using both his own ties to urban youth and Kabbah's ties to student revolutionaries. Recruits even included students from St. Edward's High School in Freetown. Sankoh's leadership changed the movement. Its base shifted from students to the most dissatisfied and marginal adults and youth in the urban and peri-urban areas of Sierra Leone. The revolutionary documents of the RUF, originally drawn up by students, were doctored with quotes from Sankoh to make it appear that Sankoh played an important role in the ideology of the movement.[78]

The Armed Forces of the Civil War

The civil war in Sierra Leone began in March 1991 and involved numerous armed forces and groups. The main parties to the conflict were the national government's Sierra Leone army and the RUF rebel forces. Various armed militias—the Civilian Defense Forces (CDF), a loose amalgam of independent ethnic militias and self-defense groups—were usually (but not always) aligned with the government against the rebels. The best-known CDF militias groups were the Kamajohs, or Kamajors (Mende), the Donsos (Kono), the Kapras (Temne), and the Tamboro (Koranko). These ethnic militias played a major role in defeating the RUF but were divided from one another by distinct local and national agendas.

Numerous other small armed factions, both political and criminal, emerged from the firestorm of civil war and the breakdown of civil government. These ranged from the Sierra Leone People's Army (an RUF faction) to a gang of ex-soldiers turned bandits known as the West Side Boys. In addition, a May 25, 1997, military coup overthrew the government of Sierra Leone and installed the Armed Forces Revolutionary Counsel (AFRC), which made common cause with the RUF rebels, inviting them to join the junta in Freetown. RUF leaders and fighters poured into the capital, creating the "People's Army" and controlling the joint RUF/AFRC junta that ruled until February 1998, when the junta was driven out by troops of the Economic Community of West African States Cease-Fire Monitoring Group.

THE SIERRA LEONE ARMY

The main armed groups had different social and political constituencies. The Sierra Leone army was and is the organized military force of the Sierra Leone state. It has a long and turbulent history, but, most important, in the decades leading up to the war it was methodically weakened in size and strength under the presidencies of Stevens (1968–1985) and Momeh (1985–1992) and their political party, the APC, so that it could not threaten the Sierra Leone government. These prewar presidents and governments steadily looted and diverted revenues; ultimately, they destroyed the basic institutions of government. As we have seen, as part of this strategy they relied on and supported private paramilitaries, which were more easily controlled through patronage politics and, unlike an army, would be too weak to initiate a military coup. At the outbreak of the civil war, the debilitated Sierra Leone army could not defeat the rebels, secure the nation state, or ensure the safety of its citizens.

THE RUF

The RUF was rooted in the aspirations of alienated and homeless children and youth and soon grew into a rebel movement. Humanitarian and media accounts of the war show little interest in the RUF's origins as a political youth movement, which was a crucial factor in its emergence. Neither has the Sierra Leone government's own role as a decades' long promoter of youth violence been subject to public scrutiny. It has also not received attention in the United Nations because the ideology and structure of the United Nations are not amenable to scrutiny of intrastate, government-sponsored violence. Even before the war, significant components of Sierra Leone's young and adult population were experienced in the use of terror against other Sierra Leoneans and were prepared to engage in political violence. The actions of the RUF during the war fascinate and repulse observers. A murderous army cloaked in revolutionary ideology, the RUF was drenched in the blood of the people for whom it claimed to be fighting. It was also an army of children and youth. Indeed, with the exception of its leader, Sankoh, virtually the entire army, including its command and control structures, was under thirty.

There was a fluid hierarchy within the RUF. Those who volunteered to join had higher status than abductees, who often became virtual slaves. Men and boys had much more power than women and girls, although women and girls attached to higher-ranking officers could sometimes wield considerable power and influence. Most women and girls were in subordinate or slavelike roles. The youngest children in the Small Boys Unit were regarded as being particularly cruel. The experiences of a sixteen-year-old girl from Kono District bear this out:

> I was hiding in the bush with my parents and two older women
> when the RUF found our hiding place. I was the only young woman
> and the RUF accused me of having an SLA [Sierra Leone Army]

husband. I was still a virgin. I had only just started my periods and
recently gone through secret society. There were ten rebels, including four child soldiers, armed with two RPGs [rocket-propelled
grenades] and AK-47s. The rebels did not use their real names and
wore ski masks so only their eyes were visible. The rebels said that
they wanted to take me away. My mother pleaded with them, saying
that I was her only child and to leave me with her. The rebels said
that "if we do not take your daughter, we will either rape or kill
her." The rebels ordered my parents and the two other women to
move away. Then they told me to undress. I was raped by the ten
rebels, one after the other. They lined up, waiting for their turn and
watched while I was being raped vaginally and in my anus. One of
the child combatants was about twelve years. The three other child
soldiers were about fifteen. The rebels threatened to kill me if I
cried.[79]

The atrocities committed by the RUF belie its alleged revolutionary beginnings, which were the initial attraction for some. Popular accounts of the
war rarely acknowledge the RUF's origins as a student movement or its original core group of relatively privileged college and high school students, mixed
with boys and youth from the poorest urban slums of Sierra Leone. The RUF
recruited dislocated and alienated youth from many segments and strata of
Sierra Leone society into the political struggle for power and resources. The
rebels simultaneously empowered and exploited children's youth and energy,
while drawing them into the vortex of violent conflict. These youth started
a war that, once underway, drew in young people from every segment of Sierra
Leone society. By pitting nearly every major social segment of Sierra Leone
society against the others, the war set immigrants against hosts, poor against
rich, slum dwellers against subsistence farmers, and ethnic group against ethnic
group. The goal: control of the Sierra Leone state and its substantial mineral
wealth.

"War Is My Food": Mobilizing Children and Youth

The war polarized and militarized the economy so that the two main centers
of economic activity—state revenues and diamonds—came under the control of opposing armed forces. The rebels controlled the diamond areas on or
near the Liberian border. The political ties between the RUF rebels and the
government of Liberia ensured that rebel mining and selling of diamonds
delivered a steady supply of weapons. Rebel control of the diamond fields also
disrupted the diverse patronage system that was the original means for attract-

ing young people to the APC strongmen.[80] The RUF stepped in to fill the vacuum. It used its control of the diamonds to lure young men away from the now-weakened patronage networks of the APC. Indeed, the RUF promised to help these young men avenge themselves and their families against the strongmen and politicians who had abandoned them.[81] But in the end it merely substituted one set of brutal patrons for another.

State revenues—aside from those obtained from diamonds—were now dedicated to the country's growing militarization. By 1992, the Sierra Leone economy was in such shambles that joining the army was commonly seen as the only way a young man could earn a decent livelihood. Young soldiers achieved near-celebrity status. The situation was so grim that protest marches were held not against war but by young men who had been turned down when they tried to enlist.[82] In response, the Sierra Leone army was expanded to include children and the unemployed.[83] By 1995 the army was consuming 75 percent of all state revenues.[84] The militarization of Sierra Leone deformed all other social institutions. In areas like Freetown, the army became the sole source of revenue, and men, women and children became dependent on the military for day-to-day survival. The thriving local trade markets, ordinarily dominated by women, were ruined; one of the few ways women could now guarantee their own economic security was by finding a soldier to be a husband or lover.[85] Military control over resources became the magnet that drew children and youth into armed forces. For many, being under arms was both safer and more economically secure than remaining in the unarmed, vulnerable, and economically ruined civilian sector. As one young soldier wrote on the stock of his rifle in red nail polish, "War is my food."[86]

"We Want Peace": Terrorizing Children and Youth

As the war deepened, the actions of the RUF grew more and more predatory. It was essentially an army of young miners and captive schoolchildren.[87] In rural areas the rebels faced increasing defiance by local militias composed largely of youth. The vast majority of rural subsistence farmers living in eastern Sierra Leone were shaken by the depravity of the movement. Although this population, primarily Kono and Mende, had strong grievances against the central Sierra Leone government, they were unprepared to join the rebels. For the Kono and Mende, the RUF, like other outsiders, was an alien gang of avaricious predators. Moreover, Mende and Kono leaders, imagining a return to power of the SLPP, were eager to control the diamond fields in their own territories. Absent local support, the RUF quickly turned on rural peoples, exploiting and terrorizing them with a frightening combination of murder, predation, and moral exhortation. The terror used against civilians and soldiers was both symbolic and pragmatic: it delivered a message that the central government was incapable of protecting the civilian population, and it pushed the population into submission or flight by showing that the rebels could kill with impunity.

A demobilized sixteen-year-old CDF fighter from Kono District spoke of the wide gap between RUF propaganda and RUF behavior. He claimed that most of the RUF combatants were students who proclaimed they were fighting for human rights, freedom of speech, education, and against the corruption and patrimonial political structures of rule and that the rebel forces made use of leaflets and other materials to explain their position. But the reality, he said, was quite different:

> If the rebels had come peacefully, if they hadn't stolen our people, hadn't burnt our villages[,] . . . if they hadn't done anything that harmed us[,] . . . we sure [would] have been glad. Because, according to their view, they are fighting for their rights. . . . But during their fight for their rights they go to the villages. They go to [persons] who don't know anything about the government. They go and kill [them] and steal [their] property. . . . Because they went and [attacked] the poor, that's why I was against them. Because when you consider the rebels the way they think about [them] in the provinces, it is that they are just armed bandits. They are just thieves.[88]

In urban areas as well there was a frightening disconnect between rebel slogans and rebel actions. Sixteen-year-old H.K. was abducted by troops allied to the rebels and forced to become a child soldier. She was at home in the Kissy area of Freetown in 1997 when AFRC troops came into her neighborhood, chanting the rebel anthem, "We Want Peace" while killing, shooting, and slaughtering people at random.[89]

Understanding the war as an extension of peacetime political violence makes it plain why the rebel forces placed thousands of women, youth, and children in a slave system that included soldiers, laborers, miners, sex slaves, and forced marriages. The politics of peacetime was itself an amalgam of patronage and violence. As the ferocity of wartime expanded, the patronage system became shaped by its brutality. With violent behavior dominating the political system, the relationship between patrons and their dependants easily devolved into a relationship between master and slave. The rebel child soldiers were part of this system. Yet at the same time the system had its own internal hierarchy, and the rebel child soldiers were more privileged and more powerful than sex slaves. Not every girl who joined the rebel ranks was a sex slave. Like boys, many joined because of the excitement, power, and material gain it offered. Some of the most powerful and violent girls, the mammy queens, were expected to play a major part in fighting and acts of terrorism. Former female combatants in child-soldier reintegration centers can still be seen saluting the one-time mammy queens.[90]

H.K.'s story shows how the boundaries between child soldier and toiler for the rebel forces were constantly shifting. Captured when her house in Kissy was set on fire with everyone else still inside, she saw AFRC soldiers cut her aunt's newborn baby in half, and then was taken to a camp and told that she would have to fight. After refusing to fight, she was placed in a "looting" contingent, was given a weapon and ammunition, and began to participate in AFRC operations. By 1999, she had become a direct combatant, and in January of that year she was part of the joint invasion of Freetown by AFRC and RUF forces and was ordered to kill people and cause as much havoc as possible. Under orders from the AFRC, she and other child combatants cut off people's arms, heads, and breasts.[91]

The story of Katmara B., a thirteen-year-old girl, is one of constant reversals. Katmara lived in a Freetown neighborhood invaded by the rebels. She and her family first tried to take refuge in a local mosque and then tried to flee the shooting. They were captured by the rebels, who then entered the mosque and killed fifteen people. Katmara also saw them hack off her uncle's hand. Within a matter of hours and days she was abducted, beaten, raped, and went from captive to combatant to being the "forced" wife of a rebel. Katmara described her "recruitment" this way: "They took us outside and told us to change our clothes and gave us combat clothes to wear. We were told that we had to do anything they told us to do. We were told that when they addressed us, we were to respond with 'Yes, sir.' At that point we were given guns and cutlasses, and told that we were to go and cut hands off." But almost as soon as she was recruited there was a reversal of fortune. "On our way to wherever they were taking us, we met up [with] another group called 'Born Naked.' The people in this group roamed the streets naked, the way they were born, and when they met people, they killed them. When the members of 'Born Naked' saw us, they told the others that they should kill us since they had been warned not to take any more hostages."[92] Then immediately another reversal:

> So, on our way to be killed, we were taken to a house with about 200 people held in it. My older cousin was sent to go and select 25 men and 25 women to have their hands chopped off. Then she was

told to cut off the first man's hand. She refused to do it, saying that she was afraid. I was then told to do it. I said I'd never done such a thing before and that I was also afraid. We were told to sit on the side and watch. . . . They chopped off two men's hands. . . . We left the two men whose hands had been cut off behind. We were then taken to a mosque in Kissy. They killed everyone in there[;] . . . they were snatching babies and infants from their mother's arms and tossing them in the air. The babies would free fall to their deaths. At other times they would also chop them from the back of their heads to kill them, you know, like you do when you slaughter chickens."[93]

War's End

The civil war in Sierra Leone wound to an end in January 2001. The RUF was finally defeated with the aid of troops from the United Kingdom. Although the immediate horrors of the war are gone, in other respects the results are mixed. In some areas the patterns of exploitation and oppression and the issues that propelled people into violent conflict have not disappeared. The peoples of eastern Sierra Leone, and especially of Kono District, suffered horribly during the war. The major displacement of the population—many of whom fled into neighboring Guinea—not only was a sign of their wartime vulnerability but also signaled their real loss of political power during peacetime. A main fear among local Kono was that the region, depopulated of its ethnic base, would continue to be exploited as it was in the prewar period and that illegal immigrant miners would squeeze out the Kono. In response, militant and politically active Kono sought not only to fight off the RUF but also to leverage themselves into position to shape the postwar peace and the inevitable issue of who would control the Kono diamonds. Once again, Kono children and youth tried to insert the issue of Kono rights into the processes of both winning the war and the reconciliation and development that are now taking place.

During the war, especially during its later stages, the Kono ethnic militia, the Donsos, fought hard against the RUF. As in the Mende ethnic militia, the Kamajors, Donso ranks were filled with children and youth. Some Kono estimate that there may have been as many as six thousand Donsos ranging in age from teenagers to young adults. The Donsos were organized by the Kono chiefs to form a resistance; they launched their movement from across the border in Guinea and from forested areas in the south. Many believed that the Donsos deserved much of the credit for defeating the RUF in eastern Sierra Leone despite the greater publicity given to the Mende ethnic militia.[94]

One of the main goals of the Donsos and other militant Kono youth was to shut down illegal mining in Kono. As the war wound down, the victorious Donso and Kono youth militants harassed immigrant miners and their financiers in Kono District. These clashes are sometimes glossed in the media as violence between the former CDF and the former RUF.[95] But they are, in fact, the continuation of the persistent conflict between immigrants and ethnic Kono. As Sahr Lebbie, a youth and militia leader, put it, his group of youth militants "maintains law and order for the traditional people of Kono."[96] Some observers see Kono District as still "sitting on a time bomb."[97] Youth-led political violence remains endemic. On July 6, 2002, militant youth destroyed houses in Koidu, which they claimed were used in drug trafficking. In addition, another group, calling itself the Tankoro Youth Group, destroyed houses in Joe Bush Town, another area of Kono.[98]

At first blush, the renewed struggles in Kono District appeared to replicate the prewar antagonism between immigrants and hosts that formed the background to the war. As in the past, the struggle over diamonds provided the context for political violence. As before, displaced youth clashed with local peoples over the control of resources. But there was a new twist: The war also created a class of infinitely exploitable slaves or slavelike persons. To be sure, the end of the war brought about the demobilization of child soldiers, and most former child combatants no longer bore arms. But the war must be seen as one of a series of episodes of terrible violence within the longer history of economic and political exploitation. The energy of children and youth remained a volatile resource to be exploited. In many respects some categories of children and youth were made more vulnerable by the war because the war created large numbers of children who were little more than armed slaves.

After the war, many of these children became disarmed and exploited laborers in the same diamond fields they worked in, protected, and fought over during the war. Today in Kono District, thousands of children and youth labor in the diamond fields, including many former child soldiers from the RUF's dreaded Small Boys Unit.[99] No longer extracted by rebel forces, these products of exploited child labor are no longer deemed "blood diamonds" and can be lawfully exported and placed in the stream of legitimate commerce. Large numbers of these children and youth, rejected by their family and kin because of the atrocities they committed during the war, are not able to return to their homes. Like slaves in the nineteenth century, torn from family and community, they are now part of the mass of diamond miners, having inadvertently traded one form of exploitation for another.

Elsewhere in Sierra Leone, attempts have been made to reintegrate child soldiers into society, with varying degrees of acceptance. The official ideology of forgiveness, which now pervades the country, is tied to the purse strings of the international agencies that control the flow of funds for the rebuilding of Sierra Leone. The distribution of funding at the grassroots level is dependent on local communities' publicly accepting the idea that former combatants are somehow "innocent." On the legal front, child soldiers have been effectively immunized from prosecution for any crimes they may have committed during the war while below the age of eighteen. Chief Prosecutor David Crane, of the Special Court, which was established to try those most responsible for atrocities during the war, has made it clear that no child will be prosecuted. In his view, the people of Sierra Leone have greeted this decision with a "collective sigh of relief."[100] And children who have committed crimes seek to be forgiven. "We started killing," said one former child soldier, "but I know it is not my fault[;] . . . this is why I believe God won't blame me—it is not my fault."[101] Abbas, whose tale of murder and mayhem opened this chapter, tells us: "We need a leader who could take care of this country. The rebellion started because of bad leadership. God must forgive boys like us. It was not our fault."[102]

Conclusion

For more than a decade the war in Sierra Leone placed child soldiers in the forefront of world attention. The war is over, and world attention has turned to other conflicts in which children are involved. But Sierra Leone haunts us. The thousands of amputees, many already abandoned and discarded symbols of the conflict, stand as human testimony to the destruction and havoc wrought by armed children and youth. Wars are said to be the affairs of adults in which vulnerable children are abused and exploited for nefarious ends. But in this case the involvement of children in war was constructed on political foundations established during peacetime. Warfare was a cruel extension of prewar conflicts in which children and youth were already integrated into an exploitive and violent political system largely ignored by the world. Children and youth have not gone away. They make up the majority of Sierra Leone's population. How their interests and concerns will be integrated into Sierra Leone society remains to be seen.

Chapter 4

Fighting for the Apocalypse

Palestinian Child Soldiers

On MARCH 29, 2002, Ayat al-Akhras, a Palestinian teenager, blew herself up outside an Israeli supermarket in Jerusalem, killing Rachel Levine, a seventeen-year-old student, and Haim Smadar, a fifty-five-year-old security guard. On the evening of March 28, Ayat videotaped her farewell address on behalf of the al-Aqsa Martyrs Brigade. She proclaimed: "I am the living martyr, Ayat Mohammed al-Akhras. I do this operation for the sake of God and fulfilling the cry of the martyrs and orphans, the mothers who have buried their children, and those who are weak on earth. I tell the Arab leaders, don't shirk from your duty. Shame on the Arab armies who are sitting and watching the girls of Palestine fighting while they are asleep. I say this as a cry, a plea. Oh, al-Aqsa Mosque, Oh, Palestine. It will be *intifada* until victory."[1] Just a few days later, in a Jerusalem cafeteria, Amneh, another Palestinian student, explained al-Akhras's act to me this way: "I think that a sixteen-year-old girl who goes out there . . . has a reason. She wouldn't just go and do that. I mean, do you know how much courage that would take?" She continued, "The thought of it. It takes so much courage to go out between people and then just blow yourself up. It takes a lot of courage." This act of suicide terrorism by a young girl was part of more than a century of conflict between Arabs and Jews over the Land of Israel. Since the closing days of the Ottoman Empire, Palestinian children and youth have been at the forefront of the conflict, often serving in the armed groups that have fought against the Jewish presence in Palestine. From the beginnings of the conflict. the conviction that young people have a duty to sacrifice themselves for the Palestinian cause has held a central place in militant forms of Palestinian political consciousness. Today, regardless of the personal pain or sense of bewilderment Palestinian parents may experience at the violent death of a child, the public expression of grief is still couched within a cultural idiom whose legitimacy has stood the test of time. No child's death is meaningless. Every dead child is a hero, a victim, and a martyr.

In recent memory the participation of children in the Palestinian cause began with the terrorist bombing of the El Al Israel Airlines office in Brussels on September 9, 1969. For this attack two thirteen-year-olds recruited by Yasir Arafat's al-Fatah faction of the Palestine Liberation Organization (PLO), threw hand grenades into the airline's office. Since then the role of children and youth in the Palestinian war against Israel has grown dramatically. Children and youth were at the forefront of demonstrations and strikes against the Israeli occupation of the West Bank in the 1970s. Beginning with the first Palestinian uprising, or intifada (1987–1993), images of rock-throwing Palestinian children and youth attacking and fleeing armed Israeli soldiers emotionally framed the drama of the conflict. The public perception of both Israelis and Palestinians, molded by the media, has evolved as well. The early image of Israel as a tiny embattled country surrounded by a hostile Arab world has been replaced by an image of Israel as an arrogant regional superpower suppressing a small people's wish for nationhood. In tandem, the image of Palestinians has shifted from a perception of them as violent airline hijackers and terrorists to the notion that they are youthful rebels.[2]

Since the onset of the second Palestinian uprising, the al-Aqsa intifada, in September 2000, children's participation in war has taken a darker turn. A long and growing list of children and youth joined Hamas (the Islamic Resistance Movement), Islamic Jihad, the al-Aqsa Martyrs Brigade, and other militant Palestinian groups to commit acts of terrorism and suicide. In January 2003, two young boys, one of whom was initially reported to be eight years old, attacked an Israeli settlement in Gaza and were shot and wounded. Ten days earlier, three fifteen-year-olds were shot and killed while trying to attack another settlement. On February 25, 2002, Noura Shalhoub, the fifteen-year-old daughter of a Tulkarm veterinarian, attacked an Israeli military checkpoint armed solely with a knife and was shot dead. On August 12, 2003, two seventeen-year-olds blew up themselves and others in an attempt to undermine the "road map" of the George W. Bush administration. The steady stream of suicide attacks and suicide bombings has valorized the ideal of personal martyrdom in the name of Palestinian nationalism.

The militarization of Palestinian children and youth began at the end of World War I, when the Balfour Declaration opened the door to increased

Jewish immigration and settlement in Palestine. From that moment, the Palestinian response to Zionism linked children, youth, and adults and propelled them into a vortex of violent conflict. In this mix, adult political leaders controlled the formal positions of power and authority as well as access to key financial resources needed to promote rebellion. But children and youth carried the banner of militancy and possessed the raw confidence and physical energy needed for violence. Children and youth may have been recruited into militant institutions and organizations created by adults, but they pushed and prodded adults into higher levels of activism, rebellion, and terrorism.

Apocalypticism and Politics

The fusion of apocalyptic visions with political movements has long been an important part of Islam.[3] The militant Palestinian response to Zionism reflected an apocalyptic and millenarian view of the Jewish presence in Palestine that imbued the Palestinian Arab struggle with meaning. The involvement of children and youth in the Palestinian national cause emerged out of the sense of cataclysm and catastrophe that permeated Palestinian nationalism. In Palestine, apocalyptic views were nourished by two nascent forms of totalitarianism then found in the Middle East, Islamism and pan-Arabism.[4] Both movements had similar goals but employed different strategies: the Islamists sought to restore Arab hegemony through the defense of Islam and the creation of a ruling religious order, while pan-Arabists sought to restore Arab hegemony in more ethnic and political terms. The competition between these rival movements was sometimes deadly, but more often they formed an adversarial partnership around the central goal of combating Zionism. In later years, both movements came under the strong influence of European fascism, creating a syncretistic worldview that penetrated and colored even the most secular Palestinian political responses to Zionism. As result the Palestinian national movement, in all its political diversity, has continually embraced a variety of religious and secular forms of authoritarianism and millenarianism.

Even under the Ottomans, many Palestinians saw the renewed Jewish presence in Palestine as the harbinger of the revival of ancient Jewish political claims to the land. Accordingly, the modern Jewish presence in Palestine created a conflict that was never solely over individual competing interests, geographic boundaries, or particular plots and parcels of land. It was, rather, a bitter existential struggle that cast a long shadow of gloom over the possibility for compromise. No matter how small, the Jewish political presence in Palestine was an affront to Islam and Arab civilization that reversed the fundamental cultural and symbolic ordering of Arab life. Given this end-of days, world-turned-upside-down view of Zionism, Palestinian Arabs sought the elimination of the Jewish political presence in Palestine and the restoration of Arab hegemony over the land and its holy sites. Individual Jews and a limited but submissive Jewish communal presence could be tolerated, but not a Jewish polity. Jewish political power, by its very existence, humiliated Palestinian Arabs and indeed the entire Arab world.

Not all Palestinian Arabs shared this uncompromising view. Even fewer were prepared to act on it. But rival political views within the Palestinian Arab community were suppressed and defeated. Militant convictions held central place in Arab political responses to the presence of Israel on the soil of Palestine, and they endure as the ideological legacy of the Palestinian nationalist movement. For Palestinians, restoring Arab hegemony is essential to the idea of "justice" for their people. As one young Palestinian television reporter, a child during the first intifada, said, "My dream is for all of Palestine. When I was little we would visit Haifa and Jaffa and Akko and walk through the Arab neighborhoods and see the Arab houses. This is Palestine for me. It might seem extreme, [but] when I think of Palestine it starts at the Lebanese border and ends at Egypt."[5] Her dream is not significantly different from the sentiments expressed in the suicide note of fifteen-year-old Noura Shalhoub, who said that by her action she wanted to send the message that "there is no safety on our soil for Jews."[6]

The fact that many Palestinians continue to dream of a Palestine without Israel or Jews does not mean that all Palestinians rule out a more pragmatic solution to the conflict.[7] But for most Palestinians "pragmatism" and "realism" are handmaidens of injustice—the surrender of some of "historic Palestine." This is one reason why many Palestinians have such admiration and respect for Hamas, Islamic Jihad, the al-Aqsa Martyrs Brigade, and other rejectionist groups. The spirit of rejectionism keeps the purity of the Palestinian dream alive.

The power of terrorism has been made amply clear. On August 19, 2003, a suicide bomber killed more than twenty Israelis on a Jerusalem bus, including many infants and toddlers. Former Palestinian prime minister Mahmoud Abbas declared his "strong condemnation of this terrible act that doesn't serve the interests of the Palestinian people."[8] The bomber, a twenty-nine-year-old former child prodigy, had memorized the Koran at age sixteen and was an imam and lecturer on Islamic law.[9] In Hebron, the bomber's hometown, Abbas's sentiments were erased by the din of the celebratory fireworks that burst over the city and by the eagerness of Hamas and Islamic Jihad to take credit for the killings.[10] When Israel retaliated and assassinated a Hamas leader, more than ten thousand Gazans attended his funeral as loudspeakers declared: "Our one constitution is the Koran. Jihad is our only road. The best ambition for us is to die as martyrs."[11]

Two Dogs and One Bone: Emerging Radicalism in the Israeli-Palestinian Conflict

"It's two dogs and one bone," Avi told me on my first day in Israel in August 1978. This was my introduction to the Israeli-Palestinian conflict. We were in Jerusalem sitting in the garden of the language-training center, or *ulpan*, where I was to study Hebrew in preparation for my new job as a lecturer in anthropology at Ben Gurion University. Avi, a teenager, was waiting for his girlfriend, who worked at the center. We started to chat, and Avi quickly decided that I was in need of some serious political socialization. I listened to Avi, but I was not in his political camp. When I started teaching at Ben Gurion, I joined the Negev Group for Civil Rights, a group monitoring local problems with Bedouin land rights. I participated in Peace Now demonstrations, subscribed to the Israleft News Service, and started listening to Jewish and Arab students talk about the prospects for peace. I still have a newspaper clipping with a photo of myself at a peace demonstration in Hebron. We were protesting the uprooting of olive trees by Israeli settlers, who were planting new trees. But among my circle of friends and colleagues the settlers seemed marginal and crazy. Peace was in the air. Anwar Sadat, the president of Egypt, had just come to Jerusalem, and Avi's theory seemed out touch with the new realities of the Middle East. I taught at Ben Gurion for several years and since then have traveled back and forth to Israel regularly, spending my sabbaticals teaching and carrying out research in Israel and trying to make sense of the conflict. While in the United States, I became an active supporter of Meretz, the left-of-center coalition of peace parties in Israel. But as I began research on child soldiers, I recalled my conversation with Avi because the child soldiers of Palestine have always been connected to the most radical Palestinian political ideologies and movements and were more likely, I believed, to embrace a zero-sum vision of the conflict. I was unprepared for how the failure of the Oslo peace process and the outbreak of the al-Aqsa intifada caused such a broad realignment of views that large numbers of people, on both sides, now sound like Avi.

Current events reveal only part of the deep support radicalism has within the Palestinian community. From the beginning, radical ideological visions shaped Palestinian responses to the human, political, and material dimensions of the conflict. Starting at the end of the nineteenth century, as Jews began to rebuild the Jewish political presence in Palestine, Jewish communities sprung to life. During the British Mandate (1918–1947) Jews created the Yishuv, or Settlement, a de facto ministate within a state from which Palestinian Arabs were excluded. The cultural understanding that developed among Palestine Arabs at this time was one of a religion (Islam) and a civilization (Arab) under siege. The Palestinian Arab community perceived the threat to its existence as overwhelming. As the conflict deepened, distinctions of social class, gender, and age within Palestinian society were muted and suppressed in the face of the external threat. At stake was the destruction of an entire way of life. A supreme struggle was required to rid the land of the criminal usurpers. Some thought that all Palestinians should serve as "soldiers" in the struggle against the Jewish presence in Palestine. The possibility that children and youth might be killed was not lightly dismissed, but this eventuality was subordinate to the greater need to defend Islam and Arab civilization.

Within this context Palestinian historical consciousness became defined by a sense of catastrophe. The mandate over Palestine formally assigned to the British at the 1920 San Remo Peace Conference was rejected and reviled by angry Palestinians as *al-Nakba,* or "the Catastrophe."[12] The 1937 British proposal that Palestine be divided into Jewish and Arab states was an additional calamity. Ten years later the emergence of the state of Israel and the creation of the Palestinian refugee crisis became the new *al-Nakba.* The Six Day War of 1967, the occupation of the West Bank by Israel, and the expansion of the Jewish settlements and Jewish population into the West Bank since 1967 have also been pivotal points in the evolution of Palestinian national consciousness. These events have imposed their own mark on Palestinian society and culture, generating a sense of anger and hopelessness.

Palestinian children and youth have responded with resistance and violence to more than thirty-five years of occupation. But the occupation is only part of the story. More striking is that from the beginning, long before there was a refugee crisis or an occupation or settlements in the occupied territories, Palestinian children and youth were expected to play a central role in violently resisting the Jewish presence in Palestine. The current situation has exacerbated and heightened this core expectation.

Those who have traveled to Israel and Palestine with their eyes and hearts even half open cannot help but be witnesses to the injustice of the occupation of the West Bank and Gaza. But in launching the second intifada Palestinians grasped a poisoned chalice. The use of suicide terrorism against Israel civilians has turned Palestinians into hostages to a process of territorial expansion that goes well beyond Israel's security needs. Jewish settlers, whose messianic visions are backed by state power, have pushed into the Palestinian heartland with every expectation that in the current chaos they can triumph over the desire of the Israeli public for peace.

The Emergence of Youth Militancy

As Jews began to immigrate to Palestine, first as a trickle and later as a flow, organized opposition to Zionism began to develop in the Palestinian Arab community. Led by the Palestinian elite, resistance first emerged in urban areas but spread to the rest of Palestine. Arab anger at the new Jewish presence crystallized around two linked issues: immigration and land purchases. The economic condition of rural Palestine had severely deteriorated under four centuries of Ottoman rule. Between 1880 and 1920 thousands of peasants left the land and migrated to urban areas. For the most part peasants left because of debt, inheritance disputes, famine, and other problems totally unconnected to land purchases. The growing poverty of the countryside and the lure of urban employment were the main economic forces in Palestine.[13] Most Jewish immigrants to Palestine settled in urban areas, but acquiring agricultural land was at the heart of the Zionist movement. When Jews began to purchase land in Palestine, they encountered a Palestinian peasantry long in deep crisis.

Palestinian peasants faced issues familiar to all peasant communities: an economic crises brought about by the commodification and sale of land and the associated processes of dislocation, migration, and urbanization; a leadership crisis, brought about by the active participation of traditional local and national leaders in the sale and alienation of land; and a demographic crisis, brought about by rising populations attempting to earn a living from smaller amounts of cultivable land.[14] As elsewhere in the world these crises led to discontent and resentment.[15] What was unique to Palestine, however, is how quickly this complex and contradictory process became incorporated into the Palestinian Arab collective consciousness as having stemmed from a single source: Zionism.[16]

Upheavals in the peasant economy directly affected Palestinian youth. Young people began to migrate to the city. They joined the rising numbers of working class and poor who lived in shantytowns on the fringes of Haifa and Jaffa and earned their living through marginal jobs and petty crime. Palestine's urban Arab population grew from less than 20 percent at the beginning of the Mandate to 33 percent at the end.[17] In this new world children and youth began to play a powerful political role. As in peasant communities worldwide, it was the children who migrated to cities, whose ties of kinship linked the city to the countryside, and who transmitted political ideas and urban unrest to the peasantry.[18] Young migrants were the prime locus of political discontent because of a newfound synergy between urban elites and energetic migrants. Young people, mostly from peasant families, formed the social networks that splayed across the urban and rural landscapes of Palestine and shaped the structure of rural discontent.

Youth militancy developed on the urban street. It was propelled forward through methods remarkably similar to those used in the modern intifada.[19] The earliest stirrings of radical nationalist sentiments were to be found in youth movements such as the Nablus Youth Society and the Jaffa Youth Society, which developed under Ottoman rule.[20] As early as 1914 Arab leaders charged that "the youth of Palestine is already inspired by the idea of assembling in order to take up the struggle against the Zionist movement."[21] During the 1920s and 1930s the urban street in Palestine saw the first appearance of organized, militant youth. The militancy of these youth cadres became a template for action and confrontation around which current events in Palestine are structured.[22]

The power of youth was also reflected within the Palestinian elite. The British appointment of Haji Amin al-Husseini as Grand Mufti of Jerusalem in 1921 was a tribute to youth and power. The Mufti was probably only twenty-two or twenty-three when he was appointed, and he gained power in a situation where leadership was normally accorded to significantly older men.[23] His appointment gave him control over the major resources of the Muslim community and facilitated his emergence as head of the Supreme Muslim Council in 1922. He was the leading religious figure in Palestine throughout the period of the British Mandate. As an Islamic jurist entitled to make decisions regarding Islamic law and to issue rulings, *fatwas*, his authority was unsurpassed.

The young Mufti transformed Palestinian Arab consciousness. As head of the Supreme Muslim Council he wove together local grievances and encoded them into a nationalist and religious narrative that reordered Arab understandings of the situation in Palestine. Early in his career, the Mufti put his energy into a major effort to renovate and rebuild Jerusalem's two most sacred Islamic sites, the Dome of the Rock and the al-Aqsa mosque. He framed these efforts as central both to the defense of Islam against Jewish efforts to rebuild the ancient Temple on Islam's holy places and to victory in the struggle over Palestine. By defining the political challenge of Zionism as a civilizational and religious struggle, the Mufti amplified opposition to Jews and Zionism in a way that resonated more deeply and widely in the Palestinian Arab community than did nationalist appeals, elite critiques of British imperialism, or specific issues of Jewish immigration and land purchases. Each of these real issues was recast as part of an assault on Islam and Arab civilization. As a *fatwa* issued by the Mufti stated: "The Judaization of the Moslem Holy Country, the expulsion of its inhabitants and the effacement of its Islamic character by the destruction of mosques, places of worship and sanctuaries has already happened in the villages sold to the Jews, and as, it is feared, will happen, God forbid, to the Mosque of Omar."[24]

The threat of the Judaization of Palestine was the central driving force of Palestinian nationalism. It pierced through divisions of class within the Palestinian movement. It animated youth from all backgrounds and drew them into the nationalist movement. The Mufti's message was not the only way Palestinian Arab nationalists framed their opposition to Zionism and the Jews, but its ominous religious tone infiltrated the peasant community, where apocalyptic visions of the world have time and again provided the ideological tinder for rebellion.[25]

By 1929, the Mufti's success in nationalizing the conflict was evident. Until 1929 opposition to Zionism was erratic and was rooted in specific local grievances. But in 1929 major violence broke out against the Jewish community. The attacks were communal: Palestinian Arabs directed their first acts of violence not against Zionists but against the Jews of the old pre-Zionist (Old Yishuv) religious communities of Hebron and Jerusalem. In the face of these attacks, Jews demanded that the Jewish community be allowed to arm itself. Jews and Arabs increasingly saw themselves as communities at war.

Young Palestinians took the lead in the spread of communal violence. On August 25, 1929, two thousand youngsters attacked the southern neighborhoods of Tel Aviv.[26] Observers at the time noted the prominent role of children and youth in the riots and massacres of Jews. The Jerusalem-based Arab Youth Association distributed a flyer printed by the Muslim Orphanage Press, the press of the Supreme Moslem Council, that defined the conflict as a historic religious struggle. The flyer, titled "Student Appeal to the Sons of the Fatherland," stated: "O Arab! Remember that the Jew is your strongest enemy and the enemy of your ancestors since older time. Do not be misled by his tricks for it is he who tortured Christ, Peace be Upon Him, and poisoned Mohammed, Peace and Worship be Upon Him. It is he who endeavors to slaughter you as he did yesterday."[27] The Palestinian Arab newspaper *El-Islamieh*, calling youth to violent action, claimed that it was "surprised that freedom loving Arab youth do not sacrifice themselves for their country in an armed defense of their existence."[28]

The rapid spread of youth political violence presented a challenge and an opportunity to Palestinian leadership. In order to meet this challenge the Mufti, the Palestinian Arab Party (the political party in Palestine allied with the Mufti and the Husseini family), and the anti-imperialist Istiqlal, or Independence, Party, began to transform the violent but largely disorganized gangs of youth militants into a centralized paramilitary force that could carry out an armed struggle against the British and the Jews. A leading article in the newspaper *El-Difaa* cited appeals to Arab institutions, parties, and organizations to arm youth and expressed concern that the available arms were not sufficiently modern.[29] But the emergence of youth-filled paramilitaries was clearly a double-edged sword because youth did not serve the interests merely of the ruling elite. As youth organizations became the local cutting edge of direct political action against both the British and the Jews, they also turned their attention to the weakness of the ruling elite.[30]

"He Laughed Like a Child": Sheik 'Iss al-Din al-Qassam and the Spread of Youth Militancy

Sheik 'Iss al-Din al-Qassam was, as Rashid Khalidi put it, "the first articulate public apostle of armed resistance" for the Palestinian cause.[31] Head of the Association of Muslim Youth in Haifa, al-Qassam inspired and organized armed groups of men and boys to carry out attacks throughout northern Palestine in the early 1930s.[32] Al-Qassam came from Syria, studied at al-Azar University in Cairo, and moved to Haifa in 1921. He first taught in an Islamic school and later was appointed imam of a Haifa mosque under the auspices of the Supreme Muslim Council. Al-Qassam stressed the purity of Islam and advocated armed struggle.[33] He demanded that the Palestinian elite and especially its religious leadership supply him with money for arms.[34]

Al-Qassam's prior military experience in Syria led him, in 1928 or 1929, to create an underground organization that used the Association of Muslim Youth as a cover. He trained youth in the use of firearms and taught them to make bombs with explosives obtained from quarry workers near Haifa. His devoted followers, the poorest and most downtrodden urban dwellers, included apprentices, kerosene venders, laborers, quarry workers, rehabilitated criminals, and displaced peasants. In 1930, al-Qassam obtained a *fatwa* from the Mufti of Damascus that authorized him to use violence against the British and the Jews.[35] Armed with this *fatwa*, al-Qassam began to target Jewish civilians in northern Palestine.

Al-Qassam began his campaign with an assault at Kibbutz Yagur, a collective farm a few miles south of Haifa on April 6, 1931. It was about 9:30 at night, before the moon had risen, and the attackers were cloaked by darkness. The assailants lay in the grass on the side of the road leading to the entrance of the kibbutz. A farm wagon carrying kibbutz members home from a visit was approaching the entrance when the assassins struck. Twelve shots were fired at point-blank range killing three—two young men and one young woman—and wounding three girls.[36] The bloody attack at Kibbutz Yagur initiated a series of strikes in northern Palestine. At the beginning of 1932 the al-Qassam group also began to throw bombs into Jewish homes in the Haifa suburbs and continued its ambushes of civilians in northern communities.[37] The last major attack took place on December 22, 1932, when a bomb was thrown into a house in the community of Nahalal, killing a father and his son.[38]

Al-Qassam's group was hunted down by the British in 1935, when he and several of his followers were killed. Yet he proved to be as important in death as in life. His death, it is said, "electrified the Palestinian people."[39] He was instantly revered as a martyr, and his death was interpreted as part of a holy war. His picture, captioned "Honor the memory of the martyr," was hung in Palestinian public buildings and was displayed at demonstrations.[40] After the death of al-Qassam, an even greater number of youths formed armed groups of guerilla fighters. Calling themselves Ikhawan al-Qassam, or the Brothers of al-Qassam, they formed armed groups and renewed attacks on the British and the Jews. In their first action, they robbed passengers and killed two Jewish passengers in a bus ambush.[41] One of the killers was reported to have said, "Go tell the police and the newspapermen that we are robbing your money in order to buy arms with which to avenge the murder of Sheikh Ez-El-Din El Kasm [sic]."[42]

Al-Qassam and his followers represented the most violent edge of the militant Islamist message in Palestine. Although his relationship with the Mufti was not always easy, they shared an identical world-view. While the Mufti trafficked in symbolism, al-Qassam trafficked in direct violence. But even within al-Qassam's group the youngest were the most violent. Pressure for violent militant action came from youth who demanded immediate armed action. The attacks on the northern communities as well as the attack at Nahalal may have been carried out by militant youth in disregard of al-Qassam's authority, and a younger faction may have attempted to seize control of the organization.

Al-Qassam, the martyr, is remembered and revered for having childlike qualities. The recasting of al-Qassam into a symbolic child forges an important cultural and emotional link between al-Qassam the adult and the children and youth of the current conflict. Al-Qassam is widely regarded as one of the most important martyrs to the Palestinian cause. In 1988, during the first intifada, the Palestinian leadership formally stressed the link between al-Qassam the martyr and his political grandchildren in the streets stating:

"O masses of our great people. O people of martyrs, grandsons of al-Qassam."[43] Hamas has named its armed units the al-Qassam Brigades.

Maryam Jameelah's hagiographic pamphlet dedicated to Palestinian youth celebrates al-Qassam as follows: "All his followers, disciples, family and friends described Shaikh Izz-u-Din [sic] as a warm, loveable person, always smiling and laughing. 'Even during the worst times,' his wife recalled, 'he would always laugh and tell us there was nothing to worry about.'" His family attributed his serene disposition to a complete faith and trust in God. One of his students in Haifa described him as a man with irresistible childlike charm. "He laughed like a child and spoke with the simplicity of a child."[44]

Other Palestinians remember al-Qassam quite differently. One Palestinian villager told of "seeing Qassam preaching jihad at the mosque and grasping a gun or sword in his hand. One of his disciples recounted a sermon in which he urged bootblacks to exchange their shoe brushes for revolvers and shoot the English rather than polish their shoes."[45] These images are not incompatible; the symbolic tie between the old warrior-child and the modern child-warrior supports the idealized purity and simplicity of the revolt. In much the same way al-Qassam is revered by contemporary Palestinian academics. As the sociologist Samih Farsoun puts it, "His martyrdom, self-sacrifice, and commitment to the national cause offered the Palestinian people a more honorable and popular model than that of the elite leadership."[46]

Seizing the Initiative: Youth and the General Strike of 1931

As al-Qassam led his armed band in rural areas, elsewhere in Palestine youth rallied to pressure the Palestinian leadership into more radical, violent action. The murders at Kibbutz Yagur and the looming sense of national conflict spread tensions throughout Palestine. Many in the Jewish community feared a reprise of the 1929 massacres.[47] In this edgy climate Palestinian youth seized the political initiative at both the national and the local level.

In Nablus in early August 1931, Palestinian youth leaders gathered with the intention of staging demonstrations and strikes. On August 15, 1931, a small demonstration took place; troops of youth paraded through Nablus beating tin cans and calling for a general strike. The demonstration was said to be in protest of the British decision to allow Jews in rural areas to create special sealed armories to store defensive weapons.[48] Although the demonstration was small, it panicked the Jewish community, which rejected the British view that the demonstrators were merely young hotheads.[49] Out of fear that Palestinian youth were calling all the shots, the Arab Executive, the leadership organization under the control of the Grand Mufti of Jerusalem, resolved to call its own general strike. Before it could take place, numerous demonstrations began to break out in Nablus. Crowds gathered around the police station shouting, "Down with the British Government, down with Zionism. Long live Arab independence." During the course of the day, demonstrations broke out all over Nablus, and the police attempted to disburse the crowds by persuasion. When that failed, they fired into the air and used their rifle butts and clubs. The crowd responded by attacking the police with stones; women actively participated and threw stones at the police from windows and rooftops.[50]

The next day violence again broke out in Nablus. Led by more than three hundred veiled women, a crowd of more than a thousand marched toward the central market shouting "Down with the Mandatory" and "Long live Arab independence." Police orders to disburse were met with a hail of stones. The superintendent of police, badly injured, ordered the police to fire their shotguns directly into the crowd; they killed three people and seriously wounded others.[51] At an official inquiry the police justified their actions by claiming that they fired into the crowd of men moving behind the front line of women. They were exonerated.[52] But this episode highlights the importance of youth-sponsored violence in the early struggle for Palestine. The Nablus youth competed with the Palestinian leadership in setting the nationalist agenda and demonstrated that they could use violence to stampede the national political leadership into action.

Nationalizing Youth Militancy

The growing power of youth presented a serious challenge to the Palestinian leaders, who wanted to control and organize youth violence. Efforts at bringing youth militants under central control began in 1932, with the emergence of the National Congress of Arab Youth and the Young Men's Muslim Association. Palestinian Arab nationalists also organized Boy Scout troops, believing that scouting, with its uniformed and organized cadre of youth, could serve as a cover for underground military activities. The National Congress quickly began to promote the formation of Boy Scout troops throughout Palestine and to bring them under its umbrella.[53]

Palestinian Boy Scouts were consciously militant and nationalistic. They rejected any link to international scouting organizations. Boy Scouts underwent paramilitary training and rallied local youth and villagers around nationalist causes.[54] Palestinian Arab scout troops quickly set to work patrolling the seashore near the Netanya coast to stop illegal Jewish immigration and forcing Palestinian merchants and shopkeepers to take part in nationalist processions.[55] Youth organizations also supported the anti-British and anti-Zionist Istiqlal Party, which was established in August 1932, and uniformed Boy Scouts bearing national flags began to appear at party meetings.[56]

Boy Scouts forged political links to other militant Palestinian youth organizations. In 1931, Boy Scout leaders helped organize a clandestine organization called Holy War (al-Jihad as Muqaddas).[57] The Rebellious Youth (al-Shabab as Thair), a secret organization with strong Boy Scout connections through the Abu Ubayda scout troop, was formed near Tulkarm. This organization was connected to the National Congress of Arab Youth and to the Mufti and was of great concern to the British because of its increasing paramilitary activity and its mixture of children, youth, and men.[58] According to British intelligence, "Some [of its members] were not the type or usual age of boy scouts, while a few others were defiantly reported to be known criminals." The authorities also noted that paramilitary drilling and other activities were taking place daily under the supervision of a Palestinian ex-police officer.[59]

All these organizations took up the call by Palestinian nationalists for Arab youth to secretly arm and form military units disguised as sports clubs and scouting troops. Boy Scouts and other groups began buying arms and engaging in military training, while calling on Palestinians to fight the British, the Jews, and those Palestinian Arabs regarded as traitors.[60] By the mid-1930s, the arming of Palestinian youth was under full steam. Arms were stockpiled, and new clandestine associations of youth, such as Young Palestine and Black Hand, began to emerge. By 1934 Holy War had sixty-three secret cells comprising four hundred youth; by 1935, the Mufti of Jerusalem had assumed personal command of the organization.[61]

Overwhelming evidence demonstrates that children and youth were active participants in the most radical violence in Palestine. A precise account is probably impossible because few records were kept, but observers in Palestine were keenly aware of the youth in the bands of Palestinian Arab fighters. Helen Wilson, an English teacher living in Bir Zeit in the 1930s, noted that her teenage students were involved in guerilla activity. Khalil al-Sakakini, the prominent Palestinian nationalist, educator, and journalist, who lived in Jerusalem during the British Mandate, noted in his diary how young the guerilla fighters were and that they even included twelve-year-old boys.[62]

"The Duty of Youth Is to Be Extremist": Creating a National Fascist Strike Force

Organized youth combatants were the most powerful expression of youth militancy in the 1930s. The emergence of youth cadres was rooted in the Palestinian desire to form a youth paramilitary along German and Italian fascist lines. In the 1930s virtually every Arab political party had one or more newspapers, each trumpeting the clarion cry for youth to take the leading role in violent resistance. Editorial comments in the Arab press lauded the role of youth in Nazi Germany and fascist Italy. These editorials used rhetorical strategies to push and cajole youth into violence. An editorial in *al-Shahab* (The Youth), a weekly newspaper of the Palestinian Arab Party, put it this way: "Arab youth, awaken from your slumber[;] . . . in every city, village and tent you should found national youth groups organized like the youth groups in Italy and Germany who will work for Arab independence and unity." The newspapers echoed the language of the political leadership. At an inaugural meeting of the Palestinian Arab Party in Tulkarm, Jamal al-Hussieni, the party leader, tried to rally youth to action and criticized youth for failing to take the lead in violent resistance. "The duty of youth is to be extremist," said al-Hussieni. "The duty of the older ones," he went on to say, was "to make the youth wait and to calm its heat." Hussieni claimed that "in Palestine the spectacle is reversed: the old ones go forth to the battle lines at the head of the camp and the youth flee from the battle lines. Youth must send the old ones back to their homes and must itself go out toward the greatness, the glory and the light."[63]

Rhetoric aside, Palestine was not Nazi Germany. In Germany, the fascist Hitlerjungend, or Hitler Youth, had its origins in Jungstrum Adolf Hitler (Adolf Hitler Boys' Storm Troops), a boys' subsidiary of the Nazi Party's Storm Troops. Hitler Youth was a nationwide phenomenon under the authority and tight control of the fascist state, whose ruling Nazi Party harnessed the power of children and youth. Mandatory Palestine, in contrast, was not a fascist state, and Palestinian Arabs had little control over the government or its resources. Moreover, Palestinian political life was a knotty web of contentious parties, personalities, and splinter groups fighting for the loyalty of youth with little prospect for national unity. The strident rhetoric of Arab national unity could not disguise the fact that many Palestinian Arabs detested party politics, seeing it as little more than a fig leaf for promotion of family and personal matters. Despite these political drawbacks, the vitality and symbolism of the fascist youth movements were immeasurably alluring. The idea that armed youth might bring an end to the hegemony of British rule in the Middle East as well as the very existence of Jewry was an irresistible but unattainable dream.

The shrill calls to take up extremist politics invoked a symbolism that glorified youth, violence, and death. By 1936 *Al Difaa*, the paper of the Istiqlal movement and the most widely read paper in the Arab community, proclaimed, in clearly fascist tones, that "youth must go out to the field of battle as soldiers of the Fatherland." Others argued that the "Land is in need of a youth, healthy in body and soul like the Nazi youth in Germany and the fascist youth in Italy which stands ready for the orders of its leaders and ready to sacrifice its life for the honor of its people and freedom of its fatherland." An *al-Shahab* editorial titled "The Strength of Youth" called on youth to "take my blood and drink it, perhaps it will heal you, give me the sword of Khalid."[64] *Al-Jamia el Islamia* called on youth to "join the flag of the nation's army[;] . . . be a pillar of fire to light up the gloom with the flaming, purifying and searing fire; be a sharp sword; take vengeance upon the usurpers."[65]

Nationalist rhetoric accompanied major efforts to build fascist-style youth organizations by recruiting young men to serve as the strike force of the nationalist movement. Throughout the 1930s the children of wealthy Palestinians returned home from European universities having witnessed the emergence of fascist paramilitary forces.[66] Palestinian students educated in Germany returned to Palestine determined to found the Arab Nazi Party of Palestine.[67] The Husseinis used the Palestinian Arab Party to established the al-Futuwwa youth corps, which was named after an association of Arab knights of the Middle Ages and which was officially designated the Nazi Scouts.[68] By 1936 the Palestinian Arab Party was sponsoring the development of storm troops patterned on the German model. These storm troops, all children and youth, were to be outfitted in black trousers and red shirts and were to be divided into three sections: below age fifteen, ages fifteen to twenty, and twenty years and older. The first troops were founded in Lod and Jerusalem.[69] The young recruits took the following oath: "Life—my right; independence—my aspiration; Arabism—my principle; Palestine—my country, and there is no room in it for any but Arabs. In this I believe and Allah is my witness."[70] The British were clearly alarmed, reporting that "the growing youth and scout movements must be regarded as the most probable factors for the disturbance of the peace."[71] The British were quite correct because the increasing levels of youth violence they were observing were merely the prelude to the outbreak of the Great Arab Revolt of 1936–1939.

The al-Futuwwa youth groups connected Palestinian youth to fascist youth movements elsewhere in the Middle East. While the Mufti was establishing youth groups in Palestine, al-Futuwwa groups were established in Iraq for boys between the ages of fifteen and twenty; they were also modeled on Hitler Youth. During the Great Arab Revolt the Mufti fled from Jerusalem and made his way first to Lebanon and then to Iraq. In Iraq he helped set up an Arab Committee to promote collaboration between Iraq and the Nazis and brought the Iraqi al-Futuwwa under its control. In sharp contrast to the groups in Palestine, Iraqi fascist youth groups operated with state sponsorship and support. They were deeply involved in the staging of deadly pogroms against Iraqi Jews. Al-Futuwwa and other youth groups continued to thrive in Iraq throughout the 1960s and 1970s. They were a precursor to the Baathist militia and were the most deadly expressions of Baathist ideology.[72] In Palestine the deadly potential of the youth groups was never fully realized. State-sponsored mass mobilization of children and youth could not take place under British rule. Nevertheless, the idea of militant youth organizations and organized youth combatants remained central to the Palestinian vision of resistance.

The Great Arab Revolt, 1936–1939

Palestinian resistance during the Mandate peaked with the Great Arab Revolt, which began in April 1936 and was led, on the urban streets at least, by Arab youth. The revolt began with the murder of three Jewish truck drivers at a roadblock outside Tulkarm and rapidly spread to the urban areas. In the early days of the revolt, violence broke out in the cities: mobs of Palestinian Arabs murdered Jews in Jaffa, and dozens of bombings occurred in both Jaffa and in Haifa. The British strategy for fighting the revolt was to seize control of the cities and drive the rebels into the countryside. Palestinian Arab activists in turn recruited from the villages, calling on Palestinian Arab youth to join the rebellion and to fight to the death. "Why," said one speaker, "should I see the youngsters of this district sleeping as if they were afraid of death and imprisonment. . . . You [must] fight your enemies, the enemies of religion, who wish to destroy your mosques, and who wish to expel you from your land."[73]

Soon after its initial outbreak the revolt was suspended while the Peel Commission met to determine a solution for resolving the violence. Its recommendation that Palestine be partitioned into two separate Jewish and Arab states resulted in the Palestinians' renewing the battle. Numerous guerilla groups attacked rural Jewish communities and police posts and otherwise destroyed and sabotaged the rural infrastructure. The Mufti of Jerusalem emerged as the leader of the revolt; some of the funding for the revolt is thought to have come from Italy and Germany.

A dramatic turn took place in September 1937, when followers of al-Qassam assassinated Lewis Andrews, the district commissioner of the Galilee. The British then exerted tremendous military and political pressure on the rebels, ruthlessly suppressing the guerilla bands and dismantling the formal Palestinian Arab leadership structure. The Mufti fled to Lebanon, joining thousands of the Palestinian bourgeoisie and political leadership in exile and leaving the rebels without unified leadership or a command structure. The rebellion began to disintegrate. Many peasants organized armed groups to fight the rebels. Some rebels also began to operate semi-autonomously and others turned to criminal activities, robbing and oppressing the peasant population they purported to represent.

Although peasant grievances provided some fuel for the rebellion, the roots of the revolt were deeply embedded in religious politics. Said Aburish, whose older brother was a loyal follower of the Mufti, argues that the revolt was "exported to the villages" by the educated bourgeoisie. For Aburish, a combination of religious persuasion and the promotion of nationalist sentiment through schooling accounted for rural discontent. The peasants, in his view, "surrendered themselves to the rebellion rather than joined it because of their feelings that the effendi, the well educated bourgeoisie, wanted it."[74]

Aburish provides a striking example of the critical disjuncture between peasant rebels and their leadership. He describes how his older brother, who had joined the Mufti in exile in Lebanon, was summoned by the Mufti and entrusted to make a perilous journey back to Jerusalem to retrieve a packet from another revolutionary. The Mufti impressed on Aburish's brother the importance and delicacy of the mission but never told him what was in the package. Aburish's brother made his way surreptitiously back into Palestine and then to Jerusalem. Under constant threat of exposure, arrest, and imprisonment, he obtained the package and brought it back to the Mufti. The Mufti opened the package, which contained the Mufti's ceremonial fez. Admiring it, the Mufti proclaimed that no one but his tailor in Jerusalem could wrap the sash of his fez so beautifully. He then dismissed the obviously bewildered youth who had risked his life for the Mufti's fez.[75]

The suppression of the Great Arab Revolt ended widespread Arab resistance in Mandatory Palestine. Despite its historic and symbolic significance, the revolt was a military, economic, and political disaster. The defeat of the rebels and the weakening of the Palestinian Arab political community paved the way for the emergence, for the first time, of an armed and vigorous Jewish nationalist movement working for the creation of a Jewish state in Palestine. Despite the 1939 British White Paper that effectively repealed the Balfour Declaration, the Palestinian Jewish community continued to flourish. Moreover, the Great Arab Revolt had reinforced the British view that the Mandate was not a viable form of government. It made clear that Great Britain would have to give up control of Palestine.[76]

Yasir Arafat: Child Soldier

The 1930s and 1940s were an important period for the political socialization of the leaders of the modern Palestinian nationalist movement. Like previous leaders the new generation looked to children and youth to participate in the fighting forces of Palestinian nationalism. Yasir Arafat, who grew up during this era, was both a youth fighter and an organizer of children and youth. Born in Cairo on August 26, 1929, Arafat was a distant cousin of the Grand Mufti. His full name was Rahman Abdul Rauf Arafat al-Qudwa al-Husseini.[77] Arafat's father was active in the Egyptian-based Muslim Brotherhood, which stressed the purity of Islam and was the organizational and ideological precursor to Hamas and Islamic Jihad. The Muslim Brotherhood took up the Palestinian cause, and its influence spread from Egypt into Gaza.

Arafat has carefully cloaked his childhood in mystery. His claims to have been born and raised in Jerusalem are demonstrably false, but even so biographers have had great difficulty in pinning down the details of his childhood.[78] Almost anything that has been said or written about him needs to treated with some degree of skepticism. Nevertheless, by age ten Arafat emerged as a militant political leader; he organized children in his neighborhood into groups, making them march and drill and beating those who did not obey.[79] He is said to have placed metal plates on the heads of children he was drilling and to have hit them with sticks if they got out of line.[80]

In the early 1940s Arafat's father, eagerly awaiting the return of the Mufti from exile, organized a fighting force in Gaza to attack Jews and Zionists. Because most of the members of the Muslim Brotherhood were too old to fight, Arafat's father needed a much younger fighting force, and he started with his own family. The nucleus of the group was Arafat himself, then almost twelve years old, and his siblings, who ranged in age from Badir, in his twenties, to Nasser, who was fourteen. Schools became the prime recruiting ground for militant youth. Their leader, Abu Khalid, was a mathematics teacher in Gaza who used his position to recruit teenage schoolboys into his group. Abu Khalid gave Arafat the name Yasir in honor of Yasir al-Berih, who succeeded to the leadership of the al-Qassam groups after the sheik was killed and who was responsible for the assassination of the district commissioner in the Galilee.[81]

With the Mufti in exile, the formal leadership of the Palestinian nationalist movement fell to the Mufti's uncle, Abdel Kader al-Husseini. Husseini wanted all fighting groups organized under the aegis of the Palestinian Arab Party. But intense internal ideological and factional conflicts prompted Abdel Kader to order the murder of Abu Khalid. To this end, a secret meeting was arranged in Jerusalem between Abu Khalid and Abdel Kader. Arafat was one of the young boys who accompanied Abu Khalid to this meeting, but before the meeting began Abu Khalid was separated from the boys, tortured, and murdered. Later that day Abdel Kader met with Arafat and other boys. He lied to them about Abu Khalid's absence and told them that Abu Khalid had been sent on a special mission. At that moment he named Arafat, then age fifteen, to be his liaison in Gaza and to ensure the integration of the Gaza group into the Palestinian Arab Party. When Arafat returned to Gaza, he was ordered to go back to school and organize his schoolmates into a secret society. Arafat proved an adept organizer of young boys. He used persuasion, violence, and intimidation to gain control of virtually all the youth groups in Gaza.[82]

The experience of World War II only exacerbated the failures of the Arab revolt. The Mufti's enthusiastic embrace of Nazi Germany and the prominence of Palestinians in the pro-Axis revolt in Iraq in 1941 alienated the British from the Palestinians. The Jewish community, which joined the war effort against Germany, prospered during the war. Jewish nationalism was also fueled by the emerging realization of the true dimensions of the Holocaust. By the end of the war, having placed their political hopes on an Axis victory, the Palestinians faced bleak prospects. The British finally decided to bring an end to British rule in Palestine and turned to the United Nations to resolve the conflict. The newly formed United Nations embraced the solution that the Palestinians had earlier declared to be catastrophic: the partition of Palestine into a Jewish state and an Arab state.

At once, Palestinian Arabs launched a guerilla war against those areas that, although still under British rule, were designated to become part of the new Jewish state. This should have been a great opportunity for Arafat. By the time World War II ended, he was about sixteen years old and had an organization of some three hundred boys, who were designated the "storm troops of Arab liberation." Moreover by 1947 the Mufti's al-Futuwwa brigades had come under the control of Abdel Kader. Arafat was ordered to integrate his youth group into al-Futuwwa but for some reason was excluded from the leadership structure in Gaza. Unhappy with this turn of events, he and his fifteen-year-old brother, Hussein, left Gaza for Jerusalem to offer their services to Abdel Kader. In his first action Arafat joined a raid on a Jewish residential neighborhood in the Old City of Jerusalem that resulted in the deaths of a number of Jews near the seven-hundred-year-old Hurva synagogue.[83] Some evidence indicates that by age seventeen he was a key figure in the smuggling of guns and ammunition from Egypt to Palestine.[84] After this time, there is no reliable record of Arafat's involvement in any militant or terrorist actions during the battles surrounding Israel's War of Independence, although he claims many heroic deeds. But if any of the autobiographical material is true, Arafat was a successful child soldier, having evolved from a ten-year-old militant to leader of the Palestinian people.

The Reemergence of Youth Militancy

Once the State of Israel was declared on May 14, 1948, and the British left Palestine, the Palestinian guerilla war against Israel became internationalized as the armies of Egypt, Iraq, and Syria, and Transjordan's Arab Legion invaded the new state. At this juncture, Palestinian Arab guerilla forces became only a small part of the conflict. The independence of Israel meant the military and political defeat of the Palestinian Arabs. Mandatory Palestine was divided among three countries: Egypt, Israel, Jordan. The vast majority of Palestinians now lived under the control of these states, but their situation had dramatically changed. Inside Israel, Palestinian Arabs continued to reside in cities, towns, and villages, but for years many Arab communities remained under Israeli military rule. Slowly, as military rule ended, the inhabitants of these communities became citizens—if only second-class citizens—of the State of Israel. Palestinians who lived under Jordanian rule were divided into two groups: those originally from the West Bank of the Jordan River, who continued to live there as before, and refugees, who were placed in camps within Jordan. Likewise, the Palestinian Arab population of Gaza, now under Egyptian administration, was composed of both native Gazans and those who were part of the mass of refugees who had left the war zones during the conflict.

The nearly twenty-year period following the War of Independence was marked by decreasing levels of violence between Palestinians and Jews, although there were frequent cross-border attacks on Israelis. During this period, the Egyptians organized the fedayeen (self-sacrificers), groups of armed Palestinians drawn largely from refugee camps who raided into Israel and who ultimately formed the nucleus of the PLO.

The Six Day War in June 1967 and the subsequent takeover of the West Bank and Gaza by Israel altered the role of the Palestinians in the conflict. The events leading up to the Six Day War are well-described elsewhere.[85] By June 8, 1967, the second day of the war, the entire West Bank, including the

Palestinian refugee camps from the 1948 war, were under Israeli control. Similarly, the Gaza Strip with its large refugee population fell under Israeli control. Just as the 1948 war sent Palestinians into exile and into refugee camps, so the Six Day War created a second, smaller wave of refugees.

Israel's conquest of the West Bank and Gaza reenergized Palestinian youth militancy. During the Mandate militant nationalists were at the forefront of Palestinian Arab political life. With Israel's West Bank occupation replacing that of Jordan, Palestinian youth again emerged as an important political force. The radicalization of youth under the Israeli occupation contrasts sharply with the political situation during the years of Jordanian occupation, when Palestinian Arab leadership was both more conservative and older. The youthful militant and nationalist radical forces of the Mandate period appeared to have disappeared.[86] Radical Palestinian political parties held little appeal for the Palestinian community as a whole. Under Jordanian occupation Palestinians, especially those in the West Bank, showed little interest in self-rule or statehood.

Palestinian politics became radicalized immediately following the Six Day War. The nationalism that had characterized Palestinian politics under the Mandate revived, coupled with a sharp turn toward international terrorism.[87] Palestinian groups such as the Popular Front for the Liberation of Palestine (PFLP), the Democratic Front for the Liberation of Palestine (DFLP), the Popular Front for the Liberation of Palestine–General Command, al-Fatah's Black September, Black June, the Syrian-based al-Saiqa, and the Iraqi-based Arab Liberation Front emerged as factions of the PLO. These groups joined forces with other international terrorist groups such as the Japanese Red Army and the German Red Army factions. Palestinian groups began a campaign of airplane hijacking and hostage taking, attacking some twenty-nine planes between 1968 and 1977.[88] Palestinians were also the first to use time bombs and altimeter bombs to blow up airliners en route and to massacre passengers at check-in counters and in waiting rooms.[89]

Palestinian terrorism was a spectacular success. It brought Palestinians international legitimacy, and it served as the prime inspiration for youth militancy.[90] The stunning political achievement of the 1972 massacre of the Israeli Olympic athletes in Munich brought the Palestinian cause recognition in the world community. In Munich's aftermath, Arafat was invited to address the United Nations, and the PLO was granted special observer status there. Terrorist operations galvanized the local population and drove a wedge between young people and the older conservative leadership that had developed under the Jordanian occupation. The PLO wanted children and youth to confront the Israeli occupation and to undermine the structures of authority that had taken root under the Jordanian occupation. Throughout 1973 and 1974 youth activists, mainly schoolchildren, held mass demonstrations, sit-ins, marches, and strikes, guided by the pro-PLO Palestine National Front.[91] The PLO youth wing, the Shabiba, organized children and youth into work committees and a network of youth-centered organizations and institutions that would enable young members to build credibility as civic leaders while demonstrating against the military occupation.[92] By 1987 tens of thousands of children and youth were members of the Shabiba.[93]

Israel's occupation of the West Bank and Gaza also paved the way for the renewal of fundamentalist Islam. The growth of the Muslim Brotherhood and the emergence of Hamas and Islamic Jihad rekindled the harsh, apocalyptic, anti-Semitic rhetoric of the Palestinian national movement during the Mandate. As one fundamentalist stated, "The resurrection of the dead at the End of Days was conditioned upon every last Jew being destroyed." The renewal of political anti-Semitism was aided by a steady supply of fundamentalist leaders from Islamic universities in Egypt. Religious fundamentalism began to spread throughout the universities and high schools on the West Bank.[94] As during the Mandate, religious and secular forms of resistance competed for the loyalty of children and youth. Fundamentalist Islam dominated the resistance movement in the Gaza Strip, while the PLO and other more secular resistance movements gained influence in the West Bank. Yet both these perspectives were found, to some degree, everywhere.

The radicalization of the Palestinian population developed out of the radicalization of its youth. The return to militant nationalism gave youth an increased stake in the political process. School strikes against the Israeli occupation were organized in 1968 and 1969. In 1975 and 1976 high school boys and other young people began to block roads, stone Israeli troops, and use explosives against Israeli targets. In May 1976 West Bank high school students took the lead in anti-Israeli street demonstrations that culminated in the throwing of rocks and Molotov cocktails at Israeli soldiers. Shimon Peres, then Israeli defense minister, mistakenly believed that these riots and demonstrations did not reflect the view of Palestinian adults because they were carried out mainly by boys and children.[95] The strategy of using children and youth was so successful that by 1980 the Youth Movement (Hareket al-Shabbibe) became the main organ by which the PLO dominated the Palestinian movement.[96] Acts of violence escalated. The 350 violent acts recorded between 1968 and 1975 doubled before 1980 and escalated further upward afterward.[97] Palestinian youth were arrested in great numbers by Israeli authorities and became the inspiration for others. The procedure for handling arrested youth was a constant source of contact and friction between Palestinian families and the Israeli military.[98]

Maya Rosenfeld's detailed historical and ethnographic study of the Dheisheh refugee camp in the West Bank provides evidence of the emergence of youth militancy.[99] In Dheisheh, opposition to Israeli occupation began immediately after the Six Day War. This opposition was organized quite differently from the manner in which West Bank politics had been organized under Jordanian rule. Then, Palestinian opposition to the Jordanian occupation was limited, passive, and led by well-educated adults with leftist, pan-Arab, and Marxist world-views. In 1967, these political groups started to fade, and independent Palestinian-oriented organizations began to predominate as the age of the political activists shifted downward toward that of teenagers and young adults. This sharp shift in age, ideology, and leadership was due in part to the absence of senior Palestinian leaders, who had fled the West Bank during the 1967 war and left a political vacuum that was quickly filled by young nationalists. Rosenfeld suggests that this group would have immediately launched a guerilla war within the occupied West Bank but for the fact that the Israeli army eliminated the option of a military response in the early stages of the occupation.[100]

But the history of Palestinian Arab militancy suggests a less radical break with the past than that suggested by comparisons with activities during the period of Jordanian rule. Children and youth, long active as militants and terrorists during the period of the British Mandate, immediately resurfaced with the onset of the Israeli occupation. The absence of activism under Jordanian occupation was a lull in the militant politics of youth. Its speedy development following the Six Day War makes plain that the identity of the occupier spurred youth into extremist politics. Once again, the threat of Jewish hegemony brought about a rebirth of the militancy that had guided Palestinian nationalism from its inception.

The Israeli occupation fell heavily on the children and youth of Dheisheh. Throughout the 1970s and 1980s Israeli suppression of Palestinian political activity was so widespread that 85 percent of Dheisheh families had at least one member who had been imprisoned by the Israelis. Within the prisons, Palestinians created a political culture informed by Palestinian national life. Prisoners returned to the community after their release as important activists and youth leaders. Centers of activism included the Palestinian Student Union and Palestinian universities such as Bethlehem and Bir Zeit. Palestinian high schools became the centers of political activity for children and youth. Inside Dheisheh, the Youth Club became a center of recruitment from the general population. The most significant youth organizations were the Givas El Amal and the Youth Movement, which organized various subgroups such as the Front for Student Work and the High School Students Committee.[101]

Young people in Dheisheh were drawn deeper into political violence by the arrest of relatives and friends. One young activist said, "At the age of 13 or 14 a person has the potential to imitate those that are older. I remember that I wanted to be like 'M' [his cousin] to participate in battle." Another informant, who was in the ninth grade when he joined the High School Students Committee, said: "We read books, we broadened our awareness through nationalist activity. We began to throw stones at Israeli patrols. We the residents of Dheisheh were among the first to use stones in confrontation with the Army." "By accident," he went on to say, "we found an old rifle and we turned into a small independent three man cell." Another young teen described his involvement as follows: "I was in a refugee camp in which everyone spoke about politics day and night and when my mother and grandmother spoke about politics how could I not speak. In the beginning my mother tried to keep me from participating in the meetings of the student committee, in demonstrations and so forth but the adults love the fight, Palestine, the revolution and suffer from the occupation . . . at the same time they fear for their children."[102]

The First Intifada: 1987–1993

The Palestinian popular uprising known as the first intifada grew out of nearly twenty years of youth radicalism. The term *intifada* means "shaking off." The first intifada broke out in the Gaza Strip in December 1987 and spread to the West Bank. Most accounts point to a traffic accident on December 8, 1987, in Gaza, in which an Israeli truck driver killed four Arab construction workers from the Jabaliya refugee camp, as the spark that ignited the intifada. But the "Battle of Balata," a mini-intifada in a refugee camp near Nablus in the spring of 1987, set the political tone for the intifada. At Balata Palestinian youth effectively took control of an entire refugee camp. At first, children under the control and direction of the Shabiba used stones as weapons, but firebombs and Molotov cocktails quickly became part of the tool kit for confronting Israeli army patrols. In May, the Israeli army moved in to arrest terrorists and militants and to confiscate weapons. Confronted by rioting women and children who gave them the choice of firing on them or withdrawing, the army withdrew, leaving Balata under Shabiba control and giving youth a clear victory over the Israeli army.[103] Balata was the first open display of the power of the Shabiba. Children and youth played a major role in initiating and sustaining the revolt, and they remained the key public face and symbol of the intifada throughout its duration.

The first intifada was a popular uprising, and the depth and intensity of the feeling caught the still-exiled PLO by surprise. From Tunis, the PLO scrambled to assert its control. Four main PLO factions—al-Fatah, the PFLP, the DFLP, and the Communist party—began to provide support, funding, and structure to the largely West Bank–based Unified Leadership of the Uprising. These organizations, based outside Palestine, constituted the "outside" leadership of the intifada. But the day-to-day operation of the intifada remained in the hands of the "inside" leadership, which was drawn from the youth movement and the organizations and institutions that mobilized youth during the 1970s and 1980s.[104]

The concentration of power and authority in the hands of children and youth during the first intifada was unmistakable. Jacques Pinto, an Israeli army officer involved in the suppression of the intifada, observed that the average age of the busloads of Palestinians who were arrested and taken into military custody for throwing Molotov cocktails and stones was seventeen. Pinto believed that the Palestinian youth were leading an intergenerational revolution as well as a war against Israel. "We are witnessing," said Pinto, "the breakdown of the whole traditional ancestral structure of society. It's a real social revolution. The peoples' committees in the villages are run by boys of fifteen, who are challenging the authority of old sheiks and imams."[105]

Palestinian youths who confronted Israelis during the first intifada were well organized. In some West Bank towns Palestinian youth would divide themselves up into small groups, each with its own commander, and lie in wait to ambush Israeli settlers driving through the town. After the settlers were attacked, the Israeli army would rush in, and the youth would draw the Israeli soldiers into the back streets of town, where they could be more easily attacked. Attack groups were supported by teenage girls, who supplied cologne, lemons, and onions to counteract the effects of tear gas. These Palestinian youth cadres garnered a great deal of media attention, much of which overlooked their clear intention to inflict physical injury on their victims.[106]

During the first intifada there were many attacks against Israelis with lethal weapons, including hand grenades, guns, and knives, but these attacks are thought to have been those of lone Palestinians rather than of organized groups. In the more coordinated youth attacks, the attackers intentionally used stones and Molotov cocktails instead of conventional weapons of war. The decision to steer clear of using arms was pragmatic rather than moral. First, Palestinians did not have access to large caches of arms. Second, at least some

Palestinians believed that by abstaining from using arms they would gain sympathy and support in the international community and within Israeli society from people repulsed by the use of Israeli military force against "civilians."[107] In all these instances the Palestinian leadership was adept at exploiting the hazy perceptual boundaries between civilians and combatants. Legally, Palestinian youth were combatants, irrespective of whether they used stones, Molotov cocktails, or rifles. Indeed, once arrested, Palestinian youth invariably demanded to be treated as prisoners of war under the Geneva Conventions. Emotionally, however, the image of stone-throwing, street-clothed youngsters confronting uniformed, armed soldiers amplified perceptions of Palestinian vulnerability.

Although the conflict was portrayed this way in the Western media, Palestinian participants understood the drama of the confrontation quite differently. Ali Qleibo, a Palestinian anthropologist, describes his own reaction to a confrontation he witnessed in Jerusalem a few days after the outbreak of the intifada. Waking up to the sound of explosions, he saw a crowd of students and young men in masks attacking a municipal van. The street, as he described it, was a battlefield. Teenagers and young men were kicking the van, smashing its windows, and trying to overturn it. They rolled a burning tire beneath the van to explode the gas tank. Israeli soldiers soon appeared shooting tear gas at the masked youths. The youth threw stones, flung the Israeli tear-gas canisters back at the soldiers, and hurled sexual insults at them to the cheers and laughter of the crowd, which grew louder and louder.[108] The symbolic power of youth militancy crystallized in one confrontation described by Qleibo:

> We began to follow the steps of a masked youth sauntering in the
> direction of the soldiers who were seeking shelter from the stones
> behind a nearby wall. [The] masked youth began walking in dance-
> like steps, coyly, ridiculing the soldiers and their bombs. . . . The
> confrontation reached a climax when the youth carried the [tear-gas]
> bomb streaming white clouds of tear gas and, like a discus thrower,
> he flung it back. He stood upright, hands on his waist, saying, "You
> come here. If you really are a man . . . show me your face." . . . The
> euphoria accompanying confrontation with the Israeli soldiers is
> contagious. The excitement moves from the street through the
> windows to us. . . . We respond with sporadic thundering applause.
> Commonplace clichés are reiterated by the throngs of men and
> women watching from the balconies. "May God's support be with
> you. May God protect your youth."[109]

Qleibo's description is not of a community exploiting its children, but of a community in ecstasy, enthralled by the power of youth.

Palestinian youth who battled Israeli soldiers during the first intifada regard that time as the glory days of Palestinian resistance. Manal, who was thirteen years old when the intifada broke out and was shot in the chest at age fifteen, states, "I miss those days a lot. They were the most beautiful days of my life. True, everyone was scared of the soldiers and their guns but we had dignity and it was our dignity that made us so defiant." Ra'at, who was jailed many times by the Israelis since his first arrest at age fourteen in 1984, states, "Nowadays, I sit around and recall the beauty of the intifada. . . . I remember the days when we were wanted by the Israelis and how we fought against a common enemy. We felt we were making a step forward, no matter how small, toward a greater goal."[110]

The intifada came to an end when Israel and the PLO entered into the Oslo Peace Accords in 1993. The Oslo Accords allowed the Palestinian leadership, including Arafat, to return to Palestine from exile in Tunis and to create formal institutions of government, namely the Palestinian Authority. In bringing the intifada to an end, the adult leadership of the Palestinians sought to curb youth violence and bring youth leadership under the control of the Palestinian Authority and the PLO.

The success of the intifada made it clear that the PLO was neither the sole relevant player nor the sole inspiration for youth violence. In Gaza and elsewhere Hamas and Islamic Jihad confirmed that for some Palestinians there could never be a political solution to the conflict. Despite their bitter differences, both these organizations had common roots in the Muslim Brotherhood, and like the religious leaders during the Mandate they defined the conflict between Israel and the Palestinians as an end-of-days struggle that could be resolved only by the destruction of Israel and the de-Judaization of Palestine. In naming its military wing the Izz a Din al-Qassam Battalion, Hamas provided a direct symbolic and military link to the earliest days of the conflict. As the intifada wound down after 1991, and prospects for peace began to emerge, both Hamas and Islamic Jihad sought to destroy such hopes by kidnapping and murdering Israeli soldiers inside Israel, murdering Palestinian collaborators, and attacking Israeli civilians. From the time of the first intifada, the Palestinian Authority was forced to share political space with a growing movement of Islamists seeking to channel the militancy of the youth who had been sidelined by the political successes of the intifada.

The al-Aqsa Intifada: Reconstructing the Apocalypse

The 1993 Oslo Peace Accords ended the first intifada. But the subsequent seven years of negotiation led to a dead end, and the peace process failed. On a late summer afternoon in 2000, I was at the home of a Palestinian family in Beit Sahur, in the West Bank near Jerusalem. Within a month, Ariel Sharon would make his famous walk onto the Temple Mount in Jerusalem, and the Palestinians would initiate the second, or al-Aqsa, intifada. My wife and I were drinking coffee and eating nuts and pastries with our Palestinian friends. My eight-year-old daughter was playing with one of the girls, and the boys were playing a computer game. Yousef, the husband, was an activist who was arrested in the 1988 Beit Sahur tax boycott, the only attempt at non-violent resistance in the history of Palestinian nationalism.[111] The atmosphere was warm and friendly, but the conversation was bleak; Yousef believed that violence was inevitable. Former right-wing prime minister Benjamin Netanyahu was better than the current Labor prime minister, Ehud Barak, Yousef told me. "At least you knew who [Netanyahu] was. You can't trust the Israeli Labor Party. They talk peace, but they are just the same as Likud."

During that summer the situation on the ground was tense. Although Israel had recently transferred additional land on the West Bank to Palestinian control, more than two hundred thousand Jewish settlers now lived on the West Bank. The PLO was fracturing, and many of its factions broke with Arafat's al-Fatah movement to join Hamas and Islamic Jihad in their rejection of the Oslo Accords. By mid-July, when negotiations at Camp David failed, mutual recriminations filled the air. On September 28, Sharon, then leader of the Israeli opposition party, visited the Temple Mount, which is adjacent to two Moslem holy sites, the al-Aqsa mosque and the Dome of the Rock. Sharon did not enter the Moslem holy sites, but most Palestinians regard his visit as the "cause" of the al-Aqsa intifada. Palestinian officials, however, acknowledge that a new intifada had been planned long in advance of Sharon's visit in order to use violence to pressure Israel at the negotiating table.[112]

With the collapse of Camp David, young leaders from al-Fatah's Tanzim (Organization) group were demanding that the Palestinian leadership move away from negotiations with Israel and toward the model of Hizbollah-style guerrilla warfare that had been directed against the Israeli occupation of south Lebanon. Although Arafat may not have ordered the beginning of the intifada, he did nothing to stop it. Rather, his strategy was to wait for the "diplomatic harvest" he believed would flow from the uprising.[113] If this was the situation, then the Sharon incident—in which a powerful Israeli who was particularly hated by Palestinians asserted political dominion over the Temple Mount—is more accurately described not as a cause of the intifada but as the occasion for a symbolic reframing of the Palestinian narrative. The event reintroduced the threatened Judaization of Palestine, the central symbolic set piece of the Islamist narrative set out by Palestinian nationalists during the Mandate. Just as the Mufti argued that the Palestinian movement was about saving the land and the holy sites from the depredation of the Jews, so Sharon's visit reenergized and revitalized this religious narrative of struggle. Once again religion and the defense of the al-Aqsa mosque became a major means of mobilizing the population and the central political idiom of the street.[114]

In 2000, the Palestinians were in a far better position to wage armed struggle against Israel than they were during the first intifada. Under the Oslo Accords, the Palestinian Authority was permitted to create a limited armed police force. For the first time in modern history Palestinians were legally allowed to arm themselves. By the time the intifada began, the Palestinians had one of the largest paramilitary forces in the Middle East with some forty thousand police under arms.[115] The new Palestinian Authority quickly began to smuggle great quantities of arms into the Palestinian-controlled territories and to place the Palestinian police and other armed groups under the command and control of Arafat. In its desire to monopolize the use of violence in the territories, the Palestinian Authority sought to push youth to the political sidelines and to control youth radicalism. The emergence of a variety of armed factions revealed the existence of both generational and ideological cleavages among Palestinians. The official Palestinian security forces were composed of older Palestinians, and the leaders and bearers of authority within these groups were former PLO exiles. But younger paramilitary forces, such as the Tanzim militia and the al-Aqsa Martyrs Brigade, were led by the former youth leaders of the first intifada and continued to draw children and youth as members.

After Oslo, the public relationship between Israelis and Palestinians reflected the officially stated assumption that political compromise between Israelis and Palestinians was both possible and desirable. But within Palestinian-controlled territories the education and training of children and youth were frequently shaped by radically different assumptions. Much of the newly developing Palestinian educational system focused on reviving the strident apocalyptic messages that the peace process should have brought to an end. Beyond the classroom, in the five-year period leading up to the outbreak of the second intifada, the Palestinian Authority established ninety paramilitary training camps for teenage youth. Training in these camps included mock kidnappings of Israeli officials by masked Palestinian commandos, mock attacks on military posts, as well as weapons training with Kalashnikov assault rifles. Practical training was combined with themes of patriotism, resistance, and a worldview that continued to call for an end to the Jewish presence in all of Palestine. As Suleiman Nubaim, age sixteen, put it, "I want my country to be free. . . . As long as Israel occupies any part of our land, in Tel Aviv, Jaffa or Haifa[,] . . . we have not liberated our homeland."[116] Similarly, Muhammad Saman, a young teenager from Beach Camp, a refugee camp in northern Gaza, who had spent two summers in a Palestinian Authority paramilitary training camp, said, "I'd give Palestinians back all their homeland, and I'd send the Israelis back to the countries they came from." If they refused to leave, Muhammad said, "Then I'd kill them."[117] Palestinian officials in charge of the camps stressed the important intergenerational political and ideological links between current youth training and the history of Palestinian resistance. One camp leader, Wajieh Affouneh, said, "We joined the Palestinian national movement when we were their age . . . and we are creating a continuum between our generation and theirs."[118]

The violence of the new intifada escalated rapidly. Stone throwing swiftly evolved into armed attacks against settlers and the military and then into suicide bombings. Suicide bombings did not begin with the intifada, but before the intifada they were the signature tool of Islamist groups. With the al-Aqsa intifada, they became a primary strategy of al-Fatah and other nationalist forces. The violence was more hierarchically structured and institutionalized than it was during the first intifada. Teen paramilitary Muhammad Saman, mentioned above, was part of a group of young children, preteenagers, teenagers, and armed adults who regularly confronted Israeli troops at the Karni junction in the Gaza Strip. The aggression at Karni was organized along generational lines. Adults usually restricted their firefights with the Israelis to the nighttime and allowed the teenagers to use rocks during the day. Israeli troops sometimes fired live ammunition at the teenagers, especially when settlers were attacked with stones and Molotov cocktails.[119] As the violence intensified, Palestinian children and youth everywhere became armed combatants and transporters and smugglers of explosives. Large numbers of young Palestinian children have been seriously injured while transporting or throwing exploding pipe bombs.[120]

THE CHILD MARTYRS: SUICIDE TERRORISM
Strikingly, children and youth have also joined the growing number of suicide terrorists whose bombs have killed and wounded hundreds of Israeli civilians. The first suicide attack took place on September 12, 1993, the day before the Oslo Peace Accords were signed on the White House lawn.[121] Following the signing of the Accords, Hamas and Islamic Jihad launched a campaign of suicide bombing in order to kill off the peace process. The campaign, which targeted buses, bus stops, restaurants, refreshments stands, and downtown areas, killed numerous civilians and soldiers.[122] Between the

signing of the Oslo Peace Accords in 1993 and August 2002, 198 suicide
bombing missions took place. Some 100 of these took place in the first ten
months of 2002.[123] Although suicide bombing was initiated by Hamas and
Islamic Jihad, its adoption by the al-Fatah–linked al-Aqsa Martyrs Brigade
declared it to be a standard tool of the Palestinian resistance.

In its 2002 report, *Erased in a Moment*, Human Rights Watch documented
the recruitment of Palestinian children and youth and noted that the al-Aqsa
Martyrs Brigade, Hamas, and Islamic Jihad had sponsored most of the bombings. Among the youngest suicide bombers were Muhammad Daraghmeh, age
seventeen, who set off a bomb in an orthodox neighborhood of Jerusalem in
March 2002; Issa Bdeir (Issan Budeir), age sixteen, who carried out his attack in Rishon Letzion on May 22, 2002; and Majd 'Atta, age seventeen, who
set off a suicide bomb in falafel shop in central Jerusalem on July 30, 2002.
In June 2002, an Israeli military court sentenced a sixteen-year-old Palestinian boy to life imprisonment for attempting to blow himself up on or near a
bus. The boy admitted to being recruited by Hamas. Islamic Jihad acknowl-
edged that it taught another child, sixteen-year-old Hamza Samudi, to drive
in order to carry out a bombing in June 2002. Similarly in April 2002 in three
separate incidents in Gaza, Palestinian boys between the ages of fourteen and
sixteen charged Israeli settlements armed with knives and crude pipe bombs
and were killed.[124]

Both Hamas and Islamic Jihad have occasionally issued public disavowals
of the recruitment of children, but the al-Aqsa Martyrs Brigade has been silent. Human Rights Watch is skeptical of these disavowals because they ob-
fuscate the issue of age and ignore the process of recruitment; they assert that
the acts of children are purely independent and voluntary. But every suicide
bombing requires a network of recruiters, logistical support, supplies, training, and assistance from the sponsoring organization. Most important, such
pro forma disavowals did not prevent bombings by children after the statements were made.[125]

The suicide bombing carried out by Issa Bdeir reveals how such acts are
organized and coordinated by different Palestinian factions.[126] Bdeir, the son
of a lawyer, was a Beit Jala schoolboy when he was recruited by the al-Aqsa
Martyrs Brigade. He was a good student, but an uncle reported that he had
written "God willing, I will be a martyr" in one of his school notebooks. Like
other suicide terrorists, his final message was recorded on video. Posing with
a black and white scarf and backpack and holding guns in each hand, he proclaimed, "I am going to commit my operation to avenge the continuous Israeli
aggression against our people. Goodbye Mother, Goodbye Father and goodbye
to my family." Just before the attack he dyed his hair blond in order to blend

in with the Russian immigrants and Israelis living in Rishon Letzion. He targeted a park where elderly men gathered to drink tea and play cards, dominoes, and backgammon, and he set off his bomb among the players.

Bdeir is dead and can no longer speak, but indirect evidence provided by a female companion who panicked and backed out at the last minute provides some insight into the organization of the attack. Joining Bdeir in the attack was Arin Ahmed, a twenty-year-old computer-programming student at Bethlehem University. She was to set off a second bomb to kill any survivors fleeing the first blast. Recruited by Tanzim, she changed her mind at the last minute, but in a cell-phone call to her and Bdeir an al-Aqsa commander prompted Bdeir to continue.

Ahmed's motivation for becoming a suicide terrorist was more personal than Bdeir's. She wanted to avenge the death of her boyfriend, Jad Salem, a member of Tanzim. Ahmed believed that Salem was killed by the Israeli Defense Forces, although he may have accidentally blown himself up while preparing a car bomb. Ahmed contacted Tanzim and volunteered for a suicide mission. Four days later she was told to prepare herself. "I thought they would take me to start preparing for it, that they would train me and teach me about weapons. . . . I was sure it was a process that took several months. Then suddenly, four days later, some Tanzim militia came and told me: 'We've chosen you. Congratulations.' . . . I never imagined it could happen so fast."

The training she and Bdeir received was short and intense. "They didn't let me think about it too much. They told me: 'You'll gain a very special status among the women suicide bombers. You'll be a real heroine. It's for Jad's memory. You'll be with him in Paradise.' They pushed me. They encouraged me. I did whatever they told me. They explained everything to Issan and me." But when they arrived at the scene of the bombing, Ahmed panicked. "I got out of the car. The place wasn't exactly like I'd seen on the map. I saw lots of people, mothers with children, teenage boys and girls. I remembered an Israeli girl my age whom I used to be in touch with. I suddenly understood what I was about to do and said to myself: 'How can I do such a thing?' I changed my mind. Issan also had second thoughts, but they managed to convince him to go ahead. I saw him go and blow himself up."

EXPLAINING SUICIDE TERRORISM

How do Palestinians understand the phenomenon of suicide terrorism, especially the active involvement of children and youth? Palestinians routinely ascribe suicide bombing to the dire situation of Palestinians under Israeli occupation. Central to the Palestinian narrative is the deep belief that Palestinians are victims. For example, the prominent Palestinian legislator Hanan

Ashrawi describes suicide bombings as largely unplanned, virtually irrational, and spontaneous acts of desperation. "The people who do it . . . ," she states, "are individuals or small groups who are driven to desperation and anger by the Israeli activities."[127] Although Ashrawi does not openly proclaim that suicide bombing is a legitimate form of Palestinian resistance, she offers little explanation beyond blaming Israel for the oppressive conditions from which these acts of Palestinian violence arise. This generic explanation shifts the blame for every act of Palestinian violence onto Israel. In the specific instance of suicide bombing, Ashrawi characterizes Palestinian suicide bombers as "double victims"—innocent victims first of the Israeli occupation and second of their own act of self-annihilation in response to the occupation. The bombers, although not necessarily heroes, are without culpability; they are as innocent as the people they kill, perhaps more so. Ashrawi spurns the notion that anything in Palestinian history or culture might provide a basis for understanding the actions of the bomber. "Our culture," she states, "is not a suicidal culture; historically, the incidence of suicide among Palestinians has been very low."[128]

There is a certain sleight of hand in Ashrawi's analysis. Islam is generally hostile to the idea of suicide. But suicide terrorists do not regard themselves, nor are they generally regarded by other Palestinians, as common suicides. Instead, like all Palestinians who have died in wars with Israel, they regard themselves as martyrs. The commonly used expression for suicide terrorists is *istashaheed* (those who kill themselves in a martyr's death), *shaheed* (martyrs), or *shaeed batal* (martyr heroes). The culturally abhorred category of suicide—otherwise forbidden in Islam—is simply not applied to these actions. In describing these acts as deviant behavior standing outside Palestinian history and culture, Ashrawi frames them within the Palestinian narrative of victimization as abnormal, "un-Palestinian" acts brought about by Israeli persecution. Suicide terrorism, like all youth violence, can be interpreted as a reaction to the calculated "invitation," embedded in Israeli acts of oppression, that tempts Palestinian youth to respond. Palestinians, in this narrative, always react to, but never initiate, acts of violence. The cycle of violence that Ashrawi so often takes pains to deplore always begins and ends with Israeli culpability and Palestinian innocence.

Although the notion of Israeli culpability for all violence is axiomatic among Palestinians, Ashrawi's view is rejected by the organizations that carry out "martyrdom" actions. Although they believe in the total criminality and culpability of Israel, they do not see young bombers as desperate and irrational. Instead, Hamas and Islamic Jihad honor and valorize the young bombers, and they celebrate their actions as an affirmative expression of the development and growth of Palestinian political consciousness; they thereby place these young people in the long history of Palestinian youth martyrs. When Salah Shehadah, a late leader of the al-Qassam Brigade, was asked about young boys' seeking martyrdom, he replied, "It is an indicator of the positive consciousness of Palestinian society and not a fault. . . . [It] is proof that the nation of Islam [*umma*] has become a *jihadist umma* that refuses disrespect and oppression." For Shehadah, the chronological age of the child was irrelevant. His only concern was that the child be mentally prepared to carry out the bombing in a manner consistent with the religious goals of the organization. "There is a need," he stated, "to instruct those children in a special military section that gives them a *jihadist* military education, so that they can distinguish right from wrong and know when they are capable of carrying out a martyrdom operation and when they should not."[129]

Hamas activists stress the idea that young martyrs must be mentally stable. Even if revenge is a motive—which it often is—their actions should not be rooted in personal anguish and distress. Osama Mzeini, a doctoral candidate in psychology at the Islamic University who was imprisoned with would-be Palestinian and Lebanese suicide bombers, states it is important "to differentiate between someone who ends his life because of mental torment, and an *istashaheed*, who is happy and loves life, a person with inner strength."[130] The view shared by Hamas activists is that the ideal martyr is exactly the opposite of the one Ashrawi describes; these activists substitute a narrative of empowerment for one of desperation. The suicide terrorist, rather than being a mentally tortured individual whose impulsive actions place him or her outside Palestinian history and culture, becomes the noble *istashaheed*, whose sacrifice takes a central place in Palestinian history and myth.

This view resonates deeply throughout the Arab world. The suicide bombing carried out by Ayat al-Akhras, referred to earlier, was widely acclaimed. Shortly after the attack the former Saudi ambassador to the United Kingdom, Ghazi al-Gosaibi, published a poem titled "The Martyrs" in the London-based Arabic newspaper *al-Hayat*. Interviewed about the reasons he had written this poem, he stated, "I saw her talking in the video broadcast on television. . . . She was young, 17, and I imagined her to be my daughter."[131] Glorifying Akhras as a "bride of heaven," the poem makes it clear that she and all the other suicide bombers and attackers are martyrs and not common suicides. "Did you commit suicide?" the poem asks. "No, we've committed suicide / preferring a life of the living-dead."[132]

These twin narratives of desperation and empowerment sometimes stand side by side as oppositional constructs and sometimes stand as complementary modes of understanding. Both views inform community understanding of the phenomenon. The honoring of child martyrdom extends beyond Islamist groups to mainstream Palestinian media and discourse. Palestinian Authority television reports extol the virtues of martyrdom, explicitly encouraging children to take part in clashes with Israeli forces. There is a fine line between a suicide attack, in which children make a hopeless assault on an Israeli settler or soldier, and a suicide bombing, in which death is inevitable.

Some Palestinians express concern about the international condemnation associated with the recruiting of children into armed combat, yet are aware of the seductive power of the child hero bearing arms. In some instances, the response has been both to publicly chide recruiters of child soldiers and to suppress information about the children involved. Human Rights Watch points to the Palestinian Journalists Syndicate's August 2002 decision that called on Palestinian armed factions to stop using children. The same decision forbade photojournalists from taking pictures of children carrying weapons or taking part in militant activities. According to the Syndicate, such images serve "the interests of Israel and its propaganda against the Palestinian people." Tawfiq Abu Khousa, deputy chair of the syndicate, argued that media coverage and the taking of the pictures was a violation of the rights of children.[133]

The idea that suicide bombing is empowering accounts for its wide support among Palestinians, despite criticism in some academic and political circles. Kalil Shiqaqi, director of the Center for Palestine Research Studies in Nablus, says that support for violence and suicide bombing is greater among young people generally than among adults and is especially high among students and professionals. Shiqaqi also reports that, among Palestinians, the more educated a person is the more likely it is that he or she will support both violence and suicide bombing.[134] Many Palestinians point to the example of Yahya Ayesh, an engineering student from Bir Zeit University who was both a leader of the al-Qassam Brigades and the first to propose that Hamas make use of "human bombs." Similarly, Nachman Tal's profile of suicide bombers shows that the main centers of recruitment for suicide bombers are al-Najah University in Nablus and the Islamic University in Gaza. Of the 149 attackers he investigated between 1993 and 2002, 53 had some higher education, 56 had a high school education, and only 40 had an elementary school education or less. Two thirds of the attacks were carried out by children and youth between the ages of seventeen and twenty-three. Islamic Jihad uses even younger attackers; they range in age from sixteen to seventeen.[135]

On the West Bank both the refugee camps and the universities, as in the first intifada, became the centers of organized attacks. At colleges and universities students came together to generate the emotional and ideological energy for direct acts of violence. The careers of some of the most prominent Palestinian terrorists are tied to the rise of Hamas and other Islamic organizations on college campuses and to their power in attracting many of the best students. For example Qeis Adwan, once regarded as one of the most dangerous terrorists, studied architecture and led the student union at al-Najah University in Nablus, the largest and most radical university in the West Bank.[136] Adwan joined Hamas when he was about twelve or thirteen. He was one of the "children of the stones" during the first intifada. During the second intifada, Adwan organized three major suicide bombings in Israel, the most well known of which was the bombing of the Sbarro Pizza restaurant in downtown Jerusalem. Adwan was killed by Israeli forces on April 5, 2002. A member of Hamas, he consciously modeled his life on the deeds of Sheik al-Qassam, becoming devout and, as a student leader, paying the most attention to the needs of poorer students. Al-Najah University became the center for Hamas's al-Qassam Brigades, and since the second intifada began, at least eleven students from al-Najah have become suicide bombers.

On November 13, 2001, Abdallah Shalah, the leader of Islamic Jihad, addressed the students at al-Najah via telephone after the student elections in which the Muslim Palestine Party, affiliated with Hamas and Islamic Jihad, increased its control of the council at the expense of the al-Fatah–linked Shuhada (Martyr's Party). He proclaimed, "Youth of Palestine, yesterday's student council elections were a vote in favor of the Intifada, a vote in favor of the Jihad and the struggle, a vote in favor of the blood of the fallen heroes, . . . a vote in favor of the heroic suicide bombers of the Izz Adin al-Qassam battalions and the Jerusalem squads. This is the righteous choice; this is the true referendum[,] . . . a test the students of Al-Najah passed with flying colors. They proved their high level of awareness and faith, and proved the depth of their connection to Islam, to Palestine and to Jihad."[137]

Under the influence of Hamas, al-Najah University emerged as a major center for bringing cultural representations of the intifada to the wider Palestinian community. It played host to a Hamas exhibition of the suicide bombing of the Sbarro Pizza restaurant in Jerusalem. The exhibition, an installation of shattered tables, faux blood, and body parts, celebrated the bombing and the al-Qassam Brigades with a sign stating: "Qassami Pizza is more delicious."[138] Likewise, after Adwan was killed, Hamas created an exhibit in his memory at the university; it commemorated his life and martyrdom as a member of the al-Qassam Brigades and celebrated the suicide attacks he organized.

For Hamas, Islamic Jihad, and other Islamist groups, suicide bombing is a sacramental act designed to restore all Palestine to the Palestinians. This

Islamist religious perspective must be taken seriously. Everyone who has spoken with or interviewed individuals involved with suicide bombing suggests that religious belief is central to the phenomenon. Nasra Hassan, a Pakistani relief worker in Gaza, interviewed almost 250 aspiring suicide bombers and recruiters between 1996 and 1999—all prior to the outbreak of the al-Aqsa intifada—and reported that she was unable to gain access to any informants until people in Gaza were convinced that she could explain the Islamic context of the suicide operations. She observed that outbreaks of suicide bombing took place whenever there was any positive momentum in the peace process. She interviewed volunteers who had been unable to complete their missions, the families of suicide bombers, and those who trained them. All Hassan's interviewees were between the ages of eighteen and thirty-eight. For some unexplained reason she did not include children in her research. Nonetheless this is the only broad study of suicide bombers currently available, and its conclusions are telling. None of the suicide bombers were uneducated, extremely poor, or depressed. Most (she doesn't give numbers) were from refugee families, but two were the sons of millionaires. All appeared to her to be "normal." Hamas activists stressed to Hassan that there was no shortage of volunteers and that the "biggest problem is the hordes of young men who beat on our doors clamoring to be sent."[139]

Hassan described a highly structured organizational system for producing martyrs. The criteria for selection of appropriate candidates from the many volunteers were a blend of religious and pragmatic conditions including an assessment of motive, family circumstances, self-discipline, and ability to pass as an Israeli Jew. Candidates who were motivated solely by personal revenge were rejected. Candidates were observed for many months and perhaps years before finally being placed in a two- or three-person "martyrdom cell." At this point, the candidate became a "living martyr" (al shaeed al hayy) and was in the final stages before the martyrdom operation took place.[140]

AYAT AL-AKHRAS: SUICIDE BOMBER

Among Palestinians, the Israelis are the "others," the "enemy," and they are invariably described as colonialists, criminals, settlers, or Zionists regardless of whether they men, women, children, or babies and irrespective of their actual political views. Individual political views are distorted to meet the needs of the narrative. For example, Dafna Spruch, who was killed in the Hamas bombing of Hebrew University, was a major activist in the Israeli protest group Women in Black, but Hamas claimed that she was a member of Women in Green, an anti-Palestinian group.[141]

The Palestinian demonization of the Zionist enemy and its reduction of that enemy to a hated abstraction is not surprising. More astonishing is that the suicide bombers themselves fare little better as their real lives and motivations are shaped and recast by the demands of the Palestinian narrative. Here again the case of Akhras serves as an example of the narrative process. Akhras is now an icon of Palestinian martyrdom; her suicide invited widespread discussion and interpretation. Eyad Sarraj, a psychiatrist and founder of the Palestinian Independent Commission for Citizens Rights, sees her death as the result of "a long history of humiliation and a desire for revenge that every Arab harbors." According to Sarraj, "Since the establishment of Israel in 1948 and the resultant uprooting of Palestinians, a deep seated feeling of shame has taken root in the Arab psyche. Shame is the most painful emotion in the Arab culture, producing the feeling that one is unworthy to live."[142] Mahdi Abdul Hadi, director of the Palestinian Society for the Study of International Affairs, explained it this way: "I believe she felt like she'd been raped. . . . She doesn't see Israelis as civilians. Every Israeli, to her, is the army. The enemy." Returning to a trope of Palestinian politics that emerged in the beginning of the last century, Hadi tells us, "Death is the only way to cleanse herself."[143] Interpreting the martyrdom of a child as an act of cleansing is part of what Jonathan Raban has called the "dialectic of purity and pollution," which leads to the "noble obligation of martyrdom." The current Mufti of Jerusalem, Sheik Ekrima Sabri, explains the power and purity of martyrdom this way: "The Muslim embraces death. . . . Look at the society of the Israelis. It is a selfish society that loves life. These are not people that are eager to die for their country and their God. The Jew will leave the land rather than die, but the Muslim is happy to die."[144]

The numerous conversations about suicide bombings that I have had with Palestinian youth make clear that despite some misgivings suicide bombing is widely supported. The reasons are varied but at bottom young people support it because they think it works and because it has made Israelis afraid. Every suicide bombing generates a palpable thrill even if at times it is accompanied by feelings of fascination, regret, and repulsion. With every suicide bombing the Islamist narrative of empowerment resonates throughout Palestinian society; the bombing conveys a sense of vicarious empowerment in a situation where Palestinians have little actual power. No young Palestinian whom I have ever spoken to has questioned the justification of suicide bombing or its morality or has showed any concern for its victims. When the issue of victimization comes up, the bomber is regarded as the victim.

Referring to Akhras, Amneh stated: "Yeah, I think she had a good reason. How would you feel if your friends are dying in front of your eyes, not being able to go to school, not being able to practice your daily life, not being able to live your life. . . . I think she had enough. It's like she said, 'I have no other choice but this.' She can't take it anymore maybe. She didn't do it out of nothing. She didn't just say, 'Okay, I'll blow myself up.' No I think she had good enough reasons." Maryam explained the same suicide bombing to me: "Yesterday . . . we were just talking about the girl who had a bomb. The sixteen-year-old girl. What got her to that point? What made her say, 'I'm going to sacrifice myself for my people?' She had nothing. She had nothing to live for. The sad thing [is that] . . . her family . . . are probably all dead. Her house is probably torn down." Mahmood explained another suicide bombing this way: "They want people to look at them. They can't do anything else. If they bomb and suicide-bomb people will look; the other governments will look and see what is happening to us. They'll think, why did he do that? They will look; they'll see the reason. I'm totally against suicide bombs, but I think it's helped. Other people and other governments are really considering this; they're looking . . . [and asking,] why did this happen? Also [he might do this] if most of his family died, most of his friends died, and he had nothing else."

Amneh, Maryam, and Mohammed explained suicide terrorism by rationalizing the bombers' motivations. Although not directly linked to Islamist movements, they are Palestinian nationalists who have participated in anti-Israeli actions. Like other Palestinians, they voiced the view that the suicide bomber had "nothing to live for." Maryam was especially worried about the repercussions of the bombing. As she said, "It's just so sad. I was so shocked and really like kind of scared. . . . A girl bombed herself, and now they [the Israelis] are going to give us hard time for it."

The language employed makes it appear as if Akhras was the only person killed. Maryam said, "A girl bombed herself." Amneh declared that she had reasons for saying, "I'll blow myself up." Although it is not surprising that Palestinians show little concern for the Israeli dead, it is remarkable that the Israeli dead are eliminated totally from the narrative. Maryam was genuinely annoyed and perplexed that the Israelis might respond negatively to the act. For her, only Akhras's death has meaning within the narrative structure. The Israeli dead were merely stage props for her act of martyrdom.

It is almost impossible to reconcile the explanations given above with the facts of Akhras's life. She was engaged to be married and was a good student; her parents were quite alive and well; her house had not been torn down; and she gave no indication to friends and family that she was ever involved in political activity. Her motives appeared so private that Israeli intelligence and the popular press claimed that she and other female suicide bombers were seduced and impregnated by male militants in order to force them into committing suicide.[145] But, in the end, the conventions of the narrative overwhelm the particulars of her life. Akhras's motives will never be known, but in most respects her personal story has been subordinated to the political construction of the narrative so that no motive is relevant other than the politically inscribed, ideological text written on the remains of her body.

Conclusion

It is unclear why suicide bombing began, and there is no way to tell whether and when it will end. But such attacks are consistent with the actions of militant children and youth since the earliest days of the British Mandate. What is remarkable are both the continuity and the novelty of the Palestinian response. Marx might as well have been thinking of the Palestinians when he remarked in the "The Eighteenth Brumaire of Louis Bonaparte," "The tradition of all the dead generations weighs like a nightmare on the brains of the living."[146] From the beginning children and youth were expected to play a leading part in the struggle against the Jewish presence in Palestine. The death of children and youth (as well as adults) was inevitable. The celebration of the martyrdom and sacrifice of the young has become an essential cultural idiom by which death is interpreted and understood in the Palestinian community.

Chapter 5 The Politics of Age

THE CASE STUDIES presented in this book challenge the dominant humanitarian concept that child soldiers are simply vulnerable individuals exploited by adults who use them as cheap, expendable, and malleable weapons of war. These studies only begin to touch the range of circumstances in which children are engaged in combat; but they make clear that no simple model can account for the presence of children on the battlefield or the conditions under which they fight. The specifics of history and culture shape the lives of children and youth during peace and war, creating many different kinds of childhood and many different kinds of child soldiers.

Age and childhood are contested domains. Chronological age has no absolutely fixed meaning in either nature or culture. Like ethnicity, age categories such as "child," "youth," and "adult" are situationally defined within a larger system and cannot be understood without consideration of conditions and circumstances.[1] Societies in which age categories are salient engage in constant struggles over who is a child and over the cultural, legal, and moral dimensions of childhood. Even the legislative determination of age provides only a deceptive appearance of permanence, which belies a constant social and political struggle. The politics of age is part of what Nancy Sherper-Hughes and Carolyn Sargent call the "cultural politics of childhood"—namely, the ideological, political, and social uses of children and the concept of the child.[2] What is new is that the struggle over age has an increasingly global dimension.

The Agency and Rationality of Children

The politics of age informs historical and ethnographic accounts of children and war, which often stand in contradistinction to legal and humanitarian accounts of war. It is as if the only two witnesses to an event could not agree on any of its details. What is the source of this clash of analysis and interpretation? The answers lie in philosophy, method, and politics. Modern studies of children begin with the premise that it is no longer appropriate to see children solely as undeveloped or incomplete adults. They assert that children have "agency"—broadly, the capacity of children to act and to exercise power, even in situations not of their own making.[3] In contrast, humanitarian accounts implicitly or explicitly draw on the orthodox developmental models of childhood set forth by Jean Piaget and his intellectual progeny. Not surprisingly, these models have widespread currency in psychology, education, social work, and other so-called helping professions. Positing that the transition from childhood to adulthood takes place in universal, naturally determined, and fixed steps, developmental models are based on the belief that children are basically immature, incompetent, and irrational. As children grow older, nature—mediated by enculturation and socialization—transforms the child into a competent, mature, and rational adult. In contrast, empirical studies in anthropology, history, and sociology offer a new paradigm for the study of childhood. This paradigm stresses the diversity of childhood and embeds the understanding of childhood in a cultural, historical, and social context. It rejects preconceived notions of children as irrational or prelogical beings. Its starting point is the premise that children are active players in the social order who dynamically shape the world around them.[4]

Ethnography—particularly the methods of participant observation—has unsettled conventional concepts of childhood and remains the best way to study children. Observing and listening to the voice of the child in natural settings, where children are not disempowered by the regimes of formal interviewing, testing, and measurement, provide the clearest portraits of the competence of children. These methods are the social science equivalent of the revolutionary field studies of primates, which forced zoologists to completely rethink conclusions that had been drawn from the study of animals in zoos and laboratories. Pioneering ethnographic work in the study of children supports the notion that children, even young ones, are far more sophisticated, knowledgeable, rational, and skillful than is assumed in the general culture or in the popular developmental models used in psychology, education, and social work.

Ethnographic and historical accounts of young soldiers stress the agency, autonomy, and independence of youth and strain to achieve common ground with humanitarian accounts that emphasize the inherent vulnerability and dependence of the young. The conflicts between these accounts are more than just a clash between old and new paradigms of childhood. Instead, for a variety of moral and political reasons, humanitarian descriptions of children provide an exaggerated version of the development paradigm. In humanitarian accounts, child soldiers are either victims or demons, or, better yet, they are demons because they are victims. Neither demons nor victims are rational actors. Most humanitarian accounts of child soldiers suggest that their behavior on the battlefield flows from their victimization; children fight because they have been kidnapped, brainwashed, physically and sexually abused, forced to take drugs. They kill because they are irrational or prerational or because their rationality has been stripped away by adults who have forced them to ingest alcohol or drugs. In this globalized version of the science fiction film *Village of the Damned*, the child soldier is portrayed as a killer automaton. Few humanitarian descriptions suggest that children, even older children, possess individual survival strategies, apply their own intelligence, strategize about situations, enter into relationships, have conversations, or do anything that ordinary soldiers might do.

Humanitarian narratives amplify the perception that children are irrational by contrasting the helplessness of children with an excessively idealized version of adult autonomy, independence, and maturity. Children are said never to be able to voluntarily join armed forces or groups even in the face of evidence to the contrary. Children are described as being prodded by economic, social, cultural, and political pressures into "volunteering" instead of exercising the "free choice" of adult soldiers. The implication is that somehow adults join armed forces by exercising free and unfettered rational choice or informed consent in the absence of any social pressure. It is hard to imagine a less authentic description of adult participation in war.[5]

Children are seen, in these narratives, to be emotional or irrational decision makers. They volunteer to be soldiers because "they *believe* that this is the only way to guarantee regular meals, clothing, and medical attention" or because "they may *feel* safer . . . if they have guns in their hands." They join because they are "*susceptible to the lure* of military life and the *sense* of power associated with carrying deadly weapons."[6] Children only believe or feel or sense. They do not know, understand, judge, or decide. In such descriptions it seems as though no person below eighteen years of age has any capacity for rational judgment. No credibility is given to the fact that volunteering for the armed forces may be the only way to survive or that armed children may be safer than unarmed civilians.

In reducing the essential characteristics of children and youth to those usually attributed to younger children, the Straight 18 position extends the concept of childhood well beyond the empirical limits of the developmental model. Even developmental models of childhood have long advanced the idea that the capacity for adult reasoning is present in teenagers as young as fourteen. Based in the central theoretical concepts of developmental psychology, these findings have been replicated in numerous empirical studies involving adolescent participation in child-custody decisions, health-care decision making, and criminal justice proceedings.[7] The evidence supports the view that adolescents have the capacity to weigh information and make decisions. Accordingly, legal scholars have increasingly argued for the recognition of adolescent decisional autonomy.[8]

The humanitarian narrative falsely assumes a consensus within Western legal traditions about the age of capacity and consent, when in fact these legal traditions comprise a multitude of confusing distinctions and doctrines. Under British common law, the age of capacity was seven. After age seven, children were deemed to have the capacity for "felonious discretion" and were subject to criminal prosecution, even in capital cases. Moreover, legal scholars have voiced considerable skepticism as to the presumed weakness of children, as well as to who benefits from imposing a fixed chronological definition of childhood. It has never been altogether clear that the true purpose of legal infancy doctrines was to protect children, and some suggest that children might have been far better off without these doctrines.[9] A considerable body of research indicates that children, certainly by age fourteen, are no less competent than adults to make major decisions concerning their own welfare.[10] In his review of legal doctrines of childhood capacity, Laurence Tribe argued that although a fully "child blind" society might not be conceivable, widespread age-based distinctions ought to be treated as "semi-suspect classifications," an idea that would invalidate all but the most compelling and justified of those distinctions.[11] Although participation in warfare could be argued to be one such compelling context, modern legal theory is generally skeptical of enduring and universal age-based distinctions and lends scant justification to creating a universal concept of childhood extending to age eighteen.

The rationale behind the Straight 18 position has little to do with scientific studies of childhood. Science is used to cover and lend support to the moral position that war is illegitimate. Humanitarian groups basically seek an end to the use of aggression. This worthy goal is consistent with the United

Nations Charter, which in its preamble weaves together human rights principles and hatred of warfare to call on the world to save future generations from the "scourge of war."[12] Clearly, the practice of states has not brought an end to war. But a legalistic approach that uses international treaties to expand the rules governing warfare does put symbolic—and in a few instances pragmatic—constraints on how war is conducted. This approach includes banning specific technologies of war, protecting civilians and combatants, controlling the behavior of combatants, and limiting the use of certain categories of persons as combatants. Dozens of treaties, protocols, conventions, and declarations ban so-called dum-dum bullets, poison gas, and land mines, among other weapons; protect civilians, prisoners of war, and the wounded; and prohibit the use of mercenaries. New prohibitions on recruiting children into armed forces and groups are part of this century-long effort to end warfare through humanitarian intervention and legal rule making. Broadening the protections for children, including redefining and expanding the definition of childhood, adds to the growing list of internationally recognized legal obstacles to war.

These legal and social changes affect the involvement of children in war in two broad ways. First, they inhibit the use and recruitment of children into armed forces and groups, and, second, they provide a mantle of protection for child soldiers by immunizing them from prosecution and absolving them from criminal liability for war crimes. These efforts have met with some success. Since the mid-1970s an international consensus that children under age fifteen should be fully protected from both recruitment and prosecution has grown. There has been less success in developing a clear international consensus on young people between the ages of fifteen and eighteen.

Ironically, these developments are taking place at the same time that elsewhere, especially in U.S. criminal law, children are assumed to have adultlike capacities and are treated like adults—including being held fully responsible for the consequences of their actions. Given the protective concerns of the Western-based humanitarian enterprise, this poses a great moral dilemma. In Western legal systems, especially in the United States, reclassifying children as adults is rarely to their benefit. Children charged with criminal acts once enjoyed the protection of the juvenile-justice system; now they can and will be treated as adults and subjected to the harshest of penalties. Children are usually reclassified as adults when the prosecutorial system intends to punish them severely. Every year in the United States, over two hundred thousand children under age eighteen are tried as adults.[13] Children who were as young as twelve when they committed a murder have been sentenced to life in prison for their crime. Protecting children from the extraordinarily punitive gaze of this brutal and unforgiving criminal justice system is one impetus for the desire to extend the concept of childhood to include older children.

But protecting children can be a Janus-faced operation, where protection and suppression work in tandem.[14] The criminal justice system and its juvenile-justice analogs exist to control and punish, so it is not surprising they also shape the concept of childhood to meet those goals. Doubtless it is far less horrific for a young person charged with a crime to be treated as a child or a juvenile instead of as an adult, but under the banner of protectionism juvenile-justice systems also subjugate and suppress children. "Children" charged with "status offenses" are routinely deprived of the civil rights of adults. The justice system regularly penalizes children for behavior that adults engage in as a matter of right. As Randy Kandel and Anne Griffiths make clear, in the name of child protection teenagers are stripped of their civil rights, placed under court supervision, assigned to foster homes and other institutions, and subjected to mandatory psychological therapy. Usually these cases involve "ordinary lawful acts and behavior that a slightly older person can freely do, such as having sex, cutting class, disobeying parents, 'trashing' one's room, or staying out late with one's friends."[15] Schools increasingly refer "disorderly" children to the criminal justice system. Students have been arrested for wearing "inappropriate" clothing, shouting at classmates, turning off bathroom lights, hiding in school and not going to class, and other forms of disorderly behavior.[16]

Broadening and solidifying the otherwise fluid boundaries among childhood, youth, and adulthood becomes especially problematic during wartime. The conditions of war often erase carefully constructed cultural, legal, and social boundaries of class, gender, and age, and reveal them as artifice.[17] Among Jewish partisans, high-status professional men with peacetime skills were often useless, while working-class men and boys with practical skills were dominant. Organized ghetto youth had better access to strategic information and weapons than did the older political leadership. The temporary leveling of status categories occasioned by war has been demonstrated time and again.

There is no doubt that in recent wars armies of children have committed horrific crimes, including innumerable acts of terrorism, murder, rape, sadism, and torture. Were they adults, they would have few, if any, legal defenses in international or domestic law. But the terrible specter of placing large numbers of children and youth on trial perhaps demands abrogating their criminal responsibility. International lawmakers may simply find it intolerable (and impractical) to place so many of the children and youth of a nation on trial, even if their justification for excluding them from prosecution rests on the flimsiest of scientific foundations.

International Law Regarding Child Soldiers

International law regulating the use of child soldiers is part of the laws of war. Usually termed *international humanitarian law*, the laws of war are articulated in both treaties and customary usages and define individual criminal culpability during wartime. The laws of war primarily govern international armed conflicts, although many provisions are also applicable to internal conflicts. War crimes are the gravest breaches of these laws.

One central concern of the laws of war is to make a clear distinction between civilians and combatants. As a general rule, combatants are privileged under the laws of war, which regulate but do not bar killing. They may lawfully kill one another with impunity. Combatants, however, may not ordinarily kill civilians. Civilians, in turn, may kill neither combatants nor one another. Such killing is not privileged—it is simply murder. The remainder of the laws of war regulate the manner and mode of killing as these have developed through custom, practice, and treaty.

The laws of war also make important legal distinctions among combatants. They may be either "lawful combatants" or "unlawful combatants." Lawful combatants are usually the regular armed forces of a party to a international conflict but may include other armed forces of a party to an international conflict that meet the following four criteria: they must be under the command and control of an individual responsible for his or her subordinates; they must display fixed and distinctive insignia or signs that are recognizable at a distance; they must carry arms openly; and they must fight according to the laws of war. Guerilla forces fighting in an international conflict may or may not be deemed lawful combatants, depending on whether they operate in a manner consistent with these criteria. Lawful combatants are especially privileged. If they are captured, they are entitled to protection as prisoners of war. As soldiers, they are entitled to kill other soldiers and cannot be punished for doing so. They can, however, be criminally liable for violating other laws of war, such as deliberately targeting civilians.

With certain exceptions, rebel groups, insurgents, or other dissident forces in an internal conflict within a state are never lawful combatants.[18] Technically, they are not combatants at all because the legal concept of combatant is reserved for armed forces and groups involved in international conflicts between sovereign states. Because of this distinction, unlawful combatants are sometimes described as offensive civilians. Terrorists are also not lawful combatants because they use the cover of their civilian status and violate other rules of war by making civilians their prime targets. If captured, unlawful combatants have none of the rights of prisoners of war. They are not war criminals per se, but they can be treated as criminals for crimes such as treason and may even be sentenced to death. Like lawful combatants, they can be considered war criminals if they commit war crimes.[19]

Regarding children, a central concern of international humanitarian law is to prevent them from serving as combatants, lawful or otherwise. In addition, international humanitarian law seeks to extend special prisoner-of-war privileges to captured children who are lawful combatants. Finally, it seeks to protect captured children who have served as unlawful combatants or committed war crimes from the severest punishments of the law.

The most important treaties encoding the laws of war are the four 1949 Geneva Conventions, which govern the treatment of the civilians, prisoners, the sick, and the wounded during wartime. In 1977, two Protocols Additional supplemented the original Geneva Conventions and have special relevance for child soldiers. Protocol Additional I enhances protections to victims of international armed conflict, while Protocol Additional II expands protections to victims of noninternational conflict. In addition, several other treaties lay out other important laws of war: the 1948 Convention on the Prevention and Punishment of Genocide and, most recently, the 1998 Rome Statute, which created the International Criminal Court.

None of the original four original Geneva Conventions addressed the issue of child soldiers. But, beginning with the Protocols Additional, prohibitions against the use of child soldiers began to emerge. Today, provisions criminalizing the recruitment of child soldiers are part of the 1998 Rome Statute as well as the 2002 treaty that established the Special Court for trying war crimes in Sierra Leone. Other international treaties also contain provisions that call for partial or total bans on the use of child soldiers, although none of these provide for criminal sanctions against violators. These include the Convention on the Rights of the Child (1989), the Optional Protocol to the Convention on the Rights of the Child on the Involvement of Children in Armed Conflict (2000), the African Charter on the Rights and Welfare of the Child (1990), and the International Labour Organization Worst Forms of Child Labour Convention 182 (1999).

INTERNATIONAL CONFLICTS AND CIVIL WARS

Beginning with the Protocols Additional, international treaties addressing the issue of child soldiers have distinguished between the two categories of conflict mentioned above and between two categories of children: international armed conflict (wars between sovereign states) and noninternational conflicts (civil wars, rebellions, and insurgencies) and younger children (below age fifteen) and older children (between the ages of fifteen and eighteen). The application of international law to each category of children depends on the type of conflict.

Conflicts between sovereign states are privileged and invoke the widest application of international humanitarian law. Treaties addressing international conflict are the product of negotiation among sovereign states that agree to be bound by treaty. The application of international treaties to noninternational conflicts is more limited. Moreover, because only sovereign states sign and ratify treaties affecting noninternational conflicts, one party is always missing—the rebel group or insurgents who are said to be bound by these treaties but have had no hand in their creation.

International conflicts are the kinds of aggression that the United Nations was established to end. The United Nations Charter prohibits aggression and confines the right to engage in war to national self-defense. However, there is no clearly defined crime of aggression under international law, which leaves the interpretation of aggression and self-defense to each state. In contrast, conflicts within sovereign states are treated, at least from each sovereign state's point of view, as treason or rebellion. Rebellions and insurgencies are criminal per se, and international law has relatively little application to them.

The dichotomy between international and noninternational conflicts remains central in the four Geneva Conventions, and the majority of provisions of the Geneva Conventions apply solely to international armed conflict. For example, the Third Geneva Convention, dealing with the treatment of prisoner of war, contains 143 articles detailing the rights and duties of prisoners of war; 142 of these are applicable only to armed conflict between sovereign states.

The dichotomy between these two types of conflict was muddied by Protocol Additional I's novel application of the rules of international conflict to internal armed conflicts "where peoples are fighting against colonial domination, and alien occupation, and against racist regimes in the exercise of their right of self-determination."[20] This provision created a class of privileged insurgents by giving them combatant status based on the political motive for the insurgency. It also puts civilians, including children, at risk from crossfire because its rules of engagement favor privileged irregulars over civilians by permitting these forces to conceal themselves among the civil population just prior launching an attack.[21] As I show below, it also gave politically privileged insurgent groups much more flexibility in the recruitment of child soldiers than ordinary rebels have.

Otherwise, only one provision, Article 3, which is common to all the Geneva Conventions, applies to noninternational combat. Article 3 outlines minimal standards of conduct toward captured insurgents and rebels, who are referred to as "persons" rather than prisoners. Article 3 protections are largely procedural. They require, among other things, that rebels be treated humanely, but—in anticipation of their usual unhappy fate—prohibit only "the passing of sentences and the carrying out of executions without previous judgment pronounced by a regularly constituted court affording all the judicial guarantees that are recognized as indispensable by civilized peoples." Despite these procedural protections, Article 3 still permits rebels to be treated as criminals.

The sharp differences in how combatants are treated in interstate conflicts and in domestic conflicts spills over into the issue of child soldiers. From the perspective of humanitarians interested in protecting children, it is odd that the level of protection should vary with the nature of the conflict. But this contradiction derives from the international law-making process, which strives to create new universal norms rather than reflect existing ones. Sometime dubbed "norm entrepreneurs," the humanitarian groups that promote the spread of the laws of war have a vested interest in elaborating and developing international law.[22] The key personnel in virtually all these organizations are from Western Europe and the United States, with only token representation from the rest of the world. As nonstate actors, humanitarian groups are completely dependent on sovereign states to sign, ratify, and implement the treaties that encode human rights and humanitarian concerns into international law. But the political interests of states often put them at odds with humanitarian groups. States, especially in the developing world, wage a continual battle to balance the desire for international legitimacy against the zealous protection of state sovereignty. They eagerly sign and ratify international treaties because they regard them as important sources of legitimacy. But they eschew international legal instruments that undermine state sovereignty.

In regard to children, this pattern of action creates both a double standard and what Jeffrey Herbst calls a "compliance gap." States make use of double standards by promoting a stringent legal rule for child protection when it comes to suppressing rebel movements but adopting a far more relaxed standard in regulating the recruitment and use of children in state armed forces. Herbst argues that compliance problems derive from the "unbreachable gap between norms and compliance when international humanitarian law is applied to children in armed conflict."[23] Although more international law has been created, the levels of compliance are increasingly low. A kind of "devil's bargain" between humanitarian groups and state actors enables the proliferation of international law as long as compliance and enforcement remain feeble. As Herbst argues, this compact might be tolerable if international laws were merely aspirational, but it is far more problematic if there is any reasonable expectation of enforcement.

Because most treaties contain feeble enforcement provisions or none at all, international humanitarian law is pragmatically weak. Many, like the Convention on the Rights of the Child, rely on "naming and shaming" mechanisms in which parties submit public progress reports concerning the measures they have adopted to implement the rights contained the treaty. The major exception to this rule is the Rome Treaty establishing the International Criminal Court (ICC) in the Hague. Under the Rome Treaty, national courts, and under some circumstances the ICC itself, may try war-crimes cases and punish those who are convicted. Moreover, because the ICC is a permanent tribunal, it can define and interpret international humanitarian law, establish precedents for future legal proceedings, and enforce its decisions.

The net effect has been to allow sovereign states and privileged insurgents greater discretion in the use of child soldiers than ordinary insurgent and rebel groups have. This was not the goal of the humanitarian groups that sought to end the participation of children in war. It may be overly critical to suggest that the child-soldier issue was hijacked by the weaker states of the United Nations in order to bolster their own sovereignty. But this result seems at least part of the implicit compact struck with state power in order to promote the ban on child soldiers.

PERSONS UNDER AGE FIFTEEN

In the Protocols Additional, the interplay between categories of war and categories of children focused on children below age fifteen. Protocol Additional I requires that state parties and privileged insurgents take all "feasible measures" so that children who have not attained the age of fifteen years do not take a "direct part in hostilities." It also requires that they "refrain from recruiting them into their armed forces." If and when such parties recruit children between the ages of fifteen and eighteen, they should "endeavour to give priority to those who are the oldest."[24]

The language of the final treaty is significantly weaker than the language of the draft treaty proposed by the International Committee of the Red Cross (ICRC). The ICRC first proposed that state parties "take all necessary measures in order that children aged under fifteen years shall not take part in hostilities and, in particular, they shall refrain from recruiting them in their armed forces or accepting their voluntary enrollment."[25] All "necessary measures" was replaced with "feasible measures," and the strictures against participation in hostilities was replaced with a ban on only "direct" participation in hostilities. The draft treaty also required states to refrain from recruiting younger children or accepting their voluntary enrollment, while the final language of the treaty is silent on the issue of voluntary enrollment. In addition, the treaty does not provide for reduction in the use of child soldiers but only for monitoring the ambiguously defined efforts to reduce their numbers.[26]

A number of factors contributed to the anemic treaty language. First, states were generally unwilling to adopt clear and obligatory language. Vague terms allow each state to determine for itself the meanings of "all feasible measures" or "direct part in hostilities." Second, the treaty met with great resistance from states that supported national liberation movements and that recognized that large numbers of children and youth were involved in these movements. Thus, from the beginning, political concerns trumped humanitarian ones. By categorizing wars of national liberation as international armed conflicts rather than as civil wars, the protocol permitted guerilla movements engaging in wars of national liberation to recruit children below the age of fifteen into their armed forces.

Not surprisingly, many of the same states took a harsher position against insurgents and rebel groups that threatened their own sovereignty. Protocol Additional II, which applies to civil wars between the armed forces of a state and dissident armed forces or other organized armed groups, makes it clear that "children who have not attained the age of fifteen years shall neither be recruited in the armed forces or groups nor allowed to take part in hostilities."[27] Here there is no parsing of the language. It is a comprehensive ban on the use of any person under fifteen years of age as a soldier in all civil wars and insurgencies other than wars of national liberation.

Protocol Additional I raises a number of complex issues, most importantly the treatment of underage combatants captured by enemy forces. It provides that when "children who have not attained the age of fifteen years, take a direct part in hostilities and fall into the power of an adverse Party, they shall continue to benefit from the special protection accorded by this Article, whether or not they are prisoners of war." Thus, children who are lawful combatants are always entitled to prisoner-of-war status. Moreover as child prisoners-of-war they are to be protected against "indecent assault" and provided with care and aid in addition to the usual protections. They are to be held in special quarters separate from adults. Finally, the protocol provides that the death penalty should not be imposed on any person who was not eighteen when the offense was committed.[28] The impact of the protocol on children who are unlawful combatants is equally important. Although not prisoners of war, they are also protected persons and immunized from the death penalty. This provision sparked debate over whether blanket immunity from the death penalty might lead child soldiers to commit the most heinous war crimes. Of equal concern was whether regular soldiers might routinely kill underage perpetrators of war crimes if they knew that those perpetrators would be treated more leniently when captured. Despite these concerns, the principle of protecting children prevailed.[29]

Like Protocol Additional I, Protocol Additional II prohibits the death penalty for offenses committed by persons under age eighteen and gives protected status to children under age fifteen. The key difference is that Protocol Additional II creates a blanket ban on recruiting children under age fifteen and on their participation in hostilities in any way: "Children who have not attained the age of fifteen shall neither be recruited in the armed forces nor allowed to take part in hostilities."[30] Like all rebel combatants in civil wars, except for the politically privileged rebels of Protocol Additional I, children of any age who participate in civil war are not eligible to be treated as prisoners of war when they are captured.

The drafters of the Protocols Additional were aware of the significant cultural variations in the ages of children, youth, and adults. But their view that the "participation of children and adolescents in combat" is an "inhumane practice" made such considerations irrelevant. Their drive to create a universal moral standard trumped any concerns about local understandings of childhood and made local practices deviant and inhumane under international law. The drafters knew that prior international agreements made age fifteen seem "reasonable" to members of civil society.[31] But because they hoped that the prohibition could be broadened beyond age fifteen in the future, they carefully crafted the protocols to hold open the possibility that the concept of childhood could be extended beyond that.

The first real opportunity to create an extended universal definition of childhood came with the Convention on the Rights of the Child (CRC) of 1989. Widely hailed as a milestone in the development of children's rights, the CRC created the first international definition of the child as "every human being below the age of eighteen years." But the CRC was a bitter disappointment to anti-child-soldier advocates because it still permits widespread use of child soldiers. The CRC merely repeats the weak language of Protocol Additional I requiring state parties to "refrain" from recruiting persons below age fifteen and to "take all feasible measures to ensure" that they do not take a direct part in hostilities.[32] It makes no direct reference to the problem of child soldiers in civil wars.

The most important development in proscribing the use of child soldiers is the 1998 Rome Statute, which gives the ICC jurisdiction over war crimes "when committed as part of a plan or policy or as part of a large-scale commission of such crimes." It is the only permanent international court in which individuals charged with war crimes can be brought to trial. Under the provisions of the statute, war crimes include "grave breaches" of the Geneva Conventions as well as "other serious violations of the laws and customs" applicable to both international and noninternational armed conflicts. In the case of younger children, the statute ends the distinction between international and domestic conflicts, creating in both instances a ban on "conscripting or enlisting children under the age of fifteen years into the national armed forces or using them to participate actively in hostilities." The Rome Statute comes closest to establishing a universal legal standard applicable to younger child soldiers, but its focus is totally on the issue of recruiting and using child soldiers. The ICC has no jurisdiction over any person who was under age eighteen at the time of the alleged commission of a war crime, thus it leaves the issue of the culpability of children who have committed war crimes unaddressed.[33]

MOVING THE AGE LINE UPWARD: THE OPTIONAL PROTOCOL
Although the Rome Statute established a universal criminal prohibition on the use of child soldiers, it did so by focusing on children below age fifteen. A new opportunity to widen the prohibitions came with the Optional Protocol to the Convention on the Rights of the Child on the Involvement of Children in Armed Conflict. The Optional Protocol grew out of widespread dissatisfaction with the CRC and represents the most recent international effort to move toward the Straight 18 position. The Optional Protocol clearly favors state parties over rebel groups. It requires that states "shall take all feasible measures to ensure that members of their armed forces who have not attained the age of 18 years do not take a direct part in hostilities." Much if the language of the Optional Protocol echoes Protocol Additional I but raises the age bar to eighteen. The weak language remains, but raising the age strengthens the earlier ban on the youngest of children by making it more difficult for field commanders to claim confusion about the age of the youngest soldiers. States must also "ensure that all persons who have not attained the age of 18 years are not compulsorily recruited into their armed forces." In addition, it requires states to raise the minimum age of voluntary recruitment above the age (fifteen) set forth for the CRC. It also makes clear that under the CRC persons under eighteen are entitled to special protection. As with

most treaties, enforcement is weak, although state parties are required to submit a binding declaration setting forth a minimum age for voluntary recruitment.[34]

The strongest language is used to squelch rebellion. The Optional Protocol provides that "armed groups, distinct from the armed forces of a State, should not, under any circumstances, recruit or use in hostilities persons under the age of 18 years."[35] The Optional Protocol's double standard permits sovereign states to recruit child soldiers but bars rebel groups from doing the same. The public-relations materials of many humanitarian groups completely ignore this distinction. But there is some ambiguity about the language. The phrase "should not . . . recruit" could be understood as moral and precatory rather than constituting a clear obligation.[36] Recall that Protocol Additional II demanded that rebels forces "shall" not recruit children under age fifteen. In addition, the practical effect of this language is unclear. The Optional Protocol provides no incentive for rebel leaders and groups, who are already subject to the harshest criminal penalties in their own countries, to adhere to a double standard for recruitment that only weakens their insurgencies.[37] The Optional Protocol also encourages the worldwide suppression of rebellion. It provides that "state parties shall take all feasible measures to prevent [rebel] recruitment and use [of children], including the adoption of legal measures necessary to prohibit and criminalize such practices."[38] This stipulation does not apply merely to states fighting a rebellion on their own soil but invites the collective international suppression of rebellion by all parties to the treaty. In this respect the Optional Protocol represents one of the first steps by an international body to criminalize rebellion and revolution. Moreover the treaty is preemptive in that it does not require the existence of an actual conflict to criminalize the efforts of nonstate armed groups to recruit children.

Testing the Laws: The Special Court in Sierra Leone

Prior to the formation of the Special Court in Sierra Leone, the tension between civil society and sovereign states over child soldiers played itself out in the language of treaties. Now, for the first time in history, criminal charges have been brought against individuals for recruiting child soldiers. Equally important, the creation of the court also raised the difficult issue of whether any of the thousands of children and youth who routinely murdered, raped, and committed acts of terror would be treated as war criminals.

The creation of the Special Court was based on a resolution of the United Nations Security Council in 2000.[39] Although the war in Sierra Leone was still raging, the resolution authorized the Secretary General of the United

Nations to negotiate an agreement between Sierra Leone and the United Nations for trying "persons who bear the greatest responsibility" for war crimes under international law as well as crimes committed under Sierra Leone domestic law. The court has the power to prosecute people for a broad spectrum of war crimes including murder, extermination, enslavement, rape, sexual slavery, forced prostitution and pregnancy, and conscripting and recruiting children into armed forces or groups or using them actively in hostilities. The determination of the age of unlawful conscription emerged from the consensus developed around similar provisions in the Rome Statute.

As of January 1, 2004, thirteen suspects had been indicted, including the principal leaders of the warring factions and their immediate subordinates. In addition to numerous other war crimes, all were charged with unlawfully recruiting children under the age of fifteen. Strikingly, on May 31, 2004, the Special Court ruled that the war crime of recruiting children under fifteen existed as a customary norm of international law even prior to the adoption of the Rome Statute for the International Criminal Court. In the court's view, the Rome Statute merely codified, but did not create, this norm.[40] Among those indicted were Foday Sankoh, the former leader of the RUF; Charles Taylor, former president of Liberia; Johnny Paul Koroma, chairman of the Armed Forces Revolutionary Council; and key field commanders such as Sam Mosquito Bockarie, Morris Kallon, Alex Tamba Brima, and Issa Hasan Sesay. Senior CDF leaders Sam Hinga Norman, Moinina Fofana, and Allieu Kondewa were also indicted. Two of the indictees are now dead. Sankoh died in custody. Bockarie fled to Liberia and is said to have been murdered by Taylor, who feared that he might testify against him. Koroma fled to Liberia and may be dead or in hiding. Taylor was allowed to leave Liberia and is living in Nigeria under a grant of asylum from the Nigerian government. The United States has offered a reward of two million dollars to anyone willing to abduct him in Nigeria and bring him before the Special Court.

The criminal culpability of children and youth was the subject of intense lobbying and negotiation by the United Nations, Sierra Leone, and international humanitarian groups. Adopting the Straight 18 position, most humanitarian groups lobbied hard against prosecuting anyone who was below eighteen at the time he or she committed a war crime. Human Rights Watch, UNICEF, Cause Canada, Save the Children, and the Coalition to Stop the Use of Child Soldiers were among many humanitarian organizations who led the opposition. The Sierra Leone government and numerous Sierra Leoneans who suffered at the hands of child soldiers felt that justice could not be served unless some children were put on trial for their crimes.

The United Nations, particularly the Office of the Special Representative of the Secretary General for Children and Armed Conflict (Office of the Special Representative), adopted a middle position that gave the court jurisdiction to try children who were between the ages of fifteen and eighteen when they committed a war crime. United Nations officials first suggested that such children would be subject to imprisonment if convicted but ultimately decided that imprisonment was inappropriate. This position was adopted by the Secretary General, who also echoed the concerns of many Sierra Leoneans that they would not look kindly on a court that failed to bring to justice children who committed terrible crimes.[41] For United Nations officials, asserting jurisdiction over these children was a positive act that allowed the Special Court to provide them a measure of justice unavailable to them in Sierra Leone's national courts. Because of the amnesty provisions of the 1999 Lome (Togo) peace accord between the government of Sierra Leone and the RUF, no child (or adult) who committed a war crime prior to 1999 could be tried in Sierra Leone's national courts. But children charged with war crimes committed after 1999 could not only be tried at a younger age but could be treated more harshly and given fewer due process guarantees in the Sierra Leone courts than in the Special Court. Because Lome's amnesty provision was not recognized by the United Nations, the Special Court may try all offenders for crimes committed since 1996. As a practical matter the court's mandate to prosecute only major war criminals made it extremely unlikely that any more than a few of the oldest children and youth could ever have been brought to trial. Nevertheless, for the first time in history an international tribunal was legally empowered to prosecute suspects who were under age eighteen at the time of the crime.

The final agreement gave the court jurisdiction to try children ages fifteen through seventeen as "juvenile offenders" but no jurisdiction over younger children. Although these juvenile offenders could be subject to a full trial, the statute granted them the presumption of rehabilitation and reintegration into Sierra Leone society and immunized them from imprisonment. The final disposition of juvenile-offender cases fell to nonpenal institutions, including child-protection agencies, foster-care institutions, approved schools, and other organizations responsible for education and vocational training. Most people anticipated that the vast majority of cases involving children would be dealt with by establishing a truth and reconciliation commission to take the testimony of all children, perpetrators and victims alike.[42] The Special Court statute specifically mandated that the prosecution of children not jeopardize the development of child rehabilitation programs and required that the court refer matters involving children to a truth and reconciliation commission where appropriate.

The Special Court was charged with prosecuting only those with the greatest responsibility for war crimes; which imposed a heavy symbolic burden on the Truth and Reconciliation Commission (TRC) once it was established. Dashing expectations that the Special Court would try more than a small number of war criminals, Ahmad Tejan Kabbah, president of Sierra Leone, stressed the need to "put an end to the speculation that the Special Court would try all or even most of those who participated in the events of the 10-year war." According to Kabbah, "the proper place for most of them and their victims will be the Truth and Reconciliation Commission."[43] Given that tens of thousands of Sierra Leoneons were killed and more than one third of the population was displaced, this was an impossible task for an underfunded commission with an institutional life span of twelve to eighteen months. In fact, the TRC was not designed to deliver much more than an official report on the horrors of war, a task already well accomplished in a nonofficial capacity by Amnesty International and Human Rights Watch.

Adding to its burden, the TRC was portrayed as the best forum for handling the issue of child soldiers. Prior to the appointment of David Crane as chief prosecutor, humanitarian groups were concerned that information about children gathered by the TRC not be given to the Special Court. But, in fact, no information gathered by the TRC will be given to the Special Court. Moreover, the entire issue of the prosecution of juvenile offenders was eliminated when Crane announced on November 1, 2003, that his office would not prosecute any juvenile offenders. As it stands now, no juvenile offenders in Sierra Leone will be tried or punished for war crimes. But they are not alone. Thousands of adults who committed war crimes will also remain unpunished. In the end, the official institutional record of the war will consist of the trial of major war criminals plus the testimony given to the TRC. The trial involves a legal process quite recognizable to the Western world. The testimony to the TRC has little connection to law or justice as these are understood in either the West or in Sierra Leone. The TRC's role is to shape an official narrative of the war in the absence of any other institution's effort to address individual criminal culpability or achieve substantive justice.

Richard Wilson, an anthropologist who participated in key technical meetings for developing the TRC's operational guidelines, makes it clear that the design of the TRC was superficial from the beginning. Most Sierra Leoneans did not want a TRC. They wanted major offenders put on trial and punished. Instead, the United Nations Mission in Sierra Leone imposed the

TRC on Sierra Leoneans because it satisfied the needs of the international community. As Wilson skeptically puts it: "Set up a truth commission, add water, stir and the international community thinks you've done reconciliation."[44]

Once the chief prosecutor determined that the court would not pursue juvenile offenders, the TRC became the only forum in which the criminal culpability of children could be addressed. But the TRC was far less capable of addressing this issue than the Special Court. Historically, victims flock to truth commissions, but perpetrators do not come unless they are under real threat of prosecution, subject to extreme community and social pressure, or hoping for amnesty. Because of the existing amnesty provisions in Sierra Leone, all perpetrators, children and adults, have few reasons to appear before the TRC.[45] Moreover, all participants in the technical meetings, anthropologists included, wanted to protect children and youth from any law, whether customary, national, or international. Sierra Leonean anthropologists invited to the technical meeting for establishing the TRC described the flogging and haranguing of juvenile offenders that routinely occur in customary courts. Wilson makes clear that these descriptions turned all participants, anthropologists included, against the customary courts and law.[46] Indeed, the view that customary law is excessively punitive bolstered the participants' conviction that children need to be protected from all law.

The TRC's mandate required it to create an impartial and official historical record of what happened to children during the war. Given the small budget and short timeframe within which the TRC functioned, it quickly distanced itself from the issue of reconciliation, referring this matter to "existing mechanisms for promoting reintegration and reconciliation of children," meaning whatever local and customary modes may exist for such matters in Sierra Leone. Under the TRC, child perpetrators were seen and treated primarily as victims.[47]

The operational guidelines developed for the TRC allowed for the limited participation of children in some in camera sessions of the TRC but excluded them from public hearings. Under the guidelines, children participated mainly by providing confidential statements to the TRC. These statements were qualitative and impressionistic and not organized around legal fact finding.[48] The participation of children was voluntary. The TRC did not use its subpoena power to compel their testimony. At public hearings, children's interests were to be represented by agents of child-protection agencies using written statements, tapes, and drawings produced by children. Under the guidelines, the structure of child interviews virtually guaranteed that they would be superficial. Interviews with children over age twelve were restricted to one hour, and interviews with children below age twelve to forty-five minutes. The children and their representatives were entitled to determine for themselves what issues they were willing to discuss with the statement takers. Unlike a court of law, the TRC did not cross-examine witnesses. In essence, those who appeared before the TRC were permitted to shape the content and structure of their own testimony. Truth was fashioned by the victims, even if many of the official "victims" were among the worst perpetrators of violence. Finally, the identities of the children will not be disclosed. Information collected will ultimately be disaggregated by age and sex in order to make it difficult to link the information with specific children. All information provided by children will be sealed, possibly for fifty years.

The TRC initiated a three-month period of statement taking in December 2002. It collected between seven and nine thousand statements before beginning a public hearing phase in April 2003. Some 450 Sierra Leoneans testified during the public hearings, which substantially concluded in June 2003. The TRC opted for broad coverage rather than in-depth investigation of any particular problem, as is done in legal proceedings. Initial indications are that 10 percent of the statements were provided by children.[49] This seems a relatively small number, given that so many children were touched by war in a country where the median age is 17.5 years.[50]

Despite the large number of people who offered statements, the TRC has probably not directly touched the lives of the vast majority of child soldiers. Some children and youth are now part of local reconciliation and integration processes that stand outside the gaze of international institutions. Many—perhaps most—are not involved in any way. Truth telling at the TRC has been hailed as nationally therapeutic, but during the public hearings there was much skepticism that the "truth" was being told. According to Tim Kelsall, four days of public hearings in Tonkolili District, in northern Sierra Leone, created intense anger and outrage in the audience. Only a hastily crafted "ritual of reconciliation" ceremony saved the day.[51]

Agreement on the truth may be less relevant to reconciliation than many believe. In Sierra Leone, as elsewhere in the world, ambiguity often serves the interest of peace. The war in Sierra Leone grew out of deep-seated inequities embedded in a corrupt and criminal state. People need safety and equitable treatment in daily life, and no amount of truth can compensate for the absence of these basic needs. Some Christian groups see the TRC as contributing to a "culture of forgiveness." Susan Shepler suggests, however, that humanitarian groups and the TRC may be contributing to a "discourse of abdicated responsibility" that allows children to portray themselves as innocent and facilitates their integration into society.[52] From this perspective, the subjective presentations and manufactured truths of the TRC may muddy the waters just enough to give children and youth enough breathing space to re-invent themselves. At least it may do no harm.

The real test for Sierra Leone is how former child soldiers are integrated into society. Here the results are mixed. Danny Hoffman's portrait of the manipulation of age categories in the disarmament process in Sierra Leone demonstrates the continuing vitality of the structures of patronage that created much of the malaise in prewar Sierra Leone.[53] In the town of Bo, former soldiers, hoping to disarm and obtain the economic benefits of demobilization, were dependent on local commanders who served as gatekeepers to international resources. These commanders made the selections as to which of their former soldiers would obtain the benefits. Those selected paid between a third and a half of their noncombatant pay packet to the commander for the opportunity to disarm and train for a job. No vetting was required for child soldiers seeking rehabilitation. But child soldiers who sought the more tangible benefits of the international community had to be categorized as adult members of regular forces, an act that required the creative energy of the gatekeeper. In Bo, rules-based bureaucratic and administrative processes created by the United Nations were converted into a system of patronage much like that of prewar Sierra Leone. Now, however, the United Nations, various international organizations, and other stand-ins for the state control the principal resources on which patronage depends.

Throughout Sierra Leone, access to development funds requires that communities accept the official view that former child soldiers are children and victims worthy of reconciliation and reintegration into society. Sierra Leoneans do not, however, fully embrace the CRC definition of the child or the cultural connotations of innocence embedded in the Western concept of the child. Many communities take on this view only because it is tied to a resource structure that enables them to rebuild lives. As Shepler puts it, "Communities organize their self-presentation around the idea of war affected youth in order to gain access to a certain amount of international aid."[54] Still, Sierra Leoneans now participate in the creation of new definitions of childhood. Many communities have prepared lists of child soldiers in hopes of attracting monies controlled by international organizations. But there is widespread resentment against former child soldiers, now recategorized as victims, who have greater access to limited postwar development funds than many of those seen as the real victims of war—including a large number of amputees—who have been left to fend for themselves.

Shepler worries that redefining youth as children may exclude young people from political processes.[55] Yet countervailing forces exist. Sierra Leone's new national youth policy defines a "youth" as any person age fifteen to thirty-five and assumes that in some instances even persons below age fifteen will participate in youth-based activities and institutions. The policy has a much more realistic view of age than the legalisms of humanitarian groups. On paper, the policy encourages the formation of youth groups and the involvement of youth in democratic political processes. Sierra Leone's president has declared that "youth empowerment is a country's best investment for a prosperous future."[56] How this policy will work in practice remains to be seen. Is it a recognition that young people are destined to play an important political role in Sierra Leone? Or does it define youth so broadly that powerful adult patrons will expropriate the resources of the young? Nothing is certain except that the politics of age continues.

Who Is a Child Soldier? The Case of Israel and Palestine

The politics of age also plays a significant role in the war between Israel and the Palestinians. In Israel and in the Western media, Palestinians have been accused of sacrificing their children. Charges of child abuse have also been leveled against Palestinian parents for their unwillingness or inability to police the behavior of children. Palestinians and Israelis accuse each other of wantonly killing each other's children. These charges are part of the mutual demonization of the other that characterizes the conflict.

The Israeli-Palestinian conflict reveals another way in which the politics of age enters the precincts of humanitarian discourse. Within the United Nations and in civil society at large, support of the Palestinian cause is enormous, and Palestinians enjoy a privileged position. Support of the Palestinian cause is a virtual litmus test for entry into the major organizations of civil society. As a result, Palestinian interests and Palestinian voices are present in almost every United Nations forum, while those of Israel are absent or muted.

The political positioning of civil society affects the analysis of the child-soldier problem by humanitarian groups. For example, in its 2001 *Child Soldiers Global Report* the Coalition to Stop the Use of Child Soldiers declares that there are "no reports of the military recruitment of children by *Fatah* militias." Likewise, it claims that there "is no evidence of child participation in Islamic Jihad." It also discounts reports that children between the ages of twelve and fifteen were recruited by Hamas, asserting that "the process of selection for the Izz al-Deen Al Quassem Brigades is . . . long and rigorous and has not to date included children."[57]

The Coalition's generally skeptical attitude toward militarized youth movements also disappears when it comes to Palestinians. "In many countries," the Coalition tells us, "military training and indoctrination is provided through schools and youth movements." But despite the clear role that Palestinian youth organizations have played in the conflict, they are the only youth organizations in the world that the Coalition describes as "voluntary." No reference is made to the Coalition's long-held view that "voluntary recruitment is often a choice not exercised freely" or that the "line between voluntary, compulsory or forced recruitment is often ambiguous." The report also uses the concepts of childhood and youth to suit its partisan position. Young Palestinians who throw rocks, burn tires, block roads, or toss Molotov cocktails are almost invariably described as "youth" or "adolescents," whether they are age ten or eighteen. However, when young Palestinians of the same age are killed by Israeli forces, they are typically described as "children." Finally, the Coalition also distorts the treaty language it otherwise champions. For example, in its comments on the al-Aqsa intifada, it claims there is "no evidence to date of children being recruited or used *systematically* by the Palestinian Authority or armed groups."[58] Aside from the fact that the Coalition draws virtually all its evidence from Palestinian sources, treaty bans on the use of child soldiers have no threshold requirement that child soldiers be used "systematically." The Coalition seems to use these qualifiers to mask the presence of child soldiers by a party to the conflict that it supports. In sum, the Coalition uncritically accepts the Palestinian interpretation of the conflict, positions itself as a partisan in the Palestinian cause, and manipulates the language of age to further that cause.

The political partisanship of humanitarian discourse, at least as it related to the Israeli-Palestinian conflict, was starkly evident during the United Nations Special Session on the Child, which I attended in May 2002.[59] Of special concern was the issue of children and armed conflict. Accordingly, the Session began with a meeting of the Security Council in which the personal experiences of several former child combatants were showcased. Many NGOs were particularly concerned with "contempt for . . . international norms on the ground" in Chechnya, Colombia, Sierra Leone, Israel, and the Occupied Territories. The leading NGOs wanted the Special Session to help consolidate and institutionalize norms and strategies already elaborated concerning children in armed conflict, tighten up systems of identifying and monitoring breaches of international norms, and sharpen tools for making parties accountable.[60]

Numerous workshops highlighted the problems of child soldiers and of other war-affected children. Among the most interesting were strategy meetings for monitoring treaty compliance and workshops for small-arms-control advocates. The workshop on children and armed conflict highlighted the tensions among civil society, the United Nations Secretariat, and the Security Council. At this workshop, experts from UNICEF, the Office of the Special Representative, the Coalition, and the newly formed Watchlist on Children and Armed Conflict (Watchlist) provided guidance as to how civil society could help implement Security Council Resolution 1379 of November 2001 on children in armed conflict. The resolution requires that the Secretary General provide the Security Council with a "list of parties to armed conflict that recruit or use children in violation of the international obligations applicable to them, in situations that are on the Security Council's agenda."[61] Put simply, whenever the Security Council is dealing with a conflict, the Secretary General advises the Council whether any of the parties to the conflict are in breach of the international laws on child soldiers. Several leading NGOs made it clear that they regarded the Security Council resolution as an opportunity to get the issue of children before the Security Council.

It is important to place this workshop in context. The Special Session, originally set for September 2001, was postponed because of the attack on the World Trade Center. It finally took place a few weeks after the incursion into Jenin, on the West Bank, by the Israel Defense Forces; at the time it was widely and falsely alleged that the Israel Defense Forces had massacred many Palestinians.[62] The large number of suicide bombings and attacks, many carried out by Palestinian children, made it evident that Palestinian children were unlawful combatants in this conflict.[63] But in this United Nations workshop, which was designed specifically to deal with the child soldier, a large portion of the time was spent on the Israeli-Palestinian conflict, and no mention was made of Palestinian child soldiers. Indeed, from the onset it was apparent that no discussion of Palestinian use and recruitment of child soldiers was possible.

The privileged position of Palestinians in the United Nations and civil society protects the Palestinian national movement from any public criticism. To my knowledge, in no other current conflict do so many humanitarian groups work to shield the use and recruitment of child soldiers from scrutiny. But not all do. Both Amnesty International and Human Rights Watch have issued reports that are critical of both Israelis and the Palestinians. However, the central symbolic moment of the Special Session, at the end of an address on May 9 by Graca Machel (the wife of Nelson Mandela and a major leader in the effort to ban child soldiers), made clear that the child-soldier issue was a creature of partisan politics. A Palestinian teenager, who claimed her name was "Jenin," asked Machel, "Children are under occupation and we are suffering—what are you waiting for to do something?" Machel responded, "I don't know what to tell you. . . . I have been haunted by a Palestinian child in a refugee camp who asked me 'How long it will take to change our lives?' It is the worst indictment of all of us. . . . The interests of big powerful countries are at stake, which overrides the interest of children."[64] When the conference session ended, Machel came down from the podium and publicly embraced "Jenin."

The central problem for anti-child-soldier advocates is that they completely sympathize and identify with the Palestinians—the only party to the conflict that uses child soldiers. To adapt to this dissonance, advocates use a number of strategies. One strategy, used by the Coalition, is simple denial. But, more commonly, humanitarian groups defer to the Palestinian narrative claim that their victimization trumps all other moral considerations. Here is how one Palestinian child advocate at the session put it: "Palestine is not part [sic] of child soldiers," she said. "They want to silence us. Do not allow the most powerful to define the struggle of a people. Sharon is talking about transfer. Sharon doesn't want peace. He has Jews coming from Argentina and I am sure there will be many atrocities in Gaza. . . .We have some militants—okay—but if you keep the murderer unpunished, don't come to the victims." Everyone in the room seemed to agree with her view that it was immoral to even raise the issue of Palestinian child soldiers in the context of Israeli aggression.

The strategies used by leading NGOs to render the Palestinian recruitment of child soldiers invisible follow suit: Watchlist, for example, was developing its own "list" as part of its efforts to monitor, report on, and advocate for children in armed conflict. This list addresses the overall protection of children in areas of armed conflict and not just the issue of child soldiers. But Watchlist's agenda at this meeting was motivated by the events in Jenin. Although it cited the suffering of both Palestine and Israeli children in the conflict, its goal was to promote the United Nations investigative mission into the Jenin incident; the make-up of this mission had brought several objections by the Israelis.[65] Comparing its list to that of the Secretary General's, Watchlist announced that it was not guided by strictly humanitarian considerations. "We are not going to create a list of the 10 worst violators," said one of its representatives. Instead Watchlist would be driven by what she termed "strategic considerations." In the case of the Israeli-Palestinian conflict, the key issue was not to be Palestinian child soldiers but the rights of children, and especially Palestinian children.

Similarly, the Office of the Special Representative turned a blind eye toward Palestinian child combatants.[66] Anticipating that the issue of Israel and Palestine would come before the Security Council, an official from the

Office of the Special Representative was equally blunt: "Most UN reports," she explained, "skirted the issue of the Israeli occupation." She continued, "We want to drive home the issue of the occupation. The focus of the UN General Secretary's report must be on Israel, and the NGOs must help shape this report." She went on denounce the "double standard" of treating Israel differently from Iraq, voiced her anger that the Israeli-Palestinian problem was the most "manipulated" issue before the United Nations, and said how wrong it would be, in the instance of Israel and Palestine, to have the Secretary General's report limited to the child-soldier issue. The remainder of the session was devoted to marginalizing the child-soldier issue so that civil society's narrative of the Palestinian problem would not be "distorted" by the politics of the Security Council.

Conclusion

The child-soldier "crisis" is a modern political crisis, which is only partly related to the actual presence of children in war. In modern discourse, it is difficult to disentangle humanitarian issues from political ones because humanitarian groups increasingly define themselves as political actors, and political groups use humanitarian rhetoric to further their own goals. The language of humanitarianism and human rights has become the language of political discourse. Little attention was paid to the presence of child soldiers in the era of national liberation movements, but it has become a significant issue now that postcolonial states face their own insurgencies. The case of Palestine is instructive here. Because the Palestinian movement is widely seen as a war of national liberation, the world community turns a blind eye to precisely the same activities it condemns in other contexts.

The child-soldier "crisis" arises from a complex set of interconnections between humanitarian and political drivers. It is not a new phenomenon, as some would claim; and it is not driven by the small-arms industry or the peculiar nature of modern warfare. Nonetheless, thousands of children and youth today are caught up in armed warfare and are committing horrible crimes. How should we see them? As innocent victims of political circumstance who should be protected and forgiven? Or as moral agents who should be held responsible for their actions?

Perhaps one impetus for seeing children as innocents in need protection is that this view gives us the ability to temper justice with mercy, particularly in the face of an adult criminal justice system that seems overly harsh and punitive. Nonetheless, the crimes these children have committed are terrible, and the systems of law designed to address them are far too inexact and weak to ever fully compensate for this evil. A more nuanced view of both the vagaries of war and the contextual definition of childhood should deepen our ability to wrestle the question. The prosecution of war crimes will always be a symbolic attempt to repair the damage of war. In this light, although crafting treaties and making pronouncements that give blanket immunity from prosecution to any person below age eighteen may satisfy the humane aspirations of the international community, its donor agencies, and human rights groups, it clearly falls short of achieving justice for the victims of war.

Notes

Chapter 1 War and Childhood

1. The source materials in this study are themselves not evenly balanced. The stories of Jewish child soldiers, for example, often come from literate individuals, many of whom survived the Holocaust and went on to rebuild their lives as adults in Israel and the United States. Some one and a half million Jewish children, almost 90 percent of the Jewish children in Europe alive in 1939, were murdered by the Germans and their allies. Deborah Dwork, *Children with a Star: Jewish Youth in Nazi Europe* (New Haven, Conn.: Yale University Press, 1992), xi. The child soldiers who survived escaped almost certain death, a fact that lends an immediate aura of heroism and poignancy to their stories. Because many of these stories are highly personal, they have a dramatic quality that is not present in more contemporary reports on child soldiers. Many Jewish child partisans also belonged to socialist or left-wing Zionist youth groups, and they made sense of their personal struggles for survival within the grand narratives of the struggle for Jewish self-determination and socialist revolution. Finally, the fact that these narratives are told largely by adults looking back at their experiences allows the narratives to achieve a coherency and depth that may not be possible in the stories of children and youth who are currently close to the battlefield.

Young people fighting in today's wars have yet to seize control of their own narratives. Much of what we know about contemporary child soldiers comes from the accounts of journalists and the investigative reports of human rights organizations. These accounts are not only shocking but are also deliberately crafted to emblematically illustrate the concerns of humanitarian and human rights groups. Accordingly, they focus exclusively on the horrors of war and reveal almost nothing of the ideologies, values, passions, daily lives, or routine experiences of children who are participating in conflict. Direct access to the experience of former child soldiers is also restricted by adult concerns that children are persons in need of protection and that the best interest of children requires either that adults speak on their behalf or that the children speak only in carefully managed and protected settings. I do not mean to imply that human rights organizations have not fairly recorded the terrible actions of children. But they provide a limited story. Indeed, as Wilson has argued, decontextualization is central to human rights reporting while the goal of anthropology is to "restore local subjectivities, values and memories as well as [to analyze] the wider global social processes in which violence is embedded." Richard A. Wilson, "Representing Human Rights Violations: Social Contexts and Subjectivities," in *Human Rights, Culture and Context*, ed. Richard

A. Wilson (London: Pluto Press, 1997), 157. Perhaps in years to come we will hear more fully from those who were children and youth in these conflicts.

Every story of child soldiers is filled with moral ambiguity. War crimes take place in every war. What distinguishes one war from another is the degree to which such crimes come to characterize and shape the conflict. U.S. soldiers clearly committed war crimes in the World War II and in Vietnam, but the deliberate targeting of civilians was not part of U.S. war policy even if the military only reluctantly prosecuted such cases. Some Jewish partisans no doubt committed war crimes. They certainly killed civilians who aided the German plan of genocide. But most partisan activity was directed at combatants. In Sierra Leone, where many young people fought as part of a criminal enterprise, there were, no doubt, many instances of individual bravery and moral and ethical behavior. Many of the children and youth who were part of the ethnic militias fought primarily to protect their homes and villages, while others fought because of their anger over economic conditions. But none of these reasons justifies the deliberate and wholesale infliction of atrocities on civilians. Similarly, few people would disagree with the legitimate rights of Palestinians to self-determination and an independent state. Yet the armed factions of the Palestinian movements have never divorced themselves from the desire to ethnically cleanse Palestine of its Jewish inhabitants, and thus civilians have been the prime target of Palestinian attacks since the beginning of the Palestinian movement in the last century. Many Palestinian children and youth have clearly been involved in activities that support these goals.

2. Francis Mading Deng, *The Dinka of the Sudan* (Prospect Heights, Ill.: Waveland Press, 1972), 68–73.
3. E. Adamson Hoebel, *The Cheyennes* (New York: Harcourt Brace, 1988), 77.
4. Afua Twum-Danso, *Africa's Young Soldiers* (Cape Town, South Africa: Institute for Security Studies, 2003), 35; see also Robert B. Edgerton, *Warrior Women: The Amazons of Dahomey and the Nature of War* (New York: Westview Press, 2000).
5. Napoleon Chagnon, *Yanomamo* (New York: Harcourt Brace, 1992).
6. Jonathan Hass, *The Anthropology of War* (Cambridge: Cambridge University Press, 1990).
7. A. W. Cockerill, *Sons of the Brave* (London: Leo Cooper, 1984), 60.
8. John C. Dann, *The Revolution Remembered* (Chicago: University of Chicago Press, 1980).
9. Dennis M. Keesee, *Too Young to Die: Boy Soldiers of the Union Army, 1861–1865* (Huntington, W.Va.: Blue Acorn Press, 2001), 19.
10. Emmy E. Werner, *Reluctant Witnesses: Children's Voices from the Civil War* (Boulder, Colo.: Westview Press, 1998), 9.
11. David B. Parker and Alan Freeman, "David Bailey Freeman," *Cartersville Magazine*, Spring 2001, <www.cartersvillemagazine.com/Spring01/whois.html> (November 20, 2001)..
12. Margaret Downie Banks, "Avery Brown (1852–1904), Musician: America's Youngest Civil War Soldier," *America's Shrine to Music Newsletter*, February 2001, <http://www.usd.edu:80/smm/AveryBrown.html> (November 20, 2001).
13. Robert Talmadge, "John Lincoln Clem," *The Handbook of Texas Online*, 2001, <http://www.tsha.utexas.edu/handbook/online/articles/view/CC/fcl26.html> (November 25, 2001).
14. Richelle Thompson, "Village Honors Its Boy Soldier," *Cincinnati Enquirer*, November 6, 1999, 00.
15. David Burke, *The Civil War: Strange and Fascinating Facts* (New York: Grammercy, 1991), 263.

16. Werner, *Reluctant Witnesses*, 2. See also Bell Irwin Wiley, *The Common Soldier in the Civil War* (1943; repr., New York: Grosset & Dunlap, 1951).

17. Werner, *Reluctant Witnesses*, 9.

18. Bernard Harrison Nadel, *The Christian Boy-Soldier: The Funeral Sermon of Joseph E. Darrow Preached in Sands Street Methodist Episcopal Church, Brooklyn, on the 27th of October, 1861* (New York: Steam Printing House, 1862); Edward P. Weston, *The Christian Soldier-Boy: An Address to the Young People of Gorham on the Death of Joseph D. Harmon of Company A, 5th Regiment Maine Volunteers, on Sabbath Evening, July 20th* (Portland, Maine: Office of Maine Teacher, 1862).

19. Susan Hull, *Boy Soldiers of the Confederacy*, 1905 (Austin, Tex.: Eakin Press, 1998).

20. Victor Silvester, *Dancing Is My Life* (London: Heinemann, 1958).

21. The narrative provided by Silvester is as follows: "We marched to the quarry out-side Staples at dawn. The victim was brought out from a shed and led struggling to a chair to which he was then bound and a white handkerchief placed over his heart as our target area. He was said to have fled in the face of the enemy. Mortified by the sight of the poor wretch tugging at his bonds, twelve of us, on the order raised our rifles unsteadily. Some of the men, unable to face the ordeal, had got them-selves drunk overnight. They could not have aimed straight if they tried, and, con-trary to popular belief, all twelve rifles were loaded. The condemned man had also been plied with whisky during the night, but I remained sober through fear. The tears were rolling down my cheeks as he went on attempting to free himself from the ropes attaching him to the chair. I aimed blindly and when the gun smoke had cleared away we were further horrified to see that, although wounded, the intended victim was still alive. Still blindfolded, he was attempting to make a run for it still strapped to the chair. The blood was running freely from a chest wound. An of-ficer in charge stepped forward to put the finishing touch with a revolver held to the poor man's temple. He had only once cried out and that was when he shouted the one word 'mother'. He could not have been much older than me. We were told later that he had in fact been suffering from shell-shock, a condition not recognized by the army at the time. Later I took part in four more such executions." ANZACs, "Boy Soldiers," n.d., <www.anzacs.net/BoySoldiers.htm> (November 20, 2001).. During World War I the British shot 306 people for desertions, some of whom were underage. British military law made no exceptions for underage soldiers and deemed all those age fourteen or older responsible for their actions. John Sweeney, "Lest We Forget the 306 'Cowards' We Executed," *Guardian Unlimited*, November 14, 1999, <http://www.guardian.co.uk/remembrance/article/0,2763,195504,00.html> (November 20, 2001).

22. Phillip Ariès, *Centuries of Childhood: A Social History of Family Life* (New York: Knopf, 1962), 411.

23. Frank Musgrove, *Youth and the Social Order* (London: Routledge, 1964), 33.

24. Aries, *Centuries of Childhood*, 202–206.

25. Ibid., 266–268.

26. Anthony Hill, *Soldier Boy* (Melbourne: Penguin, 2001).

27. "Memphis Morsels," 2001, <http://www.mecca.org/~graham/Memphis_Morsels.html> (June 30, 2001).

28. Peter Gripton, *The Arborfield Apprentice* (Arborfield, Reading, U.K.: Royal Electrical and Mechanical Engineers, Museum of Technology, 2003); D. B. Richards, "History of the Army Technical Foundation College," 2001, <http://members.lycos.co.uk/tothers/aas_history.htm> (May 1, 2004).

29. David Goodman, "Recruiting the Class of 2005," *Mother Jones*, January-February 2002, 56–61, 80–81.

30. UNICEF, "Cape Town Principles and Best Practice on the Prevention of Recruit-ment of Children into the Armed Forces and Demobilization and Social Reinte-gration of Child Soldiers in Africa," April 30, 1997, <http://www.pitt.edu/~ginie/mounzer/conventions.html#Capetown%20Principles> (January 10, 2004).
31. Martin Kohler, "From the National to the Cosmopolitan Public Sphere," in *Re-imagining Political Community: Studies in Cosmopolitan Democracy*, ed. Daniele Archibugi, David Held, and Martin Kohler (Stanford, Calif.: Stanford Univer-sity Press, 1998), 248n5, 323.
32. Ibid., 232.
33. Thomas G. Weiss, "Principles, Politics and Humanitarian Action," Tufts University Humanitarianism and War Project, November 5, 2002, <http://hwproject.tufts.edu/publications/electronic/e_ppaha.html> (January 2, 2004).
34. Robert D. Kaplan, "The Coming Anarchy: How Scarcity, Crime, Overpopula-tion and Disease Are Rapidly Destroying the Social Fabric of Our Planet," *Atlantic Monthly*, February 1994, 44–76; Paul Richards, *Fighting for the Rain Forest* (Ports-mouth, N.H.: Heinemann, 1996), provides a thorough critique of Kaplan.
35. Kenneth D. Bush and Diana Saltieri, *The Two Faces of Education in Ethnic Con-flict* (Florence, Italy: UNICEF Innocenti Research Center, 2000), vii. The use of the term *hyperpolitical* is a way of placing small-scale conflicts outside the bounds of "normal," politically based warfare. Although there have been utterly horrific postcolonial conflicts, such as the genocide of the Tutsi in Rwanda, humanitar-ian discourse reduces all contemporary postcolonial conflicts to irrational and atavistic explosions of hatred.
36. George Musser and Sasha Nemecek, "Waging a New Kind of War," *Scientific American*, June 2000, 47–53.
37. Carolyn Nordstrom, "The Backyard Front," in *The Paths to Domination, Resistance and Terror*, ed. Carolyn Nordstrom and JoAnn Martin (Berkeley: University of California Press, 1992), 260–274; Carolyn Nordstrom, *A Different Kind of War* (Philadelphia: University of Pennsylvania Press, 1997).
38. Susan Sontag, "Looking at War," *New Yorker*, December 9, 2002, 89–90.
39. Peter Mcguire, *Law and War: An American Story* (New York: Columbia University Press, 2000), 19–46.
40. John H. Bodley, "Anthropology and the Politics of Genocide," in *The Paths to Domination, Resistance and Terror*, ed. Carolyn Nordstrom and JoAnn Martin (Berkeley: University of California Press, 1992), 37–51.
41. For example, organizations such as the Quaker-based American Friends Service Committee claim that at the beginning of the twentieth century wars were fought primarily on defined battlefields between men in governmental armed forces, while today wars target civilian populations. From this perspective, past wars are seen as self-limiting and taking place in "the battlefield," understood as a zoned geographical space containing a set of uniformed adult male combatants. In con-trast, the anomie of modern warfare, its failure to be fought according to rules, results in the specific targeting of civilian populations and the resulting involve-ment of children as both combatants and victims. Sharon McManimon, "Use of Children as Child Soldiers," *Foreign Policy Focus* 4, no. 27 (1999): 1–4.
42. Graca Machel, *Impact of Armed Conflict on Children* (New York: United Nations, 1996).
43. Graca Machel, "Children in War," *Journal of the Society for International Devel-opment* 1, no. 42 (1996).
44. William Reno, "Sovereignty and Personal Rule in Zaire," *African Studies Quar-terly* 1, no. 3 (1997); William Reno, *Warlord Politics and African States* (Boulder, Colo.: Lynn Rienner, 1998).

45. Twum-Danso, *Africa's Young Soldiers*.
46. William Reno, "War and the Failure of Peacekeeping in Sierra Leone," in *SIPRI Yearbook 2000, Armaments, Disarmaments and International Security* (New York: Oxford University Press, 2001).
47. Organization of African Unity, U.S. Department of State, 2000, <http://www.state.gov/t/pm/rls/othr/rd/2000/6691.htm>, December 1, 2000.
48. William D. Hartung, "The New Business of War: Small Arms and the Proliferation of Conflict," *Ethics and International Affairs* 15, no. 1 (2001): 79–96; UNICEF, "Small Arms and Children: UNICEF Fact Sheet," 2001, <http://www.un.org/Depts/dda/CAB/smallarms/presskit/sheet5.htm> (November 25, 2001).
49. Human Rights Watch, "Facts about Child Soldiers," 2001, <www.hrw.org/campaigns/crp/facts/htm> (November 26, 2001).
50. Hartung, "The New Business of War," 80.
51. Lora Lump, "Can the Small Arms Trade Be Controlled" (speech, Carnegie Council on Ethics and International Affairs, New York, July 12, 2001).
52. Ian V. Hogg and John S. Weeks, *Military Small Arms of the 20th Century* (Iola, Wis.: Kraus, 1997), 271.
53. Daniel Hartzler, Larry Yantz, and James Whisker, *The U.S. Model 1861 Springfield Rifle Musket in the Civil War* (Piqua, Ohio: IDSA Books, 2000).
54. "Enfield Rifle," Smithsonian Institute, 2004, <http://www.civilwar.si.edu/weapons_enfield.html> (January 16, 2004).
55. "Sharps Model 1859 Carbine," in *The Weapons of Antietam: The Battle of Antietam on the Web*, 2004 <http://aotw.org/weapons.php?weapon_id=11>(January 16, 2004).
56. Canadian War Museum, Canada Museum of Civilization Corporation, "Equipment: The Lee-Enfield.303 Mark I Rifle," 2000, <http://www.civilization.ca/cwm/saw/equip/lee_e.html> (January 16, 2004).
57. D. J. Jardin, *The Mad Mullah of Somaliland* (London: Herbert Jenkins, 1923).
58. Sharon Hutchinson, *Nuer Dilemmas* (Berkeley: University of California Press, 1996), 113.
59. Hogg and Weeks, *Military Small Arms*, 291–292.
60. Scott C. Janzen, "The Story of the Rocket Propelled Grenade," S-2, 11th Armored Cavalry Regiment, Fort Irwin, Calif., April 1997, <http://leav-www.army.mil/fmso/RED-STAR/issues/APR97/APR97.HTML#STORY> (January 16, 2004); Terry S. Gander and Ian V. Hogg, eds., *Jane's Infantry Weapons* (Surrey, U.K.: Jane's Information Group, 1995), 303–304.
61. Silvester, *Dancing*, 17.
62. Tim O'Brien, *The Things They Carried* (New York: Random House, 1998).
63. Numerous scholarly and commercial sources describe the characteristics, weights, and properties of contemporary and historic small arms. See Derek Allsop, ed., *Brassey's Essential Guide to Military Arms* (Iola, Wis.: Kraus, 2000); Hogg and Weeks, *Military Small Arms*; Edward B. Williams, *Civil War Guns* (Gettysburg, Pa.: Thomas, 1977).
64. Rachel Stohl, Canadian Department of International Affairs, Ottawa, 2001 <www.international-alert.org/publications.htm> (October 25, 2001); Rachel Stohl, "Small Arms Impact Children around the World," *Weekly Defense Monitor* 5, no. 27 (2001), <www.cdi.org/weekly/2001/issue27.html> (October 25, 2001).
65. Refugees International (RI) in its promotion of the United Nations Conference on the Illicit Trade in Small Arms and Light Weapons in All Its Aspects, held in July 2001, stated that "the easy availability of small arms has been one of the major reasons for the recent increase in the use of child soldiers." RI further states

that small arms such as the AK-47 are easy to hide and their ease of operability
makes it possible for untrained children to participate in combat. RI argues that
the proliferation of these weapons makes it "advantageous" to use children in
combat. RI cites an instance in which an RI team on a mission to Sierra Leone
spoke with a thirteen-year-old member of the RUF who was apparently forcibly
recruited into the RUF and was originally given an AK-47. When the AK-47
proved too heavy for him, it was replaced with a pistol. Refugee International,
"The United Nations Sponsors Small Arms Conference," 2001, <www.refintl.org/
issues/Issue%20Spotlights/Spot_071801_smallarmsconf.htm> (August 1, 2001).
But the example really shows that the AK-47 was not light enough to be used by
young children. A pistol has far less utility in combat than an assault rifle does.
The example could just as easily be used to indicate the difficulty of finding arms
that suit young children.

66. Soldier Child International, "Uganda: Stopping the Harvesting of Children,"
1998, <http://www.soldierchild.org/history.html> (January 18, 2002).

67. A typical description of the vulnerability of children is found on the home page
of the U.S. Campaign to Stop the Use of Child Soldiers. The pages states: "More
than 300,00 children under the age of 18 are currently fighting in conflicts around
the world. Hundreds of thousands more have been recruited into armed forces
and could be sent into combat at any moment. Although most child soldiers are
teenagers, some are as young as 7 years old. Because of their emotional and physical immaturity, children are easily manipulated and can be drawn into violence
that they are too young to resist or understand. Both boys and girls may be sent
to the front lines of combat or into minefields ahead of other troops. Some have
been used for suicide missions or forced to commit atrocities against their own
family and neighbors. Others serve as porters or cooks, guards, messengers or spies.
Child soldiers also may be raped or given to military commanders as sexual slaves.
Robbed of their childhood and education, and often left psychologically scarred
or physically disabled, the future for those who survive is desperately bleak."
Available at http://www.us-childsoldiers.org (accessed on August 1, 2001).
Another example, from Amnesty International: "Youth is no protection against
torture. . . . In armed conflicts, children of an enemy group are often targeted
precisely because they represent that group's future. Children are sometimes tortured to coerce or punish their parents. In Uganda thousands of children are
recruited to the armed opposition group, the Lord's Resistance Army (LRA),
and forced to take part in ritualized killing. While all children are forced to
fight and kill, girls are allocated to LRA commanders and held as sexual
slaves." Amnesty International, Campaign against Torture, media briefing,
ACT 40/016/2000, October 18, 2000, <http://web.amnesty.org/library/Index/
ENGACT400162000?open&of=ENG-313A (July 9, 2004). At times, the rhetoric is toned down, as in a report of Secretary General of the United Nations
Kofi Annan to the Security Council: "In the armed conflicts of recent years
children have featured centrally as targets of violence and, *occasionally, even
unwillingly, as perpetrators of violence*" (my italics). United Nations, *Report of the
Secretary General: Children and Armed Conflict*, A/56/342-S/2001/852 (New
York, September 7, 2001), 1.

68. Ilene Cohn and Guy S. Goodwin-Gill, *Child Soldiers: The Role of Children in Armed
Conflict* (Oxford: Clarendon Press, 1994), 23.

69. Machel, *Impact of Armed Conflict*, 2; Nordstrom, "The Backyard Front," 271.

70. Krijn Peters and Paul Richards, "Why We Fight: Voices of Youth Combatants
in Sierra Leone," *Africa* 68, no. 2 (1998): 183, 186. For additional interviews see
Richards, *Fighting*, 87–100.

71. Harry West, "Girls with Guns: Narrating the Experience of War of Frelimo's 'Female Detachment,'" *Anthropological Quarterly* 73, no. 4 (2000).

72. Virginia Bernal, "Equality to Die For? Women Guerilla Fighters and Eritrea's Cultural Revolution," *PoLar: Political and Legal Anthropology Review* 28, no. 2 (2000): 72–73. Although the article is subtitled "Women Guerilla Fighters," Bernal explains that "a great many of EPLF's fighters, male and female joined the Front when they were not yet 18 years old. EPLF developed a school and an orphanage to meet some children's needs and EPLF did have some norms about not simply sending young people into battle. I have also heard of cases where they simply tried to turn young people away. On the other hand, I don't think 18 years of age was used by EPLF as any kind of threshold and I would guess that the end of childhood was closer to 15 or 16. Of course, this is in the context of a society where women in rural areas could be married at age twelve." Personal communication, January 7, 2002.

73. Angela Veale, *From Child Soldier to Ex-Fighter* (Pretoria, South Africa: Institute for Security Studies, 2003), 25–26, 64–65.

Chapter 2 Fighting for Their Lives: Jewish Child Soldiers of World War II

1. Galia Limor, "The Melody Plays On," Yad Vashem: The Holocaust Martyrs' and Heroes' Remembrance Authority, 2002, <http://www.yad-vashem.org.il/about_yad/magazine/data2/melody_plays_on.html> (May 15, 2002).

2. Yuri Suhl, *Uncle Misha's Partisans* (New York: Four Winds Press, 1973).

3. George P. Fletcher, *The Crime of Self-Defense* (Chicago: University of Chicago Press, 1988), 20, 21.

4. Lucy S. Dawidowicz, *The War against the Jews, 1933–1945* (New York: Holt, Rinehart and Winston, 1975).

5. Dov Levin, *Fighting Back: Lithuanian Jewry's Armed Resistance to the Nazis, 1941–1945*, trans. Moshe Cohen and Dina Cohen (New York: Homes & Meier, 1985), 50–54, 49.

6. Haim Galeen, *An Eye Looks to Zion: The Story of a Jewish Partisan* [in Hebrew] (Western Galilee, Israel: Ghetto Fighters' House, 2001).

7. Havka Folman Raban, *They Are Still with Me*, 1997; trans. Judy Grossman (Western Galilee, Israel: Ghetto Fighters' Museum, 2001); Yosef Rosin, "Memoirs" (Haifa, n.d.); Elimelech (Misha) Melamed, "Memories from the Ivye Ghetto in the Eyes of a Sixteen Year Old" (memoir, Tel Aviv, Israel, n.d.).

8. Joseph Kermish, *To Live with Honor and Die with Honor: Selected Documents from the Warsaw Ghetto Archives "O.S." [Oneg Shabbat]* (Jerusalem: Yad Vashem, 1986), 516–517.

9. Israel Gutman, "Youth Movements and the Underground and the Ghetto Revolts," in *Jewish Resistance during the Holocaust* (Jerusalem: Yad Vashem, 1971), 264.

10. Emmanuel Ringelblum, *Notes from the Warsaw Ghetto: The Journal of Emmanuel Ringelblum*, ed. Jacob Sloan (New York: McGraw-Hill, 1958), 309.

11. Hanna Krall, *Shielding the Flame: An Intimate Conversation with Dr. Marek Edelman, the Last Surviving Leader of the Warsaw Ghetto Uprising*, 1977; trans. Joanna Stasinska and Lawrence Weschler (New York: Henry Holt, 1986), 37–38.

12. Marek Herman, *From the Alps to the Red Sea*, ; trans. Judy Grossman (Western Galilee, Israel: Ghetto Fighters' Museum, 1985), 90, 5.

13. Rivka Perlis, *The Pioneering Zionist Youth Movements in Nazi-Occupied Poland* [in Hebrew] (Western Galilee, Israel: Ghetto Fighters' House, 1987), 457.

14. Israel Gutman, "Youth Movements," in *Encyclopedia of the Holocaust*, ed. Israel Gutman (New York: Macmillan, 1990), 3: 1697–1703.
15. Chana Shlomi, *L'dimuto shel Yisroel Ezreal Kozuk* (Western Galilee, Israel: Ghetto Fighters' House, 2002), 29.
16. Perlis, *The Pioneering Zionist Youth Movements*, 15.
17. Melford E. Spiro, *Kibbutz: Venture in Utopia* (Cambridge, Mass.: Harvard University Press, 1970), 44, 54.
18. Avihu Ronen, "'Youth Culture' and the Roots of the Idea of Resistance in the Ghetto (Youth Movements in Zaglembie during the Holocaust)" [in Hebrew], *Zionism: Studies in the History of the Zionist Movement and of the Jewish Community in Palestine* (Tel Aviv) 16 (1991): 142, 143, 152–153.
19. Avraham Mussinger, "'Hashomer Hatzair' in Rzeszow from 1924," Rzeszow (Poland) Community Memorial Book, JewishGen, Inc., 1967, <http://www.jewishgen.org/Yizkor/rzeszow/rzeszow.html> (May 8, 2002).
20. Sara Altman, "The Hashomer Hatzair Chapter in Rzeszow That Shaped Me," Rzeszow (Poland) Community Memorial Book, JewishGen, Inc., 1967, <http://www.jewishgen.org/Yizkor/rzeszow/rze172.html> (May 8, 2002).
21. Perlis, *The Pioneering Zionist Youth Movements*, 181.
22. Chaika Grossman, *The Underground Army*, 1965, trans. Shmuel Berri (New York: Holocaust Library, 1987), 1.
23. Melamed, "Memories from the Ivye Ghetto," 1.
24. Folman Raban, *They Are Still with Me*.
25. Michael Taussig, *Shamanism, Colonialism and the Wild Man* (Chicago: University of Chicago Press, 1987).
26. Perlis, *The Pioneering Zionist Youth Movements*, 182.
27. Rich Cohen, *The Avengers: A Jewish War Story* (New York: Vintage Books, 2000), 63–65.
28. Shalom Cholawski, *Resistance and Partisan Struggle* [in Hebrew] (Jerusalem: Yad Vashem, 2001), 41.
29. Ibid., 42.
30. Dawidowicz, *The War Against the Jews*, 223–241, 242–260, 223–260.
31. Carolyn Nordstrom, "The Backyard Front," in *The Paths to Domination, Resistance and Terror*, ed. Carolyn Nordstrom and JoAnn Martin (Berkeley: University of California Press, 1992), 261.
32. Ronen, "Youth Culture," 141.
33. Folman Raban, *They Are Still with Me*, 48–62.
34. R. Domski, "The Aims of Jewish Youth," Yad Vashem: The Holocaust Martyrs' and Heroes' Remembrance Authority, 1940, <http://www.yad-vashem.org.il/search/index_search.ht> (May 20, 2003).
35. Ronen, "Youth Culture," 142.
36. Dawidowicz, *The War against the Jews*, 264.
37. Israel Gutman, *Resistance: The Warsaw Ghetto Uprising* (New York: Houghton Mifflin, 1994), 123.
38. Grossman, *The Underground Army*, 58–59. One advantage young people had, at least in the Bialystok ghetto, was that the Germans didn't pay much attention to the young; they could thus move about more freely and talk more openly without arousing suspicion than adults could.
39. Folman Raban, *They Are Still with Me*, 316.
40. Grossman, *The Underground Army*, 65.
41. Ibid.
42. Halina Birenbaum, *Hope Is the Last to Die*, 1967; trans. David Welsh (New York: Twayne, 1971), 11.

43. Cohen, *The Avengers*, 59.
44. Ibid., 60.
45. Josh Waletzsky, *Partisans of Vilna* (film produced by the Ciesla Foundation, New York, 1986).
46. Cohen, *The Avengers*, 60.
47. Simcha Rotem, *Memoirs of a Warsaw Ghetto Fighter*, trans. Barbara Harshav (New Haven, Conn.: Yale University Press, 1994).
48. Grossman, *The Underground Army*, 175.
49. Janina Bauman, *Winter in the Morning* (New York: Free Press, 1986), 94–95.
50. Radhika Coomaraswamy, Special Rapporteur, *Violence against Women*, United Nations Economic and Social Council no. E/CN.4/2002/83/Add.2 (New York, February 11, 2002).
51. Cohen, *The Avengers*, 49.
52. Rotem, *Memoirs*, 27, 79.
53. Folman Raban, *They Are Still with Me*, 78.
54. Marek Edelman, *The Ghetto Fights* (New York: American Representation of the General Jewish Workers' Union of Poland, 1946), 28–33.
55. Rotem, *Memoirs of a Warsaw Ghetto Fighter*, 29, 29, 31, 29.
56. Grossman, *The Underground Army*, 32.
57. Shalom Cholawski, Israel Gutman, Dov Levin, and Shmuel Spector, "Partisans," in *Encyclopedia of the Holocaust*, ed. Israel Gutman (New York: Macmillan, 1990), 3: 1108–1122, 1113.
58. Ibid., 3: 1111.
59. Shmuel Krakowski, *The War of the Doomed: Jewish Armed Resistance in Poland, 1942–1944*, trans. Ora Blaustein (London: Holmes & Meier, 1984), 11, 10, 11.
60. David Boder, "Interview with Lena Kuechler," Illinois Institute of Technology, 1946, <http://voices.iit.edu/profiles/kuech_p.html> (May 1, 2002).
61. David Boder, "Interview with Nathan Schacht," Illinois Institute of Technology, 1946, <http://voices.iit.edu/profiles/schac_p.html> (May 1, 2002).
62. Ibid.
63. Michal Weilgun, Testimony of Michal Weilgun, 1992, Partisan Archives 9125, Ghetto Fighters' House, Western Galilee, Israel.
64. Berta Bertman, Testimony of Berta Bertman, 1992, Partisan Archives 9150, Ghetto Fighters' House, Western Galilee, Israel.
65. Leah Rog, Testimony of Leah Rog, 1994, Partisan Archives 9217, Ghetto Fighters' House, Western Galilee, Israel.
66. Nahum Kohen and Howard Roiter, *A Voice from the Forest: Memoirs of a Jewish Partisan* (New York: Holocaust Library, 1980), 32, 38, 55, 69.
67. Ibid., 51–52.
68. Melamed, "Memories from the Ivye Ghetto."
69. Ibid.
70. Ibid.
71. Jacob Celemenski, *Elegy for My People*, 1963; trans. Gershon Friedlan (Melbourne: Jacob Celemenski Memorial Trust, 2000), 162, 165.
72. Faye Schulman, *A Partisan's Memoir: A Woman of the Holocaust* (Toronto: Second Story Press, 1995), 127–136, 163.
73. Harold Werner, *Fighting Back: A Memoir of Jewish Resistance* (New York: Columbia University Press, 1992), 107, 114.
74. Ibid., 110, 152, 152–153.
75. Ibid., 209–210.
76. Abraham Weissbrod, "The Death of a Statle (Skalat, Ukraine)," JewishGen,

Inc., 1948, <http://www.jewishgen.org/yizkor/Skalat1/skalat.html#contents> (April 12, 2003).

77. Michael Temchin, *The Witch Doctor: Memoirs of a Partisan* (New York: Holocaust Library, 1983), 104.

78. Kopel Kolpanitzky, *Sentenced to Life* [in Hebrew] (Jerusalem: Ministry of Defense, 1999), 75, 92–111.

79. A. Romi Cohn, *The Youngest Partisan* (New York: Mesorah, 2001), 196–197.

80. Ibid., 200–202.

81. Yad Vashem, "Execution of Masha Bruskina," Yad Vashem: The Holocaust Martyrs' and Heroes' Remembrance Authority, <http://www.yad-vashem.org.il/about_holocaust/month_in_holocaust/october/october_data_images/images_7.html> (March 3, 2003).

82. Cohn, *The Youngest Partisan*, 228, 227–228, 228.

83. Waletzsky, *Partisans*.

84. Nechama Tec, *Defiance: The Bielski Partisans* (New York: Oxford University Press, 1993), 82.

85. Ibid., 157.

86. Ibid., 143.

87. Ibid., 165, 166, 164–166.

88. Rosin, "Memoirs," 110.

89. Tec, *Defiance*, 166, 165.

90. Rosin, "Memoirs," 109.

Chapter 3   **Fighting for Diamonds: The Child Soldiers of Sierra Leone**

1. Sorious Samura, "Freetown: Part 4: Memories," CNN.com., May 21, 2002, <http://www.cnn.com/2002/WORLD/africa/01/04/freetown.4/> (July 1, 2003).

2. Tom Masland, "We Beat and Killed People," *Newsweek*, May 13, 2002, 25.

3. Robert D. Kaplan, *The Coming Anarchy* (New York: Random House, 2000).

4. William P. Murphy, "Military Patrimonialism and Child Soldiers' Clientilism in the Liberian and Sierra Leonean Civil Wars," *African Studies Review* 46, no. 2 (September 2003): 69.

5. Orlando Patterson, *Slavery and Social Death: A Comparative Study* (Cambridge, Mass.: Harvard University Press, 1982).

6. Remy Ourdan, "La guerre oubliée de la Sierra Leone, au coeur des ténèbres," *Le Monde* (Paris), December 1, 1999, 14.

7. Human Rights Watch, "Sierra Leone Rebels Forcefully Recruit Child Soldiers," May 31, 2000, <http://www.hrw.org/press/2000/05/s10531.htm> (July 8, 2002).

8. Sebastian Junger, "Terror Recorded," *Vanity Fair*, October 2000, 366–369.

9. Ibrahim Abdullah and P. Mauna, "The Revolutionary United Front of Sierra Leone (RUF/SL)," in *African Guerrillas*, ed. C. Clapham (Oxford: James Currey, 1998).

10. U.S. Agency for International Development, "The Development Challenge," Washington, D.C., 2002, <http://www.usaid.gov/gn/sierraleone/background/index.html> (November 10, 2002).

11. Peter Kuyembeh, "Sierra Leone Letter of Intent to the International Monetary Fund," International Monetary Fund, July 8, 2002, <http://www.imf.org/External/NP/LOI/2002/sle/01/> (December 12, 2002).

12. R. Brett and M. McCallan, *Children: The Invisible Soldiers* (Stockholm: Radda Barnen, Save the Children, 1998), 222.

13. Krijn Peters and Paul Richards, "Why We Fight: Voices of Youth Combatants in Sierra Leone," *Africa* 68, no. 2 (1998): 186.

14. U.S. Bureau of the Census, "International Data Base: United States," and "International Data Base: Sierra Leone," 2004, <http://www.census.gov/cgi-bin/ipc/idbagg> (July 12, 2004).

15. Mamadou Diouf, "Engaging Postcolonial Culture: African Youth and Public Space," *African Studies Review* 46, no. 2 (September 2003): 9.

16. Ibid., 3.

17. Rosalind Shaw, *Memories of the Slave Trade* (Chicago: University of Chicago Press, 2002), 29, 31.

18. Walter Rodney, *A History of the Upper Guinea Coast 1545–1800* (Oxford: Oxford University Press, 1970), 259.

19. Shaw, *Memories*, 41.

20. William Reno, review of *Memories of the Slave Trade*, by Rosalind Shaw, *African Studies Review* 46, no. 1 (April 2003): 198–199.

21. Kenneth Little, *The Mende of Sierra Leone* (London: Routledge, 1967), 32–39.

22. David M. Rosen, "Diamond, Diggers and Chiefs: The Politics of Fragmentation in a West African Society" (Ph.D. diss., Department of Anthropology, University of Illinois, Urbana-Champaign, 1973).

23. Ibrahim Abdullah, "Youth Culture and Rebellion: Understanding Sierra Leone's Wasted Decade," *Critical Arts Journal* 16, no. 2 (2002): 22.

24. Ibrahim Abdullah, *"Where Did We Go Wrong?" The Youth Question and the Nation-State Project in Sierra Leone* (Freetown: Sierra Leone Campaign for Good Governance, 1997).

25. Michael Banton, *West African City: A Study of Tribal Life in Freetown* (London: Oxford University Press, 1957). Banton's study was part of a broad interest in anthropology at the time in "voluntary organizations," seen to be new urban social institutions that helped largely "tribal" African migrants adjust to urbanization and modernity. Anthropologists focused on the adaptive qualities of voluntary organizations and rarely even noted the young age of the participants or the conflicts generated by these groups.

26. Ibid., 120.

27. Leo Spitzer, *The Creoles of Sierra Leone* (Madison: University of Wisconsin Press, 1974), 184.

28. Akintola Wyse, *The Krio of Sierra Leone* (Freetown, Sierra Leone: W. D. Okrafo-Smart, 1989), 88.

29. Ibid., 88.

30. Spitzer, *The Creoles*, 196–199.

31. Ibid., 197–198.

32. Ibid., 208, 209, 214–215, 215.

33. Abner Cohen, *The Politics of Elite Culture* (Berkeley: University of California Press, 1981), 101.

34. Eugene V. Walter, *Terror and Resistance: A Study of Political Violence* (Oxford: Oxford University Press, 1969), 74–78.

35. Little, *The Mende*, 184.

36. Cohen, *The Politics*, 101.

37. Helga Kreutzinger, *The Eri Devils in Freetown Sierra Leone* (Vienna: Osterreiche Ethnologische Gesellschaft, 1966), 67.

38. Ibid., 64.

39. John N. Nunley, "Urban Ode-Lay Masquerading of Sierra Leone: A Theoretical Explanation of Failure, an Answer to Success," in *Sierra Leone Studies at Birmingham, 1983*, ed. Peter Mitchell and Adam Jones (Birmingham, U.K.: Center of West African Studies, University of Birmingham, 1983), 366.

40. Kreutzinger, *The Eri Devils*, 67, 66.

41. Ibid., 62.
42. Abdullah, "Youth Culture and Rebellion," 20.
43. Abdullah, *Where Did We Go Wrong?"*
44. Nunley, "Urban Ode-Lay Masquerading," 377.
45. Alfred B. Zack-Williams, "Child Soldiers in the Civil War in Sierra Leone" (Social Studies, University of Central Lancashire, 1999).
46. Thomas Stadelmann and Markus Meyer, *Bras and Greens and Ballheads: Interviews with Freetown "Street Boys"* (Freetown, Sierra Leone: Peoples Educational Association, 1989).
47. This quote and other unattributed quotes in this chapter are from my field notes.
48. Phil Hoose, "Musicians and Children of War: An Interview with Rashid Peters and Emile Toby," Pass It On, Spring 2002, <http://www.cmnonline.org/PassItOn/P1041Children.htm> (May 30, 2003).
49. Tom Kamara, "Diamonds, War and State Collapse in Liberia and Sierra Leone," *The Perspective,* July 18, 2000, <http://www.theperspective.org/statecollapse.html> (May 30, 2003).
50. U.S. Department of State, "Sierra Leone: Country Report on Human Rights Practices 2001," <http://www.state.gov/g/drl/rls/hrrpt/2001/af/8402.htm> (March 2, 2002).
51. Francine Dal, "European Commission Evaluation Mission: Sierra Leone," European Commission, 2001, <http://europa.eu.int/comm/echo/pdf_files/evaluation/2001/s_leone_child.pdf> December 15, 2002.
52. Typically, as in South Africa, diamonds are found in deep underground veins, or "pipes," composed of the mineral kimberlite; therefore, heavy equipment and intensive capital investment are required to recover and process the gemstones. In Sierra Leone, however, great sections of the pipes were eroded away by rivers and streams.
53. H. L. Van der Laan, *The Sierra Leone Diamonds* (London: Oxford University Press, 1965).
54. Sierra Leone Government, *Laws of Sierra Leone* (1956).
55. Maurice Dorman, Governor of the Colony of Sierra Leone (untitled address to the Kono District Council, Sefadu, October 31, 1956).
56. Sierra Leone Government, *Population Census of 1963* (1963).
57. Ken Scott Associates, *Development Proposals for Central Kono, Sierra Leone* (Freetown, Sierra Leone, 1970).
58. Sierra Leone Government, *Report of the Eastern Province Intelligence Committee to the Ministry of the Interior* (May 14, 1969).
59. Letter from Paramount Chief Bockari Torto to District Officer, Kono, July 9, 1963, Kono District Office, Yengema, Sierra Leone.
60. Fred M. Hayward, "The Development of a Radical Political Organization in the Bush: A Case Study in Sierra Leone," *Canadian Journal of African Studies* 6, no. 1 (1972): 1–28.
61. William Reno, *Warlord Politics and African States* (Boulder, Colo.: Lynn Rienner, 1998), 113–188, 116.
62. Aminatta Forna, *The Devil That Danced on the Water* (New York: Atlantic Monthly Press, 2002), 166.
63. Abdullah, "Youth Culture and Rebellion," 27.
64. Forna, *The Devil,* 172.
65. Abdullah, "Youth Culture and Rebellion," 27.
66. Forna, *The Devil,* 161–165, 174, 166.
67. Diamond mining also played a role here. It was widely rumored that the chief's official role in approving local diamond-mining licenses had resulted in corrup-

tion and cronyism that favored the SLPP. Regardless of the merits of these charges, local APC officials were determined to get rid of the chief, apparently in the hope that a pro-APC chief would funnel individual mining licenses to APC supporters. A commission of inquiry was instituted to investigate the charges, but a short time before the hearings Bona renounced his membership in the SLPP and joined the APC. This move by a prominent SLPP supporter pleased the Stevens government, but it irritated local APC officials, whose dreams of access to diamonds and control of local patronage began to fade. When the commission of inquiry finally arrived in Nimi Koro Chiefdom, it announced that it would not entertain formal charges against the chief. Its real function, the members asserted, was no longer to get rid of the chief but to heal the rift between the chief and the people. As a sop to local APC officials, the commission agreed to allow the airing of all the charges against the chief. Bona, although denying most of the charges, was quite candid as to how people were chosen for the office of village chief in Kono. "It is the normal way of elections here," the chief stated in court. "People choose the chief in a corner and bring him into the courtroom. He who does not want him is beaten up."

68. Abdullah, "Youth Culture and Rebellion," 36.
69. Hilton E. Fyle, *Sierra Leone: The Fighter from Death Row* (Parkland, Florida: Universal, 2000), 8.
70. Rosen, "Diamond, Diggers and Chiefs," 83–111; David M. Rosen, "The Politics of Indirect Rule: Political Leadership among the Kono of Sierra Leone 1896–1983," in *Sierra Leone Studies at Birmingham, 1983*, ed. Peter Mitchell and Adam Jones (Birmingham, U.K.: Center of West African Studies, University of Birmingham, 1983), 320–352.
71. David M. Rosen, "Dangerous Women: 'Ideology,' 'Knowledge' and Ritual among the Kono of Eastern Sierra Leone," *Dialectical Anthropology* 6 (1981): 151–163; David M. Rosen, "The Peasant Context of Feminist Revolt in West Africa," *Anthropological Quarterly* 56, no. 1 (January 1983): 35–43.
72. Richard Fanthorpe, "Neither Citizen nor Subject? 'Lumpen' Agency and the Legacy of Native Administration in Sierra Leone," *African Affairs* 100 (2001): 363–386; Patrick Mauna, "The Kamajoi Militia: Civil War, Internal Displacement and the Politics of Counter-Insurgency," *African Development* 22, no. 3/4 (1997): 77–100.
73. The description of the development of the radical student movement that follows is drawn primarily from the account of Ibrahim Abdullah, a sociologist who was a student at Fourah Bay College at the time: Ibrahim Abdullah, "Bush Path to Destruction: The Origin and Character of the Revolutionary United Front/Sierra Leone," *Journal of Modern African Studies* 36, no. 2 (1998): 203–235. See also Zack-Williams, "Child Soldiers."
74. Abdullah, "Youth Culture and Rebellion," 33, 31.
75. Abdullah, *"Where Did We Go Wrong?"*
76. David Pratt, *Sierra Leone: Danger and Opportunity in a Regional Conflict* (Ottawa, Canada: Ministry of Foreign Affairs, July 27, 2001), 44.
77. Ibid., 44.
78. Abdullah, *"Where Did We Go Wrong?"*
79. Louise Taylor, "'We'll Kill You If You Cry,'" Human Rights Watch, January 2003, <http://hrw.org/reports/2003/sierraleone/>, (June 3, 2003).
80. Reno, *Warlord Politics*, 24.
81. Paul Richards, *Fighting for the Rain Forest* (Portsmouth, N.H.: Heinemann, 1996), 48–52.
82. Shaw, *Memories*, 196.

83. Zack-Williams, "Child Soldiers," 12.
84. Reno, *Warlord Politics*, 126.
85. Shaw, *Memories*, 195–196.
86. Molly Bingham, "Twenty-Five Year Old Kamajor Fighter Holds His Gun That Reads 'War is My Food' Which He Painted on with Red Nail Polish," photograph, Human Rights Watch, 2000, <http://www.hrw.org/campaigns/sleone/photo-essay/photo13.html> (June 10, 2003).
87. Paul Richards, "Are 'Forest' Wars in Africa Resources Conflicts? The Case of Sierra Leone," in *Violent Environments*, ed. Nancy Lee Peluso and Michael Watts (Ithaca, N.Y.: Cornell University Press, 2001), 66.
88. Quoted in Peters and Richards, "'Why We Fight," 190.
89. Radhika Coomaraswamy, Special Rapportur, *Violence against Women*, United Nations Economic and Social Council no. E/CN.4/2002/83/Add.2 (New York, February 11, 2002), 5.
90. Allison Bennet, "The Reintegration of Child Ex-combatants in Sierra Leone with Particular Focus on the Needs of Females," University of East London, 2002, <http://www.essex.ac.uk/armedcon/story_id/000025.doc.> (June 15, 2003).
91. Coomaraswamy, *Violence*, 5.
92. Physicians for Human Rights, "War-Related Violence in Sierra Leone," 2002, <http://www.phrusa.org/research/sierra_leone/report.html#1> (June 5, 2003).
93. Ibid.
94. International Crisis Group, *Sierra Leone: Managing Uncertainty* (Freetown, Sierra Leone, 2001), 11.
95. Tim McKinley, "Sierra Leone Diamond Town Seeks Alternative," *BBC News*, April 2, 2002, <http://news.bbc.co.uk/1/hi/world/africa/1908691.stm> (November 9, 2002).
96. Ibid.
97. UNAMSIL, Press Briefing, Freetown/UNAMSIL Public Information Office, January 25, 2002, <http://www.un.org/Depts/dpko/unamsil/DB/250102.htm> (October 1, 2002).
98. United Nations Office for the Coordination of Humanitarian Affairs, "Sierra Leone: Humanitarian Report 01–03 July 2002," July 31, 2002, <http://www.reliefweb.int/w/rwb.nsf/0/1040ca394feaea2685256c0e00636c56?OpenDocument> (July 12, 2004).
99. Lansana Fofana, "UN Envoy Stunned by Magnitude of Child Slavery," Inter Press Service News Agency, February 28, 2003, <http://www.ipsnews.net/africa/interna.asp?idnews=16367> (August 25, 2003).
100. David Crane, Chief Prosecutor, Sierra Leone Special Court, "Remarks," Friends of Sierra Leone, Washington, D.C., May 27, 2003, <www.fosalone.org/crane.htm> (August 24, 2003).
101. Ron MuCullagh (producer/director), *Cry Freetown* (film produced by Insight News Television, 2000).
102. Masland, "We Beat," 28.

Chapter 4   Fighting for the Apocalypse: Palestinian Child Soldiers

1. Joshua Hammer, *A Season in Bethlehem* (New York: Free Press, 2003), 160. For a general study of female suicide bombers, see Barbara Victor, *Army of Roses: Inside the World of Palestinian Women Suicide Bombers* (Emmaus, Pa.: Rodale, 2003).

2. Samih Farsoun, *Palestine and the Palestinians* (Boulder, Colo.: Westview Press, 1997), 9.
3. Said Amir Arjomand, "Islamic Apocalyptism in the Classic Period," in *The Encyclopedia of Apocalyptism*, ed. Bernard McGinn (New York: Continuum, 1998), 238–283.
4. Paul Berman, "Totalitarianism and the Role of Intellectuals," *Chronicle Review*, May 9, 2003, B12; Paul Berman, *Terror and Liberalism* (New York: Norton, 2003).
5. Wendy Pearlman, *Occupied Voices: Stories of Everyday Life in the Second Intifada* (New York: Thunder's Mouth Press and Nation Books, 2003), 57.
6. "Teenage Martyr," *Daily Star*, February 26, 2002, <http://www.lebanonwire.com/news/02022609DS.htm> (October 17, 2003).
7. Palestinian Center for Survey and Policy Research, "Palestinian Public Opinion Poll No. 9," October 15, 2003, <http://www.pcpsr.org/survey/polls/2003/p9epressrelease.html> (October 16, 2003).
8. James Bennet, "Bombing Kills 18 and Hurts Scores on Jerusalem Bus," *New York Times*, August 20, 2003, A1.
9. Don Van Natta Jr., "The Terror Industry Fields Its Ultimate Weapon," *New York Times*, August 24, 2003, Late Edition, 4: 7.
10. James Bennet, "The Illusions of Progress," *New York Times*, August 23, 2003, A6.
11. Frank Bruni, "At Gaza Funeral, Arab Anger Boils Up; Israel Tightens Checkpoints," *New York Times*, August 23, 2003, A6.
12. Baruch Kimmerling and Joel S. Migdal, *The Palestinian People* (Cambridge, Mass.: Harvard University Press, 2003), 84.
13. Benny Morris, *Righteous Victims: A History of the Zionist-Arab Conflict, 1881–2001* (New York: Random House, 2001), 123, 128.
14. Eric Wolf, *Peasant Wars of the Twentieth Century* (New York: Harper & Row, 1969); Eric Wolf, "On Peasant Rebellions," *International Social Science Journal* 21, no. 2 (1969): 286–293.
15. Wolf, *Peasant Wars*.
16. Morris, *Righteous Victims*, 123.
17. Rosemary Sayigh, *Palestinians: From Peasants to Revolutionaries* (London: Zed Books, 1979), 39.
18. Wolf, *Peasant Wars*, 292.
19. Morris, *Righteous Victims*, 129.
20. Farsoun, *Palestine*, 59.
21. Morris, *Righteous Victims*, 64.
22. Kimmerling and Migdal, *The Palestinian People*, 111.
23. Zvi Elpeleg, *The Grand Mufti: Haj Amin al-Hussaini, Founder of the Palestinian National Movement*, 1988; trans. David Harvey; ed. Shmuel Himelstein (London: Frank Cass, 1993), 1–14.
24. U.K. Foreign Office, Criminal Investigative Department, FO 371, February 5, 1935, Periodic Appreciation Summary No. 4/35, Public Record Office, London.
25. Wolf, *Peasant Wars*, 295.
26. Morris, *Righteous Victims*, 115.
27. Frederik H. Kisch, *Palestine Diary* (London: V. Gollanscz, 1938), 267–268.
28. "The Terror," Central Zionist Archives, Jerusalem, S25, 10499, 1936.
29. Ibid.
30. Kimmerling and Migdal, *The Palestinian People*, 111.

31. Rashid Khalidi, "Palestinian Peasant Resistance to Zionism before World War I," in *Blaming the Victim*, ed. Edward Said and Christopher Hitchens (London: Verso, 2001), 227.

32. Yehoshua Porath, *The Emergence of the Palestinian-Arab National Movement: 1918–1929* (London: Frank Cass, 1974), 289.

33. Shai Lachman, "Arab Rebellion and Terrorism in Palestine: The Case of Sheikh al-Din al-Qassam and His Movement," in *Zionism and Arabism in Palestine and Israel*, ed. Elie Kedourie and Sylvia Haim (London: Frank Cass, 1982), 60, 62.

34. Farsoun, *Palestine*, 105.

35. Lachman, "Arab Rebellion and Terrorism in Palestine," 64, 77, 63.

36. Kisch, *Palestine Diary*, 400–402; Kibbutz Yagur, "History," 2002, <www.yagur.com/files/history.asp> (November 18, 2003).

37. Lachman, "Arab Rebellion and Terrorism in Palestine," 65.

38. Tom Segev, *One Palestine, Complete*, 1999; trans. Haim Watzman (New York: Henry Holt, 2000), 361.

39. S. Abdullah Schleifler, "The Life and Thought of 'Izz-Id-Din al-Qassam," *Islamic Quarterly* 22, no. 2 (1979): 61–81.

40. "The Terror."

41. Farsoun, *Palestine*, 104–105.

42. "The Terror."

43. Zacharey Lochman and Joel Beinin, *Intifada: The Palestinian Uprising against Israeli Occupation* (Boston: South End Press, 1989), 329.

44. Maryam Jameelah, *Shaikh Izz-Ud-Din Al-Qassam Shaheed: His Life and Work* (Lahore, Pakistan: Mohammad Yusuf Khan & Sons, 1990), 10.

45. Ted Swedenburg, *Memories of Revolt: The 1936–1939 Rebellion and the Palestinian National Past* (Minneapolis: University of Minnesota Press, 1995), 2.

46. Farsoun, *Palestine*, 105.

47. Joseph M. Levy, "Palestine Tension Reported Growing," *New York Times*, August 11, 1931, 6.

48. Joseph M. Levy, "Protest by Arabs Fails to Develop," *New York Times*, August 16, 1931, 13.

49. Ibid.

50. Joseph M. Levy, "General Strike Set by Arab Executive," *New York Times*, August 18, 1931, 5.

51. Joseph M. Levy, "Seven Hurt in Riot in Palestine Town," *New York Times*, August 24, 1931, 10.

52. "Cleared in Palestine Riot," *New York Times*, September 9, 1931, 8.

53. Yehoshua Porath, *The Palestinian Arab National Movement: 1929–1939* (London: Frank Cass, 1977), 212, 22.

54. Lachman, "Arab Rebellion and Terrorism in Palestine," 58.

55. Zvi Elpeleg, *The Grand Mufti*, 37; Porath, *The Palestinian Arab National Movement*, 122–123.

56. Porath, *The Palestinian Arab National Movement*, 125–126.

57. Ibid., 131.

58. Lachman, "Arab Rebellion and Terrorism in Palestine," 58–59; Porath, *The Palestinian Arab National Movement*, 132.

59. U.K. Foreign Office, Criminal Investigative Department, FO 371, August 6, 1935, Periodic Appreciation Summary No. 12/35, Public Record Office, London.

60. Porath, *The Palestinian Arab National Movement*, 130, 132.

61. Lachman, "Arab Rebellion and Terrorism in Palestine," 57–58.

62. Segev, *One Palestine*, 365, 363.

63. "Imitation of Nazi and Fascist Methods in the Education of Youth," Central Zionist Archives, Jerusalem, S25, 10499, 1936.
64. Ibid.
65. Royal Palestine Commission, Letter, Central Zionist Archives, Jerusalem, S25, 10499, January 27, 1937.
66. Thomas Kiernan, *Arafat: The Man and the Myth* (New York: Norton, 1976), 42.
67. "Imitation."
68. Morris, *Righteous Victims*, 124.
69. "Imitation."
70. Morris, *Righteous Victims*, 124.
71. U.K. Foreign Office, Criminal Investigative Department, FO 371, November 16, 1935, Periodic Appreciation Summary No. 17/35, Public Record Office, London.
72. Kanan Makiya, *Republic of Fear* (Berkeley: University of California Press, 1998), 178, 179, 180, 76, 178.
73. Morris, *Righteous Victims*, 128–135, 131.
74. Said Aburish, *Children of Bethany* (London: I. B. Tauris, 1988), 42.
75. Ibid., 52–53.
76. Segev, *One Palestine*, 442.
77. Kiernan, *Arafat*, 33.
78. Janet Wallach and John Wallach, *Arafat: In the Eyes of the Beholder* (New York: Carol, 1990).
79. Alan Hart, *Arafat: A Political Biography* (Bloomington: Indiana University Press, 1989), 70.
80. Andrew Gowers and Tony Walker, *Arafat: The Biography* (London: Virgin Books, 1994), 10.
81. Kiernan, *Arafat*, 85–86, 86, 117.
82. Ibid., 112, 118–119, 123, 132.
83. Ibid., 133, 136–137, 139.
84. Hart, *Arafat*, 71.
85. Michael B. Oren, *Six Days of War* (Oxford: Oxford University Press, 2002).
86. Moshe Maoz, *Palestinian Leadership on the West Bank* (London: Frank Cass, 1984), xi, xii.
87. Ibid., xii.
88. Morris, *Righteous Victims*, 377.
89. Ibid.
90. Ibid., 378.
91. Arabi Awwad and Jiryis Qwwas, "Resistance in the Occupied Territories," *Journal of Palestine Studies* 3, no. 4 (1974).
92. Joost R. Hilterman, *Behind the Intifada* (Princeton, N.J.: Princeton University Press, 1991), 46.
93. Morris, *Righteous Victims*, 563.
94. Ibid., 564.
95. Maoz, *Palestinian Leadership*, 88, 117, 155, 134.
96. Hilterman, *Behind the Intifada*, 51.
97. Kimmerling and Migdal, *The Palestinian People*, 297.
98. Hilterman, *Behind the Intifada*, 53.
99. Maya Rosenfeld, "Ways of Life, Division of Labor and Social Roles of Palestinian Refugee Families: The Case of the Dheisheh Refugee Camp" (Ph.D. diss., Sociology and Anthropology, Hebrew University of Jerusalem, 1997). I relied on Rosenfeld's doctoral dissertation, in Hebrew, for this section of the argument. Since I did my research, a revised version of Rosenfeld's dissertation has appeared

in English: Maya Rosenfeld, *Confronting the Occupation: Work, Education and Political Activism of Palestinian Families in a Refugee Camp* (Stanford, Calif.: Stanford University Press, 2004).

100. Ibid., 283.
101. Ibid., 279.
102. Ibid., 293, 294 [my translation].
103. Morris, *Righteous Victims*, 572–573.
104. Hilterman, *Behind the Intifada*, 53.
105. Jacque Pinto, *Judean Journal* (London: Quartet Books, 1990), 43, 42.
106. Andrew Rigby, *The Living Intifada* (London: Zed Books, 1990), 56.
107. Ibid., 57, 58.
108. Ali H. Qleibo, *Before the Mountains Disappear: An Ethnographic Chronicle of the Modern Palestinians* (Cairo: Al Haram Press, 1992).
109. Ibid., 58–59.
110. Muna Hamzeh-Muhaissen, "Remembering the Glory of the Intifada," *Palestine Report* 3, no. 27 (December 12, 1997), <http://www.jmcc.org/media/report/97/Dec/2.htm#four> (May 28, 2003).
111. Joharah Baker, "How to Fight Back," *Palestine Report* 8, no. 34 (February 2, 2002), <http://www.jmcc.org/media/report/02/Feb/2.htm#feature> (May 28, 2003).
112. Morris, *Righteous Victims*, 662.
113. Graham Usher, "Facing Defeat: The Intifada Two Years On," *Journal of Palestine Studies*, no. 126 (Winter 2003).
114. Rima Hammami and Salim Tamari, "The Second Intifada: End or New Beginning," *Journal of Palestine Studies* 118 (Winter 2001).
115. Ibid.
116. John F. Burns, "Palestinian Summer Camp Offers the Games of War," *New York Times*, August 3, 2000, A1, A16.
117. Michael Finkel, "Playing War," *New York Times Magazine*, December 24, 2000, 46.
118. Burns, "Palestinian Summer Camp."
119. Finkel, "Playing War," 32.
120. "Abu Mazan: 40 Children in Rafah Who Received Money to Throw Bangalore," Spokesperson's Unit, Israel Defense Forces, June 27, 2002, <http://www.idf.il/english/announcements/2002/june/mazen.stm> (May 25, 2003).
121. Christopher Reuter, *My Life Is a Weapon: A Modern History of Suicide Bombing* (Princeton, N.J.: Princeton University Press, 2004); Morris, *Righteous Victims*, 622. Some evidence indicates that the Lebanese movement Hizbollah, which, like Hamas and Islamic Jihad, is existentially opposed to the existence of a Jewish state, trained Palestinians in suicide bombing. Jessica Stern, *Terror in the Name of God: Why Religious Militants Kill* (New York: Ecco Press, 2003), 47. For a complete discussion of Hizobollah's theological opposition to a Jewish polity in the Middle East, see Amal Saad-Gorayeb, *Hizbu'llah: Politics and Religion* (London: Pluto Press, 2003).
122. Morris, *Righteous Victims*, 626.
123. Avishai Margalit, "The Suicide Bombers," *New York Review of Books*, January 16, 2003, 36.
124. Human Rights Watch, *Erased in a Moment: Suicide Bombing Attacks against Israeli Civilians* (New York, 2002), 90.
125. Ibid., 91, 92.
126. The following account of the suicide attacks by Arin Ahmed and Bdeir is taken from Vered Levi-Barzilai, "A Near Death Experience," *Haaretz* Internet, June 28,

2002, http://www.haaretzdaily.com.hasen/pages/ShArt.jhtml?itemNo=178487 (June 15, 2003).

127. "Palestinians Condemn Bombing," BBC News, May 30, 2002, <http://news.bbc.co.uk/1/hi/world/middle_east/1997672.stm> (May 25, 2003).

128. Gaylen Byker, "The Darkest Hour of the Soul: A Conversation with Hanan Ashrawi," *Books and Culture: A Christian Review* 8, no. 2 (March 2002), 17.

129. Human Rights Watch, *Erased in a Moment*, 92.

130. Amira Hass, " Driven by Vengeance and a Desire Driven by Vengeance and a Desire to Defend the Homeland," *Haaretz* Internet, May 27, 2003, <http://www.haaretzdaily.com/hasen/pages/ShArt.jhtml?itemNo=187074 & contrassID=2&subContrassID=5&sbSubContrassID=0&listSrc=Y&itemNo=187074> (June 15, 2003).

131. "Leaky Event behind New Saudi Water Minister?" *Saudi Arabia News*, October 23, 2002, <http://www.najaco.com/travel/news/saudi_arabia/2002/october/23.htm> (June 25, 2003).

132. "Martyrs vs. War Criminals," *Milli Gazette*, May 5, 2002, <http://www.milligazette.com/Archives/01052002/0105200257.htm> (June 25, 2003).

133. Human Rights Watch, *Erased in a Moment*, 92–93.

134. Khalil Shiqaqi, "The View of Palestinian Society on Suicide Terrorism," in *Countering Suicide Terrorism* (Herzliya, Israel: International Policy Institute for Counter-terrorism, 2002), 163.

135. Nachman Tal, "Suicide Attacks: Israel and Islamic Terrorism," *Strategic Assessment* 5, no. 1 (June 2002), <www.tau.ac.il/jcss/sa/v5n1p6Tal.html> (May 5, 2003).

136. Elizabeth Rubin, "The Most Wanted Palestinian Terrorist," *New York Times Magazine*, June 30, 2002, 28.

137. "Hamas and Islamic Jihad Triumph in al-Najah University Student Elections," Israel Defense Forces, 2001, <http://www.idf.il/newsite/english/alnajah/alnajah.stm> (June 26, 2003).

138. Rubin, "The Most Wanted Palestinian Terrorist," 28.

139. Nasra Hassan, "An Arsenal of Believers," *New Yorker*, November 11, 2001, 37.

140. Ibid.

141. Margalit, "The Suicide Bombers," 36.

142. Eyad Sarraj, "Why We Blow Ourselves Up," *Time*, April 8, 2002, 39.

143. Isabel Kershner, "Death Wish," *Jerusalem Report.Com*, 2002, <http://www.jrep.com/Palaffairs/Article-7.html> (June 27, 2003).

144. Jonathan Raban, "My Holy War," *New Yorker*, February 4, 2002, 28–36.

145. Intelligence and Terrorism Information Center, "Palestinian Women: A Study of the Bethlehem Area (2000–2002)," Center for Special Studies, 2002, <http://www.intelligence.org.il/eng/bu/women/women.htm#d> (June 27, 2003).

146. Karl Marx, "The Eighteenth Brumaire of Louis Bonaparte," in *Karl Marx: Political Writings*, vol. 2, ed. David Fernbach (New York: Vintage Books, 1974), 146.

Chapter 5 The Politics of Age

1. J. Clyde Mitchell, *The Kalela Dance* (Manchester: Manchester University Press, 1956), 31. Mitchell was among the first anthropologists to describe "tribalism" and ethnicity from an interactionist perspective.

2. Nancy Sherper-Hughes and Carolyn Sargent, "Introduction: The Cultural Politics of Childhood," in *Small Wars: The Cultural Politics of Childhood*, ed. Nancy Sherper-Hughes and Carolyn Sargent (Berkeley: University of California Press, 1998), 1–33.

3. Vered Amit-Talai and Helena Wulff, eds., *Youth Cultures: A Cross-Cultural Perspective* (London: Routledge, 1995); Myra Bluebond-Langner, *The Private Worlds of Dying Children* (Princeton, N.J.: Princeton University Press, 1978); Myra Bluebond-Langner, *In the Shadow of Illness* (Princeton, N.J.: Princeton University Press, 1996); Helen Schwartzman, ed., *Children and Anthropology: Perspectives for the 21st Century* (Westport, Conn.: Bergin & Garvey, 2001); Sharon Stephens, ed., *Children and the Politics of Culture* (Princeton, N.J.: Princeton University Press, 1995). For a general review of the anthropological literature on the role of violence in the lives of children, see Jill Korbin, "Children, Childhoods, and Violence," *Annual Review of Anthropology* 32 (2003): 431–446.

4. Alan Prout and Allison James, "A New Paradigm for the Sociology of Childhood?" in *Constructing and Reconstructing Childhood*, ed. Allison James and Alan Prout (London: Falmer Press, 1990), 8.

5. The humanitarian view of consent is based on legal notions of consent as these exist within a peacetime legal regime. Classic definitions of consent in modern legal discourse rest on the elements of mental capacity and voluntariness. Consent encompasses the capacity to reason as well as to be free from duress and compulsion in the reasoning process. In the law, consent is defined as "an act of reason, accompanied with deliberation, the mind weighing with a balance the good or evil on each side. It means a voluntary agreement by a person in the possession and exercise of sufficient mental capacity to make an intelligent choice to do something proposed by another. It supposes a physical power to act, a moral power of acting, and a serious determined and free use of these powers. . . . It is an act unclouded by fraud, duress, or sometimes even mistake." *Black's Law Dictionary*, abridged 5th ed. (St. Paul, Minn: West, 1983), 160.

6. Graca Machel, *The Impact of War on Children* (London: Hurst, 2001), 11; italics mine.

7. Ellen Greenberg Garrison, "Children's Competence to Participate in Divorce Custody Decisionmaking," *Journal of Clinical Child Psychology* 20 (1991): 78–87; Kenneth Ginsberg et al., "Adolescents' Perceptions of Factors Affecting Their Decisions to Seek Health Care," *Journal of the American Medical Association* 273 (1995): 1913, 1917; David G. Scherer, "The Capacities of Minors to Exercise Voluntariness in Medical Treatment Decisions," *Law and Human Behavior* 15 (1991): 431–445; Thomas Grisson, "Juveniles' Capacity to Waive Miranda Rights: An Empirical Analysis," *California Law Review* 68 (1980).

8. Rhonda Gay Hartman, "Adolescent Autonomy: Clarifying an Ageless Conundrum," *Hasting Law Review* 51 (Fall 2000): 1–100.

9. In the area of child labor a set chronological age may not function for the benefit of the child but for someone else. A father, for example, might be entitled to the earnings of an unemancipated child and might be entitled to disaffirm the child's contract when he feels the child is spending foolishly. Robert Edge, "Voidability of Minor's Contract: A Feudal Doctrine in a Modern Economy," *Georgia Law Review* 1 (1967): 204–267.

10. Lois A. Weithorn, "Involving Children in Decisions Affecting Their Own Welfare," in *Children's Competence to Consent*, ed. Gary B. Melton et al. (New York: Plenum, 1983), 235–260.

11. Laurence Tribe, "Childhood, Suspect Classifications, and Conclusive Presumptions: Three Linked Riddles," *Journal of Law and Contemporary Problems* 39, no. 7 (1975): 8–66, 32.

12. Mary Ann Glendon, *A World Made New: Eleanor Roosevelt and the Universal Declaration of Human Rights* (New York: Random House, 2001), 18.

13. S. Grisso et al., "Juveniles' Competence to Stand Trial: A Comparison of Adolescents' and Adults' Capacities as Trial Defendants," *Law and Human Behavior* 27 (2003): 333–363; Thomas Grisso and Laurence Steinberg, "The MacArthur Juvenile Adjudicative Competence Study," John D. and Catherine T. MacArthur Foundation, 2003, <http://www.mac-adoldev-juvjustice.org/competence%20study%20summary.pdf> (May 1, 2004).

14. The Anglo-American legal system long justified the suppression of women's rights as a form of protection of the "gentler" sex. Apologists for slavery in the United States celebrated the protective paternalism of the slave master and the civilizing mission of the slave system. Similarly, the language of protection can easily be used to justify forms of control that go well beyond safeguarding the child. Therefore, when it comes to children, the language of protectionism needs to be thoroughly queried.

15. Randy F. Kandel and Anne Griffiths, "Reconfiguring Personhood: From Ungovernability to Parent Adolescent Autonomy Conflict Actions," *Syracuse University Law Review* 53 (2003): 995–1065. Anne Griffiths and Randy F. Kandel, "Hearing Children in Children's Hearings," *Child and Family Law Quarterly* 12, no. 3 (2000): 283–299.

16. Sara Rimer, "Unruly Students Facing Arrest, Not Detention," *New York Times*, January 4, 2004, Late Edition, 17.

17. Women participating in the labor force during World War II resisted returning to the roles and routines of domestic life. A cultural assault followed on women who chose work over domestic roles because their doing so challenged the authority of men and the conventions of family life. Stephanie Coontz, *The Way We Never Were* (New York: Basic Books, 1992), 31–32.

18. Article 1(4) of Protocol Additional I, discussed below, provides the main exception. A second, and rare, exception is when the state involved gives formal recognition to the belligerency, as during the Civil War in the United States.

19. Simon Chesterman, ed., *Civilians in War* (Boulder, Colo.: Lynn Rienner, 2001); Yoram Dinstein, "The Distinction between Unlawful Combatants and War Criminals," in *International Law at a Time of Perplexity: Essays in Honor of Shabtai Rosenne*, ed. Yoram Dinstein and Mary Tabory (London: Martinus Nijhoff, 1989), 103–116; Judge Advocate Generals' School, *A Treatise on the Juridical Basis of the Distinction between Lawful Combatant and Unprivileged Belligerent.* (Charlottesville, Va., 1959); Jenny Kuper, *International Law Concerning Child Civilians in Armed Conflict* (New York: Oxford University Press, 1997); Colm McKeogh, *Innocent Civilians: The Morality of Killing in War* (New York: Palgrave, 2002); Karma Nabulsi, *Traditions of War: Occupation, Resistance, and the Law* (New York: Oxford University Press, 1999); .

20. "Protocol Additional I to the Geneva Conventions of 12 August 1949 and Relating to the Protections of Victims of International Armed Conflict," Article 1(4), June 8, 1977, <http://www.unhcr.ch/html/menu3/b/93.htm> (December 15, 2003).

21. Ibid., Article 44 (3); Kenneth Anderson, "Who Owns the Rules of War?" Crimes of War Project, April 24, 2003, <http://www.crimesofwar.org/special/Iraq/news-iraq6.html>(January 14, 2004). This special case of noninternational conflict was widely understood as applying to the African National Congress in its armed insurgency against South Africa. Some argue that the Palestinian uprising in Israel also fits this model, although there is considerable controversy over this matter. Israel regards the Palestinian uprising as a noninternational conflict, while many Palestinians regard it as an international conflict in that it is a struggle for self-

determination. Israel has no legal sovereignty over the West Bank and Gaza, but neither do these territories constitute a sovereign state. However, as a matter of international law the Palestinian argument is weak because Israel is not a party to Protocol Additional I, and novel interpretation of international conflict embedded in the treaty cannot rest on international customary law. Resolutions of the General Assembly have repeatedly endorsed the Palestinian right of self-determination, but the General Assembly is not a law-making body. In any event, as has frequently been pointed out, "the General Assembly's extension of the right of self determination to the Palestinians and the inhabitants of South Africa, coupled with its failure to extend that right to other 'non-colonial' peoples, has increased rather than reduced the problem of double standards." Peter Malanczuk, ed., *Akehurst's Modern Introduction to International Law* (London: Routledge, 1997), 333.

22. Martha Finnemore and Kathryn Sikkink, "International Norm Dynamics and Political Change," *International Organization* 52 (Autumn 1998).
23. Jeffrey Herbst, "International Laws of War and the African Child: Norms, Compliance and Sovereignty," Princeton University Center for Research on Child Well Being, 2002, <http://crcw.princeton.edu/workingpapers/WP00-02-Herbst.pdf> (January 2, 2004).
24. "Protocol Additional I," Article 77 (2).
25. International Committee of the Red Cross, "Commentaries on the Protocol Additional to the Geneva Conventions of 12 August 1949, and Relating to the Protection of Victims of International Armed Conflicts (Protocol I), 8 June 1977," Sections 3204–3208, 1987, <http://www.icrc.org/ihl.nsf/COMART?OpenView (August 15, 2003).
26. Daniel Helle, "Optional Protocol on the Involvement of Children in Armed Conflict to the Convention on the Rights of the Child," *International Review of the Red Cross* 839, September 30, 2000, <http://www.icrc.org/web/eng/siteeng0.nsf/iwpList520> (August 14, 2003).
27. "Protocol Additional II to the Geneva Conventions of 12 August 1949 and Relating to the Protections of Victims of Non-International Armed Conflict," Article 4(3)(c), June 8, 1977, <http://www.unhcr.ch/html/menu3/b/94.htm> (August 15, 2003).
28. "Protocol Additional I," Article 77 (3) and Article 77 (5).
29. International Committee of the Red Cross, "Commentaries on the Protocol Additional," Sections 3204–3208.
30. "Protocol Additional II," Article 5.
31. International Committee of the Red Cross, "Commentaries on the Protocol Additional," Sections 3183, 3179.
32. "Convention on the Rights of the Child," United Nations High Commission on Human Rights, Article 1 and Article 38 (2), November 20, 1989, <www.unhchr.ch/html/menu3/b/k2crc.htm> (February 11, 2002).
33. Rome Statute of the International Criminal Court, 17 July 1998, Articles 8(1), 8(2)(b)(xxvi), 8(2)(e)(vii), http://www.un.org/law/icc/statute/romefra.htm (July 15, 2003).
34. "Optional Protocol to the Convention on the Rights of the Child on the Involvement of Children in Armed Conflict," United Nations Office of the High Commissioner for Human Rights, Articles 1, 2, 3, and 8, February 12, 2002, <http://www.unhchr.ch/html/menu2/6/protocolchild.htm> (August 14, 2003).
35. Ibid., Article 4.
36. Helle, "Optional Protocol."
37. Ibid.

38. Shara Abraham, "Child Soldiers and the Capacity of the Optional Protocol to Protect Children in Conflict," *Human Rights Brief* 10, no. 3 (2002), <http:// www.wcl.american.edu/hrbrief/10/3child.cfm> (August 8, 2003).
39. United Nations, Security Council Resolution 1315, S.RES/315 (2000).
40. *Prosecutor v. Sam Hinga Norman*, Decision on Preliminary Motion Based on Lack of Jurisdiction (Child Soldiers), Case No. SCSL–2004–14–AR72(E), Special Court for Sierra Leone, Freetown, May 31, 2004.
41. Ilene Cohn, "The Protection of Children and the Quest for Truth and Justice in Sierra Leone," *Journal of International Affairs* 55, no. 1 (Fall 2001)" 9, 13.
42. The creation of a truth and reconciliation commission was part of the 1999 Lome peace accord. The agreement provided that "a Truth and Reconciliation Commission shall be established to address impunity, break the cycle of violence, provide a forum for both the victims and perpetrators of human rights violations to tell their story, get a clear picture of the past in order to facilitate genuine healing and reconciliation." "Peace Agreement between the Government of Sierra Leone and the Revolutionary United Front," Sierra Leone Web, July 7, 1999, <http://www.sierra-leone.org/lomeaccord.html> (December 1, 2003). The current Truth and Reconciliation Commission was established by an act of the Sierra Leone Parliament on February 10, 2000, in order to "create an impartial historical record of violations and abuses of human rights and international humanitarian law related to the armed conflict in Sierra Leone, from the beginning of the Conflict in 1991 to the signing of the Lome Peace Agreement; to address impunity, to respond to the needs of the victims, to promote healing and reconciliation and to prevent a repetition of the violations and abuses suffered." "Truth and Reconciliation Act of 2000," Special Court for Sierra Leone, 2000, <http://www.sc-sl.org/> (December 1, 2003). With respect to children, the act provided that the Commission should "work to help restore the human dignity of victims and promote reconciliation by providing an opportunity for victims to give an account of the violations and abuses suffered and for perpetrators to relate their experiences, and by creating a climate which fosters constructive interchange between victims and perpetrators, giving special attention to the subject of sexual abuses and to the experiences of children within the armed conflict." "Truth and Reconciliation Act of 2000," Part III 6(2)(b). In addition the act provided that "the Commission shall take into account the interests of victims and witnesses when inviting them to give statements, including the security and other concerns of those who may wish to recount their stories in public and the Commission may also implement special procedures to address the needs of such particular victims as children or those who have suffered sexual abuses as well as in working with child perpetrators of abuses or violations." "Truth and Reconciliation Act of 2000," Part III 7 (4).
43. Ahmad Kabbah, "Address by the President His Excellency Alhaji Dr. Ahmad Kabbah at the Start of Public Hearings of the Truth and Reconciliation Commission," Sierra Leone Web, April 14, 2002, <http://www.sierra-leone.org/ kabbah041403.html>(December 1, 2003).
44. Richard A. Wilson, "Children and War in Sierra Leone: A West African Diary," *Anthropology Today* 17, no. 5 (2001): 22.
45. Cohn, "The Protection of Children," 25, 26.
46. Wilson, "Children and War in Sierra Leone," 22.
47. Natalie Mann and Bert Theuermann, eds., *Children and the Truth and Reconciliation Commission for Sierra Leone: Recommendations for Policies and Procedures for Involving Children in the TRC* (New York: UNICEF, 2001), 2, 9–13.

48. Wilson, "Children and War in Sierra Leone," 22.
49. Truth and Reconciliation Commission for Sierra Leone, April 8, 2003, <http://www.sierra-leone.org/trc-trcforsierraleone.html> (March 1, 2004).
50. U.S. Central Intelligence Agency, "Sierra Leone," 2003, <http://www.cia.gov/cia/publications/factbook/geos/sl.html> (August 15, 2003).
51. Tim Kelsall, "Truth, Lies and Ritual. Preliminary Reflections on the Truth and Reconciliation Commission in Sierra Leone" (paper, African Studies Center, Leiden, January 14, 2004).
52. Susan Shepler, "Child Soldiers and the Ambivalent Effectiveness of Discourses of Abdicated Responsibility" (paper, African Studies Association, Boston, October 30, 2003), 10. Forthcoming as "The Rights of the Child: Global Discourses of Youth and Reintegrating Child Soldiers in Sierra Leone," *Journal of Human Rights*.
53. Danny Hoffman, "The Benefits of Youth: The Disarmament of Child Soldiers in Sierra Leone," in *Youth Overcoming Political Violence* (Paper delivered at the African Studies Association, Boston, October 30, 2003). The following discussion is drawn from Hoffman's account.
54. Shepler, "Child Soldiers," 19.
55. Ibid., 23.
56. Republic of Sierra Leone, "National Youth Policy of Sierra Leone," June 30, 2003, <http://www.statehouse-sl.org/policies/youth.html> (January 7, 2004).
57. Coalition to Stop the Use of Child Soldiers, *Child Soldiers Global Report* (London, 2001), 288.
58. Ibid., 22–23, 288, 41, 22–23, 289.
59. Thirty-seven hundred NGOs accredited with UNICEF or the United Nations Economic and Social Council were invited to attend the Special Session, which was held at United Nations headquarters in New York from May 6 to May 10, 2002.
60. NGO Caucus on Children and Armed Conflict, "Oral Statement," in *Second Substantive Session of the Preparatory Committee for the Special Session of the General Assembly in 2001* (New York: United Nations, January 31, 2001).
61. United Nations, Security Council Resolution 1379: Children and Armed Conflict, S.RES/1379, 2001, Paragraph 16.
62. I was in Israel at the time of the event and watched a televised CNN report in which a weeping Palestinian woman falsely alleged that she had personally observed the Israel Defense Forces line up and execute a large group of Palestinian men.
63. Amnesty International, *Without Distinction: Attacks on Civilians by Palestinian Armed Groups*, tech. rept. MDE/02/003/2002 (New York, 2002); Human Rights Watch, *Jenin: IDF Military Operations* (New York, May 2002).
64. This and all other unattributed quotes in the remainder of this chapter are from my field notes.
65. Watchlist on Children and Armed Conflict, "West Bank and Gaza Strip and Israel" (fact sheet, Women's Commission for Refugee Women and Children, 2002).
66. As of June 2002, 530 Israelis had been killed in the al-Aqsa intifada, while 1,460 Palestinians had been killed. Israeli fatalities consisted of almost 80 percent noncombatants, while among Palestinians 55 percent were combatants. The age and sex distribution of Israelis killed showed a basic random pattern, which reflected the effects of terrorist attacks on the Israeli civilian population as a whole. Palestinian fatalities, both combatants and noncombatants, tended to be skewed

toward young men and boys, including many teenagers; these deaths arose from confrontations at flash points at which largely young male Palestinians—combatants, noncombatants, and violent protestors—confronted Israeli troops. Don Radlauer, "An Engineered Tragedy: Statistical Analysis of Casualties in the Palestinian-Israeli Conflict September 2000–June 2002," June 20, 2002, <http://www.ict.org.il/researchreport/researchreport.htm> (June 24, 2002).

Selected Bibliography

Abdullah, Ibrahim. "Bush Path to Destruction: The Origin and Character of the Revolutionary United Front/Sierra Leone." *Journal of Modern African Studies* 36, no. 2 (1998): 203–235.

Abdullah, Ibrahim, and P. Mauna. "The Revolutionary United Front of Sierra Leone (RUF/SL)." In *African Guerrillas*, ed. C. Clapham, 173–193. Oxford: James Currey, 1998.

Abu-Lughod, Ibrahim. *Transformation of Palestine*. Evanston, Ill.: Northwestern University Press, 1971.

Aburish, Said. *Children of Bethany*. London: I. B. Tauris, 1988.

Allsop, Derek, ed. *Brassey's Essential Guide to Military Arms*. Iola, Wis.: Kraus, 2000.

Alon, Gedalia. *The Jews in Their Land in the Talmudic Age*. 1984. Trans. Gershon Levi. Cambridge: Harvard University Press, 1989.

Amit-Talai, Vered, and Helena Wulff, eds. *Youth Cultures: A Cross-Cultural Perspective*. London: Routledge, 1995.

Anderson, Benedict. *Imagined Communities*. London: Verso, 1991.

Ariès, Phillip. *Centuries of Childhood: A Social History of Family Life*. New York: Knopf, 1962.

Arjomand, Said Amir. "Islamic Apocalypticism in the Classic Period." In *The Encyclopedia of Apocalypticism*, ed. Bernard McGinn, 238–283. New York: Continuum, 1998.

Atran, Scott. "Genesis of Suicide Terrorism." *Science* 299 (March 7, 2003): 1534–1539.

Awwad, Arabi, and Jiryis Qwwas. "Resistance in the Occupied Territories." *Journal of Palestine Studies* 3, no. 4 (1974).

Banton, Michael. *West African City: A Study of Tribal Life in Freetown*. London: Oxford University Press, 1957.

Bauman, Janina. *Winter in the Morning*. New York: Free Press, 1986.

Bayart, Jean-Francois, Stephen Ellis, and Beatrice Hibou. *The Criminalization of the State in Africa*. Bloomington: Indiana University Press, 1999.

Becker, Howard. *German Youth: Bond or Free*. New York: Oxford University Press, 1946.

Berman, Paul. *Terror and Liberalism*. New York: Norton, 2003.

Bernal, Virginia. "Equality to Die For? Women Guerilla Fighters and Eritrea's Cultural Revolution." *PoLar: Political and Legal Anthropology Review* 28, no. 2 (2000): 61–76.

Birenbaum, Halina. *Hope Is the Last to Die*. 1967. Trans. David Welsh. New York: Twayne, 1971.

Bluebond-Langner, Myra. In the Shadow of Illness. Princeton, N.J.: Princeton University Press, 1996.
———. The Private Worlds of Dying Children. Princeton, N.J.: Princeton University Press, 1978.
Bodley, John H. "Anthropology and the Politics of Genocide." In The Paths to Domination, Resistance, and Terror, ed. Carolyn Nordstrom and JoAnn Martin, 37–51. Berkeley: University of California Press, 1992.
Bornstein, Avram S. Crossing the Greenline between the West Bank and Israel. Philadelphia: University of Pennsylvania Press, 2002.
Brett, R., and M. McCallan. Children: The Invisible Soldiers. Sweden: Radda Barnen, Save the Children, 1998.
Brown, Ian. Khomeini's Forgotten Sons: The Story of Iran's Boy Soldiers. London: Grey Seal, 1990.
Celemenski, Jacob. Elegy for My People. 1963. Trans. Gershon Friedlan. Melbourne: Jacob Celemenski Memorial Trust, 2000.
Chagnon, Napoleon. Yanomamo. New York: Harcourt Brace, 1992.
Chesterman, Simon, ed. Civilians in War. Boulder, Colo.: Lynn Rienner, 2001.
Cholawski, Shalom. "Yeheskel Atlas." In Encyclopedia of the Holocaust, ed. Israel Gutman, 1: 106. New York: Macmillan, 1990.
Cholawski, Shalom, and Dov Levin. "Partisans: Belorussia and Lithuania." In Encyclopedia of the Holocaust, ed. Israel Gutman, 3: 1113–1118. New York: Macmillan, 1990.
Coalition to Stop the Use of Child Soldiers. Child Soldiers Global Report. London, 2001.
Cockerill, A. W. Sons of the Brave. London: Leo Cooper, 1984.
Cohen, Abner. The Politics of Elite Culture. Berkeley: University of California Press, 1981.
Cohen, Rich. The Avengers: A Jewish War Story. New York: Vintage Books, 2000.
Cohn, A. Romi. The Youngest Partisan. New York: Mesorah, 2001.
Cohn, Ilene. "The Protection of Children and the Quest for Truth and Justice in Sierra Leone." Journal of International Affairs 55, no. 1 (Fall 2001): 1–34.
———, and Guy S. Goodwin-Gill. Child Soldiers: The Role of Children in Armed Conflict. Oxford: Clarendon Press, 1994.
Dann, John C. The Revolution Remembered. Chicago: University of Chicago Press, 1980.
Davis, Archie K. Boy Colonel of the Confederacy: The Life and Times of Henry King Burgwyn, Jr. Chapel Hill: University of North Carolina Press, 1985.
Dawidowicz, Lucy S. The War against the Jews, 1933–1945. New York: Holt, Rinehart and Winston, 1975.
Deng, Francis Mading. The Dinka of the Sudan. Prospect Heights, Ill.: Waveland Press, 1972.
Dinstein, Yoram. "The Distinction between Unlawful Combatants and War Criminals." In International Law at a Time of Perplexity: Essays in Honor of Shabtai Rosenne, ed. Yoram Dinstein and Mary Tabory, 103–116. London: Martinus Nijhoff, 1989.
Diouf, Mamadou. "Engaging Postcolonial Culture: African Youth and Public Space." African Studies Review 46, no. 2 (September 2003): 1–12.
Dwork, Deborah. Children with a Star: Jewish Youth in Nazi Europe. New Haven, Conn.: Yale University Press, 1992.
Elpeleg, Zvi. The Grand Mufti. 1988. Trans. David Harvey. London: Frank Cass, 1993.
Fanthorpe, Richard. "Neither Citizen nor Subject? 'Lumpen' Agency and the Legacy of Native Administration in Sierra Leone." African Affairs 100 (2001): 363–386.

Farsoun, Samih. *Palestine and the Palestinians.* Boulder, Colo.: Westview Press, 1997.
Ferme, Mariane C. *The Underneath of Things: Violence, History, and the Everyday in Sierra Leone.* Berkeley: University of California Press, 2001.
Finnemore, Martha, and Kathryn Sikkink. "International Norm Dynamics and Political Change." *International Organization* 52 (Autumn 1998).
Fletcher, George P. *A Crime of Self-Defense.* Chicago: University of Chicago Press, 1988.
Folman Raban, Havka. *They Are Still with Me.* 1997. Trans. Judy Grossman. Western Galilee, Israel: Ghetto Fighters' Museum, 2001.
Forna, Aminatta. *The Devil That Danced on the Water.* New York: Atlantic Monthly Press, 2002.
Fyle, Hilton. *Sierra Leone: The Fighter from Death Row.* Parkland, Fla.: Universal Publishers, 2000.
Glass, James M. "German Treatment of Jewish Children during the Holocaust." In *Resisting the Holocaust,* ed. Ruby Rohrlich, 239–255. Oxford: Berg, 1998.
Glendon, Mary Ann. *A World Made New: Eleanor Roosevelt and the Universal Declaration of Human Rights.* New York: Random House, 2001.
Granatstein, Yecheil. *The War of a Jewish Partisan.* New York: Mesorah, 1986.
Griffiths, Anne, and Randy F. Kandel. "Hearing Children in Children's Hearings." *Child and Family Law Quarterly* 12, no. 3 (2000): 283–299.
Grossman, Chaika. *The Underground Army.* 1965. Trans. Shmuel Berri. New York: Holocaust Library, 1987.
Gutman, Israel. "Partisans." In *Encyclopedia of the Holocaust,* ed. Israel Gutman, 3: 1109–1113. New York: Macmillan, 1990.
———. *Resistance: The Warsaw Ghetto Uprising.* New York: Houghton Mifflin, 1994.
———. "Youth Movements." In *Encyclopedia of the Holocaust,* ed. Israel Gutman, 3: 1697–1703. New York: Macmillan, 1990.
———. "Youth Movements and the Underground and the Ghetto Revolts." In *Jewish Resistance during the Holocaust,* 260–284. Jerusalem: Yad Vashem, 1971.
Hamill, H. M. [Howard Melancthon]. *Sam Davis, a True Story of a Young Confederate Soldier: Who Was Hanged after Capture because He Would Not Betray a Secret of His Commander.* Kennesaw, Ga.: Continental Books, 1959.
Hammer, Joshua. *A Season in Bethlehem.* New York: Free Press, 2003.
Harkabi, Yehoshafat. *Arab Strategies and Israel's Response.* New York: Free Press, 1977.
Hart, Alan. *Arafat: A Political Biography.* Bloomington: Indiana University Press, 1989.
Hass, Amira. *Drinking the Sea at Gaza: Days and Nights in a Land under Siege.* Trans. Elana Wesley and Maxine Kaufman-Lacusta. New York: Henry Holt, 1996.
Hass, Jonathan. *The Anthropology of War.* Cambridge: Cambridge University Press, 1990.
Hayward, Fred M. "The Development of a Radical Political Organization in the Bush: A Case Study in Sierra Leone." *Canadian Journal of African Studies* 6, no. 1 (1972): 1–28.
Herman, Marek. *From the Alps to the Red Sea.* Trans. Judy Grossman. Western Galilee, Israel: Ghetto Fighters' Museum, 1985.
Hill, Anthony. *Soldier Boy.* Melbourne: Penguin, 2001.
Hilterman, Joost R. *Behind the Intifada.* Princeton, N.J.: Princeton University Press, 1991.
Hirsh, John L. *Sierra Leone: Diamonds and the Struggle for Democracy.* Boulder, Colo.: Lynn Rienner, 2001.
Hoar, Jay S. *Callow, Brave and True: A Gospel of Civil War Youth.* Gettysburg, Pa.: Thomas, 1999.
Hoebel, E. Adamson. *The Cheyennes.* New York: Harcourt Brace, 1988.

Hogg, Ian V., and John S. Weeks. *Military Small Arms of the 20th Century.* Iola, Wis.: Kraus, 1997.

Hull, Susan. *Boy Soldiers of the Confederacy.* 1905. Austin, Tex.: Eakin Press, 1998.

Human Rights Watch. *Children in Sudan: Slaves, Street Children, and Child Soldiers.* New York, 1995.

———. *Erased in a Moment: Suicide Bombing Attacks against Israeli Civilians.* New York, 2002.

Hutchinson, Sharon. *Nuer Dilemmas.* Berkeley: University of California Press, 1996.

Kandel, Randy F., and Ann Griffiths. "Reconfiguring Personhood: From Ungovernability to Parent Adolescent Autonomy Conflict Actions." *Syracuse University Law Review* 53 (2003): 995–1065.

Kaplan, Robert D. *The Coming Anarchy.* New York: Random House, 2000.

Keesee, Dennis M. *Too Young to Die: Boy Soldiers of the Union Army, 1861–1865.* Huntington, W. Va.: Blue Acorn Press, 2001.

Kehoe, Thomas Joseph. *The Fighting Mascot, the True Story of a Boy Soldier, by the Boy Soldier Himself, Thomas Joseph Kehoe, with Illustrations by Clyde Forsythe.* New York: Dodd, Mead, 1918.

Kermish, Joseph. *To Live with Honor and Die with Honor: Selected Documents from the Warsaw Ghetto Archives "O.S." [Oneg Shabbat].* Jerusalem: Yad Vashem, 1986.

Khalidi, Rashid. "Palestinian Peasant Resistance to Zionism before World War I." In *Blaming the Victim,* ed. Edward Said and Christopher Hitchens, 207–233. London: Verso, 2001.

Khalidi, Walid. *From Haven to Conquest: Readings in Zionism and the Palestinian Problem until 1948.* Beirut: Institute for Palestinian Studies, 1971.

Kiernan, Thomas. *Arafat: The Man and the Myth.* New York: Norton, 1976.

Killbride, Phillip, Colette Suda, and Suda Njeru. *Street Children of Kenya.* Westport, Conn.: Bergin & Garvey, 2000.

Kimmerling, Baruch, and Joel S. Migdal. *The Palestinian People.* Cambridge, Mass.: Harvard University Press, 2003.

Kohen, Nahum, and Howard Roiter. *A Voice from the Forest: Memoirs of a Jewish Partisan.* New York: Holocaust Library, 1980.

Korbin, Jill. "Children, Childhoods, and Violence." *Annual Review of Anthropology* 32 (2003): 431–446.

Krakowski, Shmuel. *The War of the Doomed: Jewish Armed Resistance in Poland, 1942–1944.* Trans. Ora Blaustein. London: Holmes & Meier, 1984.

Krall, Hanna. *Shielding the Flame: An Intimate Conversation with Dr.Marek Edelman, the Last Surviving Leader of the Warsaw Ghetto Uprising.* 1977. Trans. Joanna Stasinska and Lawrence Weschler. New York: Henry Holt, 1986.

Kreutzinger, Helga. *The Eri Devils in Freetown Sierra Leone.* Vienna: Osterreiche Ethnologische Gesellschaft, 1966.

Krohn-Hansen, Christian. "The Anthropology and Ethnography of Political Violence." *Journal of Peace Research* 34, no. 2 (1997): 233–240.

Kuper, Jenny. *International Law Concerning Child Civilians in Armed Conflict.* New York: Oxford University Press, 1997.

Laffin, John. *Boys in Battle.* London: Abelard-Schuman, 1967.

Levin, Dov. *Fighting Back: Lithuanian Jewry's Armed Resistance to the Nazis, 1941–1945.* Trans. Moshe Cohen and Dina Cohen. New York: Holmes & Meier, 1985.

Little, Kenneth. *The Mende of Sierra Leone.* London: Routledge, 1967.

Lochman, Zacharey, and Joel Beinin. *Intifada: The Palestinian Uprising against Israeli Occupation.* Boston: South End Press, 1989.

Lockwood, James D. *Life and Adventures of a Drummer-Boy; or, Seven Years a Soldier. By James D. Lockwood: A True Story.* Albany, N.Y.: J. Skinner, 1893.

Lubetkin, Zivia. *In the Days of Destruction and Revolt.* 1979. Trans. Ishai Tubbin. Tel Aviv: Am Oved, 1981.

Machel, Graca. *Impact of Armed Conflict on Children.* New York: United Nations, 1996.

Makiya, Kanan. *Republic of Fear.* Berkeley: University of California Press, 1989.

Malanczuk, Peter, ed. *Akehurst's Modern Introduction to International Law.* London: Routledge, 1997.

Maoz, Moshe. *Palestinian Leadership on the West Bank.* London: Frank Cass, 1984.

Mcguire, Peter. *Law and War: An American Story.* New York: Columbia University Press, 2000.

McKeogh, Colm. *Innocent Civilians: The Morality of Killing in War.* New York: Palgrave, 2002.

Mishal, Shaul. *The PLO under 'Arafat.* New Haven, Conn.: Yale University Press, 1986.

Mitchell, J. Clyde. *The Kalela Dance.* Manchester: Manchester University Press, 1956.

Morgenstern, Arie. "Dispersion and the Longing for Zion, 1240–1840." *Azure* 12 (Winter 2002).

Morris, Benny. *Righteous Victims: A History of the Zionist-Arab Conflict, 1881–2001.* New York: Random House, 2001.

Murphy, William P. "Military Patrimonialism and Child Soldiers' Clientilism in the Liberian and Sierra Leonean Civil Wars." *African Studies Review* 46, no. 2 (September 2003): 61–87.

Musgrove, Frank. *Youth and the Social Order.* London: Routledge, 1964.

Musser, George, and Sasha Nemecek. "Waging a New Kind of War." *Scientific American,* June 2000, 47–53.

Nabulsi, Karma. *Traditions of War: Occupation, Resistance, and the Law.* New York: Oxford University Press, 1999.

Nagengast, Carol. "Violence, Terror, and the Crisis of the State." *Annual Review of Anthropology* 23 (1994): 109–136.

Nordstrom, Carolyn. "The Backyard Front." In *The Paths to Domination, Resistance and Terror,* ed. Carolyn Nordstrom and JoAnn Martin, 260–274. Berkeley: University of California Press, 1992.

———. *A Different Kind of War.* Philadelphia: University of Pennsylvania Press, 1997.

Oren, Michael B. *Six Days of War.* Oxford: Oxford University Press, 2002.

Pearlman, Wendy. *Occupied Voices: Stories of Everyday Life in the Second Intifada.* New York: Thunder's Mouth Press and Nation Books, 2003.

Peters, Krijn, and Paul Richards. "Why We Fight: Voices of Youth Combatants in Sierra Leone." *Africa* 68, no. 2 (1998), 183–210.

Pinto, Jacque. *Judean Journal.* London: Quartet Books, 1990.

Porath, Yehoshua. *The Emergence of the Palestinian-Arab National Movement: 1918–1929.* London: Frank Cass, 1974.

———. *The Palestinian Arab National Movement: 1929–1939.* London: Frank Cass, 1977.

Qleibo, Ali H. *Before the Mountains Disappear: An Ethnographic Chronicle of the Modern Palestinians.* Cairo: Al Haram Press, 1992.

Reuter, Christopher. *My Life Is a Weapon: A Modern History of Suicide Bombing.* Princeton, N.J.: Princeton University Press, 2004.

Richards, Paul. *Fighting for the Rain Forest.* Portsmouth, N.H.: Heinemann, 1996.

Rigby, Andrew. *The Living Intifada.* London: Zed Books, 1990.

Ringelblum, Emmanuel. *Notes from the Warsaw Ghetto: The Journal of Emmanuel Ringelblum.* Ed. Jacob Sloan. New York: McGraw-Hill, 1958.

Rosen, David M. "Dangerous Women: 'Ideology,' 'Knowledge' and Ritual among the Kono of Eastern Sierra Leone." *Dialectical Anthropology* 6 (1981): 151–163.

————. "The Peasant Context of Feminist Revolt in West Africa." *Anthropological Quarterly* 56, no. 1 (January 1983): 35–43.

Rosenfeld, Maya. *Confronting the Occupation: Work, Education and Political Activism of Palestinian Families in a Refugee Camp.* Stanford, Calif.: Stanford University Press, 2004.

Rotem, Simcha. *Memoirs of a Warsaw Ghetto Fighter.* Trans. Barbara Harshav. New Haven, Conn.: Yale University Press, 1994.

Saad-Gorayeb, Amal. *Hizbu'llah: Politics and Religion.* London: Pluto Press, 2003.

Said, Edward. *The Question of Palestine.* New York: Vintage Books, 1992.

Sayigh, Rosemary. *Palestinians: From Peasants to Revolutionaries.* London: Zed Books, 1979.

Schleifler, S. Abdullah. "The Life and Thought of 'Izz-Id-Din al-Qassam." *Islamic Quarterly* 22, no. 2 (1979): 61–81.

Schulman, Faye. *A Partisan's Memoir: A Woman of the Holocaust.* Toronto: Second Story Press, 1995.

Schwartzman, Helen, ed. *Children and Anthropology: Perspectives for the 21st Century.* Westport, Conn.: Bergin & Garvey, 2001.

Segev, Tom. *One Palestine, Complete.* 1999. Trans. Haim Watzman. New York: Henry Holt, 2000.

Shaw, Rosalind. *Memories of the Slave Trade.* Chicago: University of Chicago Press, 2002.

Shehadeh, Raja. *Samed: Journal of a West Bank Palestinian.* New York: Adama Books, 1984.

Sherper-Hughes, Nancy. "Who's the Killer? Popular Justice and Human Rights in a South African Squatter Camp." *Social Justice* 22, no. 3 (1995): 143–164.

Sherper-Hughes, Nancy, and Carolyn Sargent. "Introduction: The Cultural Politics of Childhood." In *Small Wars: The Cultural Politics of Childhood,* ed. Nancy Sherper-Hughes and Carolyn Sargent, 1–33. Berkeley: University of California Press, 1998.

Silvester, Victor. *Dancing Is My Life.* London: Heinemann, 1958.

Sontag, Susan. "Looking at War." *New Yorker,* December 9, 2002, 82–98.

Spiro, Melford E. *Kibbutz: Venture in Utopia.* Cambridge, Mass.: Harvard University Press, 1970.

Spitzer, Leo. *The Creoles of Sierra Leone.* Madison: University of Wisconsin Press, 1974.

Stephens, Sharon, ed. *Children and the Politics of Culture.* Princeton, N.J.: Princeton University Press, 1995.

Stern, Jessica. *Terror in the Name of God: Why Religious Militants Kill.* New York: Ecco Press, 2003.

Suhl, Yuri. *Uncle Misha's Partisans.* New York: Four Winds Press, 1973.

Swedenburg, Ted. *Memories of Revolt: The 1936–1939 Rebellion and the Palestinian National Past.* Minneapolis: University of Minnesota Press, 1995.

Talmon-Garber, Yonina G. *Family and Community in the Kibbutz.* Cambridge, Mass.: Harvard University Press, 1972.

Temchin, Michael. *The Witch Doctor: Memoirs of a Partisan.* New York: Holocaust Library, 1983.

Thamm, Gerhardt B. *Boy Soldier: A German Teenager at the Nazi Twilight.* Jefferson, N.C.: McFarland, 2000.

Tiger, Lionel, and Joseph Shepher. *Women in the Kibbutz.* New York: Penguin Books, 1975.

Twum-Danso, Afua. *Africa's Young Soldiers.* Cape Town, South Africa: Institute for Security Studies, 2003.

Van der Laan, H. L. *The Sierra Leone Diamonds*. London: Oxford University Press, 1965.

Vered, Amit, and Nigel Rapport. *The Trouble with Community*. London: Pluto, 2002.

Victor, Barbara. *Army of Roses: Inside the World of Palestinian Women Suicide Bombers*. Emmaus, Pa.: Rodale, 2003.

Wallach, Janet, and John Wallach. *Arafat: In the Eyes of the Beholder*. New York: Carol, 1990.

Walter, Eugene V. *Terror and Resistance: A Study of Political Violence*. Oxford: Oxford University Press, 1969.

Walzer, Michael. *Just and Unjust Wars*. New York: Basic Books, 1977.

Werner, Emmy E. *Reluctant Witnesses: Children's Voices from the Civil War*. Boulder, Colo.: Westview Press, 1998.

Werner, Harold. *Fighting Back: A Memoir of Jewish Resistance*. New York: Columbia University Press, 1992.

West, Harry. "Girls with Guns: Narrating the Experience of War of Frelimo's 'Female Detachment.'" *Anthropological Quarterly* 73, no. 4 (2000).

Wilson, Richard A. "Representing Human Rights Violations: Social Contexts and Subjectivities." In *Human Rights, Culture and Context*, ed. Richard A. Wilson, 134–160. London: Pluto Press, 1997.

Index

AFRC. *See* Armed Forces Revolutionary Counsel
African Charter on the Rights and Welfare of the Child (1990), 139
age: of population in Africa, 62; and status boundaries, 62, 132, 135–137
Akhras, Ayat al-, 91, 128–131
Akiva youth movement, 26, 32, 40
al-Aqsa intifada, 91, 96, 118–121, 154
al-Aqsa Martyrs Brigade, 91, 92, 120, 122
al-Aqsa mosque, 98, 119
al-Futuwwa youth groups, 106, 107, 110
All People's Congress (APC), 76–80, 85
Alluvial Diamond Mining Ordinance, 74, 75
al-Qassam Brigade, 100–102, 108, 109, 126
Amnesty International, 149, 155
APC. *See* All People's Congress
APC Youth, 78–80
Arab nationalism, 93–96, 105, 106
Arab Revolt (1936–1939), 29, 107–109
Arafat, Yasir, 109–112, 118–120
Armed Forces Revolutionary Counsel (AFRC), 82, 86
Armia Ludowa (People's Guard), 31, 41, 48, 50
Article 3, Geneva Conventions, 141
Association of Muslim Youth, 100

Balfour Declaration, 92, 108

Bamako Declaration on Small Arms Proliferation (2000), 14
Betar youth movement, 26, 32, 50
Bielsky, Tuvia, camp of, 53–55
Bona, Dudu, 78, 170n67
Boy Scouts, 27, 103, 104
Bright, Herbert Christian Bankole, 67
British Mandate, 29, 96, 98, 103–113
British military, 4–6, 8, 15

Cape Town Principles (1997), 9. *See also* UNICEF
childhood: boundaries of, 4, 7, 62, 132, 133, 135, 137, 165n72; definition of, 2–4, 7, 8, 132, 144, 152; and military culture, 6–8; paradigms of, 134, 135. *See also* Straight 18
child labor, 89, 90
children: age of legal capacity, 135; developmental models of, 133, 135; moral agency of, 24; reasoning capacity of, 134, 135; special vulnerability of, 8, 16–17, 47, 48, 132, 134, 157, 164n67; status offenses, 137; as suicide bombers, 121–131. *See also* criminal culpability, of children
child soldiers: and African Charter on the Rights and Welfare of the Child, 139; in African cultures, 4, 8, 17, 64; under age fifteen, 142–144;

About the Author

DAVID M. ROSEN is a professor of anthropology and law at Fairleigh Dickinson University, College of Florham, Madison, New Jersey. He received his Ph.D. in anthropology from the University of Illinois, Urbana-Champaign, and his J.D. from Pace Law School and is a member of the Bar of the State of New York. He has carried out field research in Kenya, Sierra Leone, and Israel. His research interests are the connections between law and culture. He lives in Brooklyn, New York.

Printed in the United States
71953LV00005B/322-348